Photographing and "Videoing" Horses Explained—Digital and Film

Photographing and "Videoing" Horses Explained—Digital and Film

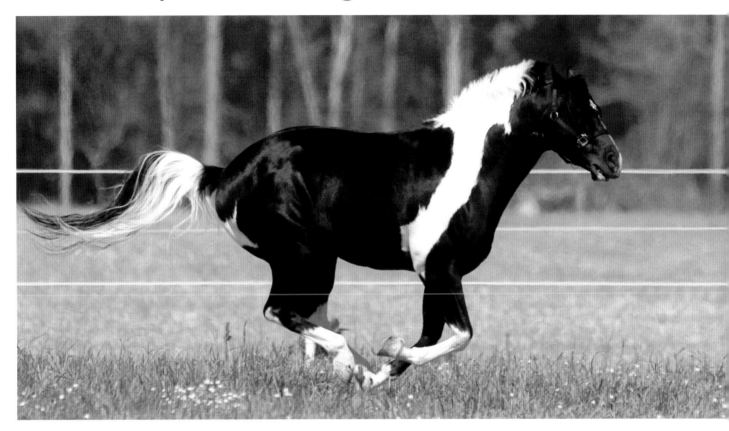

The Horse Owner's Manual for Improved Portraits,
Schooling Tools, Sales and Promotions

Charles Mann

Photography by Charles Mann

with contributions by Ami Hendrickson
and Stormy May

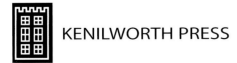

KENILWORTH PRESS

Published in Great Britain in 2007 by
Kenilworth Press, an imprint of Quiller Publishing Ltd
Wykey House, Wykey, Shrewsbury, SY4 1JA

First published in 2006 in America by
Trafalgar Square Books
388 Howe Hill Road
North Pomfret
Vermont 05053, USA

ISBN 978-1-905693-15-3

British Library Cataloguing in Publication Data
A catalogue record for this book is available from the British Library

Jacket design by Heather Mansfield
Book text design by Carrie Fradkin
Typefaces: Myriad MM

Printed in China

KENILWORTH PRESS
An imprint of Quiller Publishing Ltd
Wykey House, Wykey, Shrewsbury, SY4 1JA
tel: 01939 261616 fax: 01939 261606
e-mail: info@quillerbooks.com
website: www.kenilworthpress.co.uk

Contents

Acknowledgments

First of all, I would like to thank Martha Cook and everybody else at Trafalgar Square Publishing for giving me this opportunity and for working with my schedule and me.

I cannot begin to thank Stacey Wigmore enough for her help and support during this project. Without her there would be no book. She has gone out of her way and has put in many a late hour taking my ramblings and organizing them into a more structured format. She has gone with me on many photo shoots and has done everything from grooming a horse to carrying equipment. Stacey, thanks!

I have the good fortune to have many friends, friends of friends, and horse owners who were willing to participate in the making of this book. I thank you all.

Special thanks go to my girlfriend, Emily Daignault, for being a willing model, and for letting me use some (not so good) photos that she took to illustrate some key points.

Thanks to Kathleen Murphy, who asked for some photos of her and her horses after working the booth one weekend for Amy McCool, McCool Photography, and me. And thank you, Sarah Phelps, director of Great & Small at the Rickman Farm, for letting me photograph their horses and facilities.

I can't exclude the many top riders whose images grace the pages of this book, like Laura Kraut, Todd Minikus, David O'Connor, Bob LaPorta, Margie Engle, Brandee Broch, Megan Young, John Lyons, and Megan Eldrick. I am sure that I have missed someone. I'm sorry if I did, but thank you.

Jim Duley, of Penn Camera, has been a great help with technical tips and general advice. He's been an all around resource for information and props. He also has this knack of draining my bank account whenever Nikon comes out with a new camera. Thanks, Jim!

In addition, I would like to thank all the editors, art directors, and publishers of the publications that I have worked with for allowing me to reproduce the magazine covers and articles featured throughout this book.

Over the years, I have come in contact with many people who have helped me become the photographer that I am today. One of those people that stands out is Barry O'Brian of Adelaide, Australia. Barry was the equestrian venue photo manager at the 2000 Sydney Olympics.

When I received my Olympics credentials two weeks before the start of the games, I was excited. Then I realized that they were for a journalist and not a photographer. This presented a big problem. First, I would not have admittance to the field of competition. Second, I would not have access to the Kodak and Nikon services that are provided during such big events.

I immediately started the phone calls and e-mails trying to get my credentials changed before I left for Sydney, to no avail. Once in Sydney, the USET press officer, Marty Bauman, and I tried going directly to the IOC and the USOC, only to be told that there was nothing that they could do.

Marty then introduced me to Barry and explained my situation. Barry was very understanding, but said he could not do anything—his hands were tied. He did explain to me which areas I had access to and where I could shoot. I had no choice at that point, because I had already spent a lot of money to get there, so I decided to concentrate my energy into producing the best images I could with what was available to me.

Every day, Barry would come over and ask how things were going and I would show him what I was able

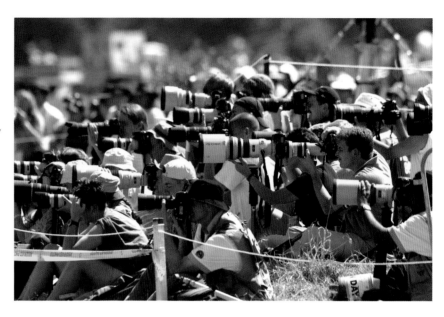

Photo i: When covering the Olympics, you are literally elbow to elbow with hundreds of other photographers from around the world, all trying to capture the emotions of the games, the moments of victory, and even those of failure. The photo positions can get very cramped.

to get from my position. He was always very complimentary and encouraging me to do more. Every day, I would try to find a more interesting vantage point that none of the other photographers had. This proved difficult at times, because of my credentials' limitations, but I always managed to find something new, and Barry would come over and ask to see it.

After the first week of shooting dressage, cross-country, team show jumping, and medal ceremonies, eventing's individual show jumping round was approaching and David O'Connor had a very good chance of winning the gold medal. I knew that I needed to have better access if I was going to be able to capture the emotions of the medal ceremonies. So that morning, I walked into Barry's office and pleaded one more time to see if he could do anything. He said he would try.

The day went on. David won his gold medal and circled the arena carrying a US flag attached to a riding crop. As I rushed back to the press tent to download and send my images, Barry walked up behind me, as he had

done everyday, and asked how my day went. I showed him the victory lap image I had captured of David on Custom Made with the flag (see p. 1).

Barry said that I did a good job and he guessed I "did not need this," as he dropped an official photographer's vest in my lap. He told me that he had a long talk with the photo chief of the Olympics where he had explained my situation and told him how I was playing by the rules and not causing any trouble.

The following week, Barry approached me while I was photographing the dressage competition from outside the arena. He asked me why I was not on the field, and said he had lobbied hard for my vest. I assured him that I would use it, but I had learned the prior week that not being with all the other photographers allowed me to have unique images that nobody else had. He patted me on the shoulder and said he had faith in me and he was not surprised to find me here.

I can't thank Barry enough for the support and for everything he did for me during those games. I came

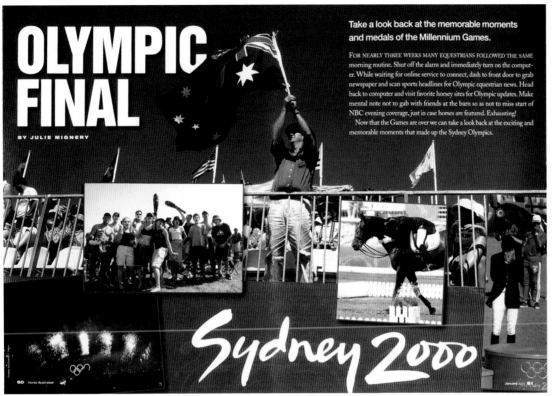

OLYMPIC FINAL

BY JULIE MIGNERY

Take a look back at the memorable moments and medals of the Millennium Games.

FOR NEARLY THREE WEEKS MANY EQUESTRIANS FOLLOWED THE SAME morning routine. Shut off the alarm and immediately turn on the computer. While waiting for online service to connect, dash to front door to grab newspaper and scan sports headlines for Olympic equestrian news. Head back to computer and visit favorite horsey sites for Olympic updates. Make mental note not to gab with friends at the barn so as not to miss start of NBC evening coverage, just in case horses are featured. Exhausting!

Now that the Games are over we can take a look back at the exciting and memorable moments that made up the Sydney Olympics.

Sydney 2000

60 Horse Illustrated

Photo ii: Moira Harris, editor of *Horse Illustrated,* told me that during the 1996 Olympics, she could get all the action photos she wanted from any of the other photographers. What she wanted for her magazine was the "feeling of being there at the 2000 Olympics," both as a spectator and a competitor. With that in mind, and having to work from areas that other photographers were not in, I was able to capture some unique moments that nobody else had. These were exactly what she was looking for to open their Olympic article.

away from that experience with a better understanding of how important it is to know how to make the best of a difficult situation.

Having the best access does not always mean that you will get the best pictures. In creating unique images, you set yourself apart from all the other photographers. The hardest part is keeping that kind of energy up and thinking creatively week after week—whether at the Olympics or at a local horse show.

I'd like to thank my mother and sister for all the encouragement they gave me over the years. My mother, Shirley Mann, who passed away during the writing of this book, always wanted to know everything about all of my trips, whether I was going around the corner to the local show or halfway around the world to cover the Olympics. And I am especially grateful to my sister, Deborah, for not letting me feel guilty about leaving town for weeks on end during Mom's long illness. I am lucky to have a sister like her.

Finally, I can't forget Buddy, who has missed way too many trips to the P-A-R-K (don't say it out loud!) He is always there when I need him, whether as a stand-in before a horse shows up, or when leading the horse to the shoot. He is always ready to go.

Introduction

The horse is one of nature's most beautiful animals, so it is surprising that so many photographers—both amateur and professional—fail to portray the horse well. This book will give you some hints and suggestions on how to improve the quality of your photos and capture better images of horses at leisure or in competition. If you are a breeder wanting to promote your stallion or stock, or someone who just wants to sell a horse, knowing how to take an image that really captures the buyer's attention is paramount.

Equipment for film and digital still cameras and video recorders, features to look for (both good and bad), and tips on selecting lenses, film, and accessories are covered. I will also touch on some basic photography rules and techniques, and provide some tips on how to set up and shoot portraits of horses with and without people. In addition, I will discuss the things you need to know how to do once you have captured your images, including dealing with a photo lab, making prints from home, and archiving your images for years to come. "Videoing" lessons and shows as well as videography and photography for sales and promotion are all covered extensively at the end of the book.

Most importantly, I hope to show you how to develop your photographic eye. You will learn how you can make a not-so-good image into a better one with very little effort. You will learn how the camera sees things, and you will come to understand how different photographic techniques can affect the look of your equine subject.

So let's get started. You have a horse to capture—on film that is.

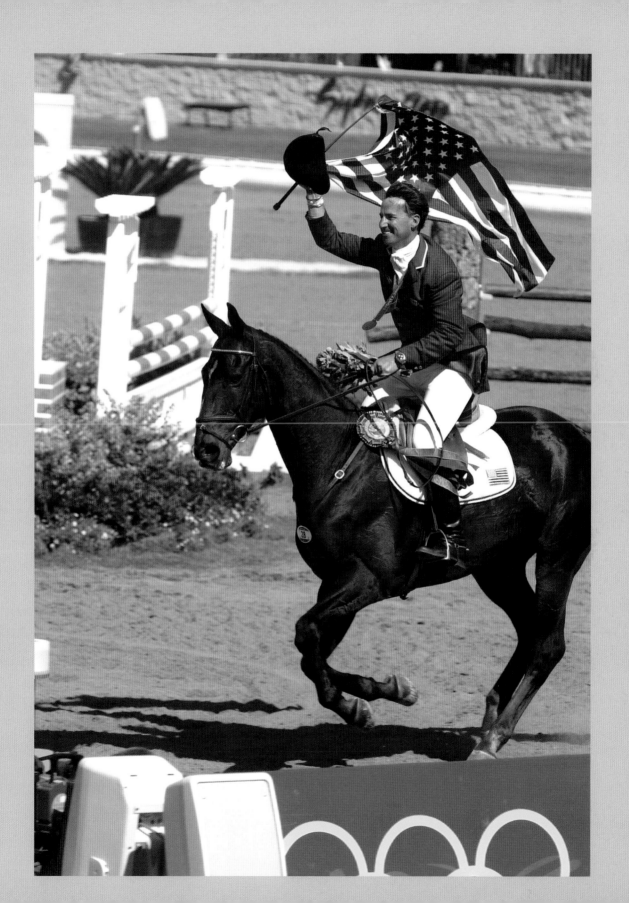

1
The Basics

So many cameras, so little time. The market is filled with numerous types and brands of cameras that can be used for a variety of situations (Photo 1.1). All cameras will take a picture. The question is: what kind of picture do you want to take? It is important that you know what kind of image you wish to capture.

I'm not going to debate the pros and cons of different brands of cameras such as Canon versus Nikon. That's like arguing about Macs versus PCs, Ford versus Dodge, or Quarter Horses versus Thoroughbreds. As you familiarize yourself with what is available, you will develop your own preferences. Instead, I will focus on what equipment you will need to get the job done.

Before you get started, you need to ask yourself these questions:

▶ *What am I going to do with the photos I take? Am I going to use them for reproduction in a book or magazine; for Web sites, e-mail, or other online images; or to make prints?*

▸ *What kind of budget do I have?*
▸ *Do I want a system that can be expanded as my interests and abilities progress?*

Knowing the answers to these questions will help you begin your camera search.

A Visit to the Camera Store

When you walk into a tack shop to buy a new saddle, it's helpful to know what kind of riding you plan to do. Different disciplines, such as dressage, barrel racing, show jumping, trail riding, sidesaddle, or saddle seat, require different tack. Granted, just because you regularly ride hunters using a flat jumping saddle doesn't mean you can never go on the occasional trail ride in that saddle. It will do the job. If you're going to spend a lot of time working cattle on a ranch, however, a Western-style saddle might be more comfortable and appropriate for the job.

The same reasoning holds true when deciding what kind of camera you need.

The Internet is a great resource when camera shopping. Do your research before going to the store. Write down any questions you have, so you can ask the salesperson if a particular camera model will perform the way you would like it to.

An important question for you to ask is, "Is it easy to use?" A camera that is easy to use will be one that you want to take with you all the time. If it is too complicated or confusing, it will sit in a drawer and collect dust.

Before buying any camera, make sure that you can comfortably and easily work all of the controls. (One consideration I have to keep in mind, for instance, is that my big hands make it difficult to use a camera with tiny buttons and controls.)

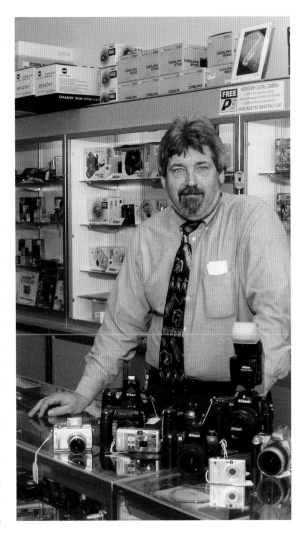

1.1 Jim Duley, store manager of Penn Camera, Laurel, MD, shows a small sampling of the wide range of cameras available.

Other things to consider include custom settings, lens selection, attachments, battery type and life, and—particularly for digital cameras—storage media and whether or not the camera is compatible with your computer. You should also try to determine whether or not the camera you are considering can be upgraded or accessorized as your skills grow.

When researching your options, don't necessarily confuse "simple" with "spare." Some point-and-shoots have a wide range of features available. Features you may want to consider—which will be explained in detail later—include:

▸ Manual aperture setting ability,

▸ Manual shutter speed options,

▸ Exposure compensation,

▸ Program settings that take the guesswork out of certain situations, and

▸ Manual as well as automatic focus. (Even if you are the type of person who wants a camera to do everything automatically, you may still want the option to override some of the automatic settings from time to time—or later, once you get more comfortable with your camera and abilities.)

Before you set foot in a camera shop, be honest about what you plan to do with your camera. Make a wish list of features. Take that list to your camera or electronics store and see which cameras will perform the functions you want. Just as importantly, see which ones feel comfortable to you.

The best thing to do is go to a camera or electronics store and play—and I do mean *play*—with different cameras. See what feels comfortable in your hands and to your eye. Experiment with a wide variety of cameras that might fit your needs.

Film vs. Digital

The great debate over the merits of film and digital cameras continues. Ask a roomful of photographers which is better, and you'll get a number of very strong opinions and arguments from both sides.

In essence, the decision of using film or shooting digitally comes down to your personal preference. When photographing with film, your images end up on film. When you shoot digitally, your images are captured on a photo sensor and stored as files (each image is considered a "frame"). From the photographer's point of view, however, the process of shooting is the same.

Most major camera manufacturers make both film and digital cameras. The models are usually designated with either an "F" for film or a "D" for digital cameras.

Film comes in a variety of ISO speeds. What speed you choose depends upon factors such as available light, whether you are shooting indoors or outdoors, and how quickly your subject will be moving (for a more complete explanation, see "Film Speed" p. 14). Though digital cameras do not use film, many models feature a dial or electronic readout that provides you with a way of setting the film ISO equivalent. (See "Types of Cameras," p. 6.)

After shooting over 500 rolls of film at the 1996 Olympic Games in Atlanta, Georgia (Photo 1.2), I spoke to a sales rep at my local camera store. He declared that I would be shooting digitally by the following Olympics in 2000. I laughed at him. Not only did I not see digital as the medium that I would be using, but at the time, the price of a good digital camera was around $19,000, and was a prohibitive issue.

When the new Nikon D1 digital camera came out at the end of 1999, I decided to see what the fuss was about. At $5,000, I thought it was still a little pricey, but it was much more affordable than four years earlier.

The same camera store rep made me apologize to him before he would let me see the camera! After I'd read many articles about the advances in digital photography, both the speed that the cameras were able to achieve and the reality that my clients wanted—and needed—images faster and faster, convinced me to give the digital medium a try.

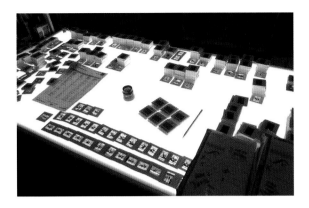

1.2 My light table during the editing process of some of the 500 rolls of slide film I took at the 1996 Olympics. Every one of the slides received a label with an ID number and caption that included the name of horse and rider, as well as what country they represented.

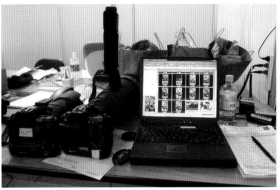

1.3 My work area at the 2000 Olympics. No wonder I decided to go digital! I liked the ability to see the images instantly, instead of waiting for several hours—or until the next day—to pick up my film.

I stepped into the digital age with one foot and bought my first digital camera in April, 2000.

At the Rolex Kentucky Three-Day Event, I started the weekend shooting dressage with both my Nikon F5 film camera and my new digital Nikon D1. After downloading my morning images during the lunch break, I put down the F5, and started shooting digital exclusively. I have never looked back. After I returned home from the event, I ordered my second D1 camera body.

My mind was made up during the event when the editor of a weekly magazine said, "I hear you went digital. Can you provide us with images from each day for our Web site?"

The mental gears started turning—this was something I hadn't even considered. And I have to say the camera store sales rep was right: I photographed almost all of the 2000 Olympics in Sydney with my digital cameras (Photos 1.3 & 1.4).

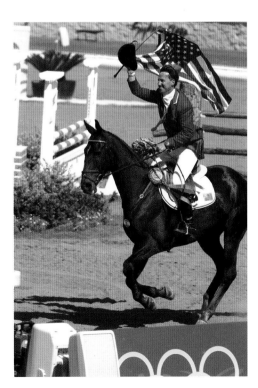

1.4 David O'Connor riding Custom Made after they won the Individual Eventing Gold Medal at the 2000 Sydney Olympics. I was able to post this image on the USET (United States Equestrian Team) Web site within five minutes after I took the photograph.

While, in the end, the decision between film and digital ended up being a no-brainer for me, I am not saying that digital is right for everyone. Remember that a good photographer makes the best of the camera. Just as buying a $100,000 show horse will not make you a better rider, a digital camera will not make you a great photographer.

You need to evaluate how you plan to use your camera and your photographs in order to choose what is right for you. I am a firm believer that you should use the camera with which you are most comfortable.

If you like film and want someone else to do the printing for you or you are not comfortable using a computer to handle your photographs, then stay with film.

On the other hand, if you like the instant gratification of seeing your images right away—which is what appeals to me—and love to send pictures to friends and family over the internet, then digital is the way to go.

There is also a middle ground. If you don't want to invest in a digital camera, but still wish to have photos in a digital format, most photo labs offer the option of scanning your film at the time of processing. They will then put your images on a photo CD or on the Internet, in addition to making traditional prints.

Though digital photography has many parallels to film photography, both mediums also have distinct differences.

Digital photography has three main components: (1) the camera, (2) the computer with the software, and (3) your output—this can be your printer or any other way of printing your images, plus the storage of files (Photo 1.5). When these three segments do not mesh correctly, your final image may not look very good. The color could be off, the image may be flat, or you might see *pixels* (the "picture elements," or tiny dots that make up a digital image) in the final print.

I use the following analogy to illustrate the knowledge needed to produce quality digital images:

If I gave you an Ansel Adams negative and asked you to make a print from it (assuming that you knew the basics of how to print black-and-white images from a negative), could you produce a print that looked exactly like one Adams did himself?

Chances are that you would be able to produce an okay print, but not one with the detail and the mood of an Ansel Adams print. That is because Adams was a master of his photographic techniques and could manipulate the processing in the darkroom to give him exactly the images he wanted.

The same principle holds true for digital photography. Unless you understand the digital workflow and color management process, your final images may not be of a consistent quality.

Types of Cameras

Disposable

If you only like to ride once in a while, you probably don't want to buy a brand new bridle. Similarly, you don't have to own a fancy, expensive camera to go out and take pictures. Today, disposable cameras are almost everywhere. These single-use cameras contain a roll of film, a lens, a shutter, and (sometimes) a flash (Photo 1.6).

Several different types of disposable film cameras are available. Options include the basic model, with or without flash; panoramic format, with a higher width to height ratio (Photo 1.8); and waterproof units.

Disposable digital cameras are also available. In order to access the images stored on them, you must turn in the camera to a lab with printing facilities and software compatible with the camera's digital requirements.

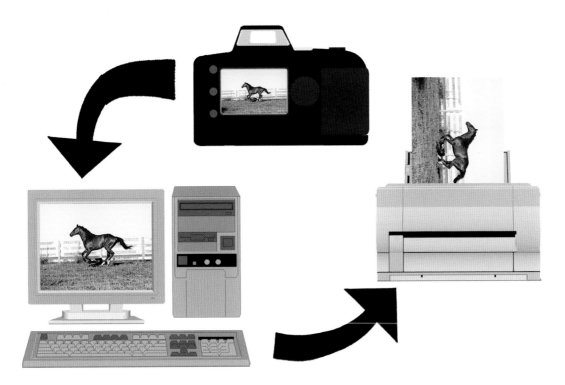

1.5 The three parts of digital photography: (1) the camera, (2) the computer and software, and (3) the output (a printer or CD). Knowing color management and the digital workflow is essential in order to produce consistent, accurate digital quality and color (see chapter 5).

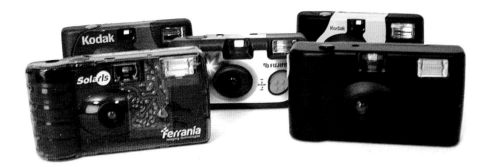

1.6 Some examples of disposable cameras from various manufacturers.

1.7 The image on the left is the original, 640 kb, unretouched, digital photo. The one on the right is the image on a 24- by 60-foot banner on the side of the SunTrust Building in Washington, DC.

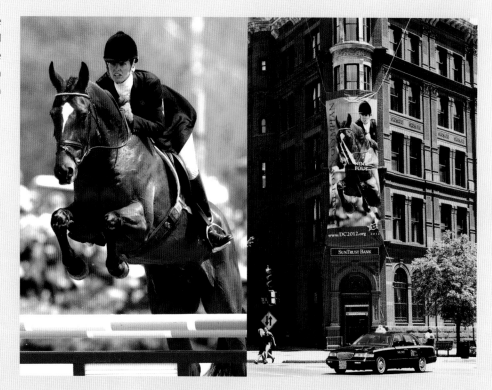

RESOLUTION: HOW BIG IS BIG ENOUGH?

The pixel density of a digital camera's image sensor chip is measured in *megapixels*. One megapixel is equal to one million pixels. In general, the more megapixels, the higher the camera's resolution capability.

But bigger isn't always better. Today's cameras boast 5, 10, or more megapixels. When looking to purchase a digital camera, it's easy to get caught up in the megapixel sales pitch. When purchasing a camera, however, it's often better to pay more attention to things such as camera weight, battery life, manual control capability, and shutter lag (see p. 15) than to fall prey to the megapixel hype.

You don't need huge electronic files to take crisp, clear, digital images. When I was first getting into digital, Jim Duley, the store manager of Penn Camera told me, "You have to ask yourself, 'How big is big enough?'"

For example, I have a picture I took at the Rolex Kentucky Three-Day Event with my first digital camera, a Nikon D1—a 2.7 megapixel camera. Shooting in normal (.jpg) mode, the camera generated a 640 kilobyte (kb) file for a single image frame. A 640 kb file is very small compared to the size of files I shoot now. That image was later blown up to a 24-foot by 60-foot banner that hung on the side of a building (Photo 1.7).

The point is, having many megapixels is not essential for taking an image that will enlarge well. Quantity is not always an indicator of quality.

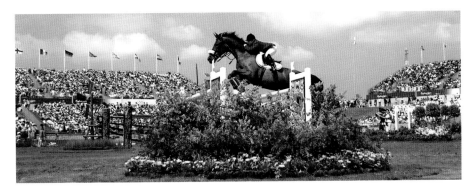

1.8 Panoramic photographs, like this, are significantly wider than they are high.

Some disposables and point-and-shoots (see below) are twin lens reflex (TLR) cameras. They use two lenses—one for taking the picture and a second for the viewing lens. In other words, the image you see is not necessarily the image you will take.

Disposable cameras typically come loaded with higher speed film, which may negatively affect the quality of your images, so double check what is available before you buy (for a better understanding of film speeds, see p. 14).

Point-and-Shoot

If you are primarily interested in trail riding, there is no need to go buy a top-of-the-line show saddle with intricate tooling and silver trim. You just want something comfortable and dependable. The same goes for buying a camera that you will only use occasionally for basic purposes.

"Point-and-shoot" average consumer-grade cameras—both film and digital—are popular choices (Photo 1.9). They offer more features than disposables, but are considerably less complicated than the lens and flash options that come with single lens reflex (SLR) cameras.

Single Lens Reflex (SLR)

If you ride often, you probably don't go out and buy all new brushes and equipment every time you get a new horse. Likewise, if photography is more than just a passing hobby, you will want an expandable camera system—either film or digital—with components that you can add on as you need them. Some of these components include:

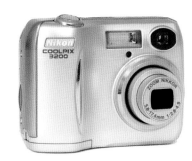

▶ A wide variety of lenses,
▶ Flashes for better light control,
▶ Data backs that provide such options as date stamping or text printing on your images, and
▶ Remote cables that enable you to capture an image without being in direct contact with the camera.

1.9 A sampling of the point-and-shoot cameras that are available.

Many accessories are interchangeable between different cameras, which means that if you decide to upgrade your camera, you don't have to go out and buy all new components.

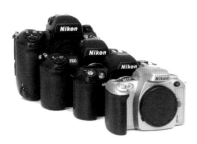

1.10 Samples of the variety of SLR cameras that are available, including models for the general consumer, advanced amateur, prosumer, and professional photographer.

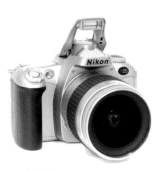

1.11 Consumer-grade SLR cameras can cost as little as $200 for a film body and lens and $700 for a digital body.

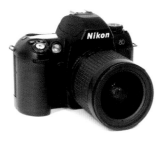

1.12 For around $400 to $500 for film bodies and $1,000 for digital bodies, the advanced amateur can spend a little more money and get a few more options. Cameras for the advanced amateur, such as this model, have more accessories available than the consumer models.

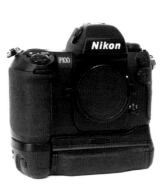

1.13 For between $150 and $1,500, the prosumer can have almost all the features of the professional photographer without the cost of true professional-grade equipment.

The single-lens reflex (SLR) is a good example of an "upgradable" camera that can grow with you. Most manufacturers have several different grades of SLR cameras. These range from the least complicated models for the average consumer, through units with features that appeal to the advanced amateur and the mid-range "prosumer" (or sophisticated hobbyist), to high-end cameras for professional photographers (Photo 1.10).

The consumer's camera has just the basic features and may include a line of inexpensive lenses (Photo 1.11). Cameras for advanced amateurs give the photographer a little more control over the final image (Photo 1.12). Models for prosumers have even more functions, custom settings, and accessories (Photo 1.13). Finally, there are the professional cameras with all the "bells and whistles" you could ask for.

No matter which manufacturer's camera system you consider, there are several levels of SLR cameras that should fit your needs. If you are not sure how involved in photography you will become, you can always start at the bottom and work your way up as you get more comfortable with the camera.

Make sure the components you purchase for a lower end camera are compatible with a camera the next level up. This advice applies to both film and digital cameras within a manufacturer's line.

Another advantage of an SLR system is that you can often rent components that you don't use on a regular basis—such as a motor-drive that will trip the shutter faster than you can do manually, allowing for continuous shooting, or specialty lenses like a fish-eye, or a 400mm telephoto lens that would cost anywhere from $1,000–$8,000 to buy. You can rent a higher end camera body for special occasions and use your own lenses. You could even rent a digital body to try.

Necessary Accessories

Lenses

Choosing the right lens options for your camera is important. Whether you are looking at a disposable, a point-and-shoot, or an SLR camera, make sure you choose a lens with the proper range of *focal length* for the pictures you want to take.

Focal length simply refers to the distance from a lens to its focus.

A lens' focal length determines the size of the image captured on film. If you were to take two pictures of the same subject from the same distance, then the lens with the longest focal length would form the largest image on the film. A long focal length also focuses more attention on your subject, and less on the surroundings. For much more information on understanding how focal length relates to your photography, see chapter 3: Getting Up Close and Personal.

When it comes to choosing lenses, you must first have some idea of where you will be in relation to your subjects. A lens with a relatively short focal length is not a good choice for shooting subjects that you can't get close to, such as horses and riders in competition, or a mare and foal way out in a field. On the other hand, a lens with a long focal length (like a telephoto lens), will not be able to capture the entire subject when you are standing too close to it.

A staggering selection of camera lenses is available. To many photographers, choosing the right lens can be more difficult than finding a camera they like. The best way to determine what lens is best for you is to try as many as possible. Experiment. See what aspects you like, and what you can live without.

Lenses generally fall into one of the following categories: standard, wide-angle, or telephoto.

Standard camera lenses are intended to capture an image similar in perspective to what the human eye observes. These lenses generally have a 50mm or 55mm focal length. A standard camera lens is best suited for taking general, informal photographs.

Most *wide-angle* lenses have a focal length of 18mm to 35mm. These indispensable lenses have many uses. Because they expand both perspective and depth of field (see p. 30), they are essential when covering a large subject area, such as a side view of a six-horse hitch, or hunters in the field. They are well suited for landscape photography, and other nature scenes. They also lend themselves to photographing large groups of people or horses. Wide-angle lenses aren't just for outdoor use. They can also be employed for indoor photography, and used for close-ups.

Just as buying a $100,000 show horse will not make you a better rider, a digital camera will not make you a great photographer.

Telephoto camera lenses are the opposite of their wide-angle counterparts. The image, when seen through a telephoto, appears to narrow. Telephotos generally have focal lengths of 80mm to 500mm. The focal lengths may be fixed (or constant). *Zoom* lenses, however, allow you to change the focal length and magnify the image. Telephoto lenses are necessary for getting good shots from long distances. They are invaluable when photographing shows and other sporting events.

Some specialty lenses, like macros and fish-eyes, can provide you with additional image options—but they will probably not find regular use in your photographic endeavors. *Macro* lenses enable you to obtain extremely sharp focus and image clarity at very short distances. They lend themselves to detailed, close-up nature photography. *Fish-eyes* are extreme wide-angle lenses with focal lengths of 6mm to 16mm. They create obvious image distortion, making the final photograph appear "domed" or convex.

> Buying a camera that requires an unusual or uncommon battery can lead to trouble when your battery dies in the middle of shooting.

ADVANCED TIP: POWER TO GO

A power inverter is an easy and inexpensive solution to getting power on the go. The power inverter plugs into the cigarette lighter in your car and converts that power to AC current that you can then use to recharge your camera or laptop batteries. Power inverters are often a much more economical choice than purchasing specialized car adaptors for individual electronic items.

The wattage of all the items that you might want to recharge or use while on the road will determine the size of the power inverter you will need. For example, my laptop draws 70 watts and my camera battery charger draws 23 watts for a total of 103 watts. The 400-watt inverter that I have works just fine—with power to spare. It comes with two AC outlets and automatically shuts itself off when the car battery gets too low.

Batteries

With all the electronics in cameras today, having a consistent, convenient power source is critical. Ideally, your camera will use readily available batteries (AA is a common battery size) that can be purchased almost anywhere.

Buying a camera that requires an unusual or uncommon battery can lead to trouble when your battery dies in the middle of shooting. You must be prepared to carry fully charged spares of the special battery or have a recharger plug and power source available in the field.

Regardless of what type of batteries you use, find out how many photos can be taken before changing or recharging the batteries is necessary. If you plan to take a lot of pictures and a camera has a low ratio of photos to battery life, consider a different model. In addition, bear in mind that viewing images on the liquid crystal display (LCD) screen of a digital camera can quickly wear down the batteries.

Choosing Your Medium

Choosing the right film or digital media all depends upon how you plan to use your images. If you will need to make

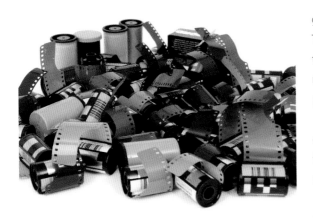

1. 14 Various color, black and white, negative and slide films.

generally calibrated for people and places—not horses. The operator knows that the grass should be green and the sky should be blue, but doesn't know how much red is in your chestnut horse's coat or how golden your palomino is.

If you intend to use negative film regularly, and the color of your horse is critical, I suggest that you become friends with your local photo lab and talk to the person doing your printing.

If you plan on submitting your photographs for publication in a magazine, newspaper, or advertisement, prints—even prints with perfect color—may not reproduce as well as slide film.

When a print is finally scanned so it can be used in the publication, the final image is several generations removed from your original. The first generation is the original negative. The print comes next, then the scanned image. The final, printed page is the fourth—or even fifth—generation, depending on the printing process. Each generation loses a little bit of information, color sharpness, and contrast. Furthermore, if the photograph was printed on textured paper, it further adds to the degradation of quality in the scanned image.

Slides/Transparencies

Slide film (or positive image) is typically used when photos are taken for slide presentations or reproduction in print, including magazines and advertising. Since using slide film eliminates the need for several generations of copies when preparing an image for publication, it results in a sharper, cleaner image on the printed page.

The colors in a properly exposed transparency will reproduce more accurately than those in a negative film. Slides also tend to have a sharper, finer grain than negatives. This makes them ideal for projecting large images while maintaining detail.

prints, then negative film is probably best. If you intend to send the images off to be reproduced in a magazine, you may prefer to use slide film. If you want to send the images as e-mails or place them on your Web site, digital imaging may make the most sense.

Film Options

When it comes to film, you have two choices: negatives or slides (also known as transparencies). Film is available in color or in black and white (Photo 1.14).

Negatives

Negative film, in which the image is captured in reverse tones, is best used if you plan to make prints from your photographs. Negative film also allows you to easily make photographic enlargements.

When working with negative film, bear in mind that when you have your negatives printed, the person or machine that prints your photographs has no idea what the actual colors are in that image. The lab relies on averages for the film type used, and the machine is

If you intend to use negative film regularly, and the color of your horse is critical, become friends with your local photo lab and talk to the person doing your printing.

Prints may be made from slides, but these typically cost more than those made from negative film, because some labs will make an inter-negative that is then used to make the final prints.

Black and White

Black and white film is not just for arty photography students. In certain conditions, black and white may be your film of choice.

In extremely difficult lighting situations, shooting in black and white can be a life-saver. It can produce enough contrasts to produce acceptable images in strongly back-lit conditions, with bright sun that would either wash out or overly darken images on color film. Also, if filming in mixed light (using a flash under neon, sodium, halogen, and fluorescent lights, with natural sunlight streaming through a window, for instance), black and white film offers a much more dependable outcome than color film.

An additional advantage to shooting black and white film is that it tends to produce the most flattering portraits. This is why actors and actresses often have their promotional photographs done in black and white. It evens out skin tones, minimizes blemishes and other skin defects, hides veins, and even softens the appearance of wrinkles. Slightly overexposing the film will result in a less detailed image—something many people "of a certain age" are pleased to see.

Film Speed

A film's "speed" relates to its light sensitivity. Both negative and slide film comes in various ISO (International Standards Organization) speeds from as low as 50 to as high as 6400. The lower the ISO number, the slower the speed, and the less sensitive the film is to light. The higher the ISO number, the faster the film speed and the more sensitive it is to light.

The size of the film grain has a direct relationship to film speed. The grain is typically finer and color saturation is better in slower speed films. The grain gets larger and color saturation tends to drop as the film speed increases.

As a general rule, ISO 400 color negative or black and white film is a good choice for an all-around film. It has a medium grain that allows for good close-ups and portraits.

If you want fine detail with vibrant colors in your photographs, or if you want to make very large prints, then a slower speed film is needed. On the other hand, if you are looking to stop action—such as during a sliding stop or when a horse jumps a fence—or if you have to shoot in low levels of light, a high speed film is indicated.

There is a direct relationship between the film speed and exposure. ISO 400 film is twice as fast as ISO 200, which is equal to one f-stop (see p. 19) of light (i.e., going from f/5.6 down to f/4 or 1/1000 to 1/500. As a rule, the slower the film speed, and the more light needed, the better the quality of the photographs produced. For a detailed explanation of exposure, aperture and f-stops, see chapter 2: Seeing the Light).

Going Digital

Digital "film" can be any kind of media that stores digital images, including compact flash, smart media, memory sticks, memory cards, secure digital/multimedia cards, XD media, CDs, or DVDs. Most digital cameras can only use one type of media, but some can use several different types.

Many digital cameras allow you to adjust the picture resolution of your images. This enables you to determine image quality to some degree. If, for instance, you are just taking a picture to remind yourself what something looks like, and have no intention of printing the photograph, it may make sense to set the resolution lower. But if you are shooting images that you intend to print and frame, use the highest resolution available.

Picture resolution is important when storing images on the camera's memory card. As a rule of thumb: the higher the image quality, the bigger its file size. This means that you can fit more lower quality images than higher quality images on a memory card. The bigger the card in your camera, the more images you can store on it before downloading to your PC becomes necessary.

Like film, all digital media is not created equal. Just because you find a 1 gigabyte card that is half the price of another does not mean it will perform in the same way. Digital media differs in how quickly information can be read, how fast it can be written to and from your camera, and in the speed that images may be transmitted to your computer.

Most digital cameras have a *buffer*, a place to store information for a certain number of files (frames) before writing the image information to the media. Media with a slow write time will take longer to write. This can prevent you from taking more photos until the writing has freed up space in the buffer.

Understanding Shutter Lag

If you want your horse to stop on a dime, you need him to give you an immediate response to your aids. The same holds true for trying to capture that peak-of-action photo: your camera needs to capture the image at the moment you press the button (Photo 1.15).

One question I'm commonly asked is why the user can't stop the action at a given instant. This is known as *shutter lag*, or the time that elapses between pushing the shutter release and the moment when the camera

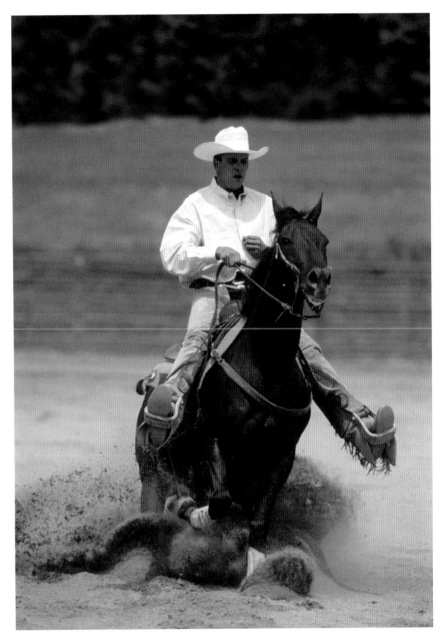

1.15 Cameras with little or no shutter lag allow you to capture the exact moment on film.

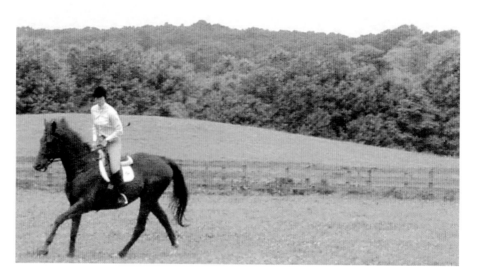

1.16 As you can see from this photo, the horse is almost running out of the frame due to the shutter lag on this point-and-shoot digital camera.

actually records the picture. The delay can mean not capturing the moment you were looking for or, worse yet, missing it entirely (Photo 1.16).

To illustrate, how many times have you tried to take a photo of a horse jumping a fence but only managed to get a really ugly picture of the horse with both front legs on the ground and the hind legs just inches from landing? Yet you pushed the button just as the horse was perfectly arced over the apex!

If the timing of your photographs is important to you, look for a camera with the shortest shutter lag. Ask the sales rep if you can take the camera outside and photograph a moving car to get an idea of what the lag time is for the camera you are interested in buying.

With some cameras, shutter lag can be reduced significantly if you depress the shutter release button halfway before actually taking the picture. This can "wake up" the camera and activate its autofocus system in order to capture a critically timed photograph.

Turning off the flash red-eye reduction feature will also make some cameras a little more responsive.

If you know how long the lag time is, you can sometimes anticipate when to push the shutter release button before your subject reaches the defining moment. But this is an imprecise method at best, and I would highly recommend testing it before you use it for any critical images.

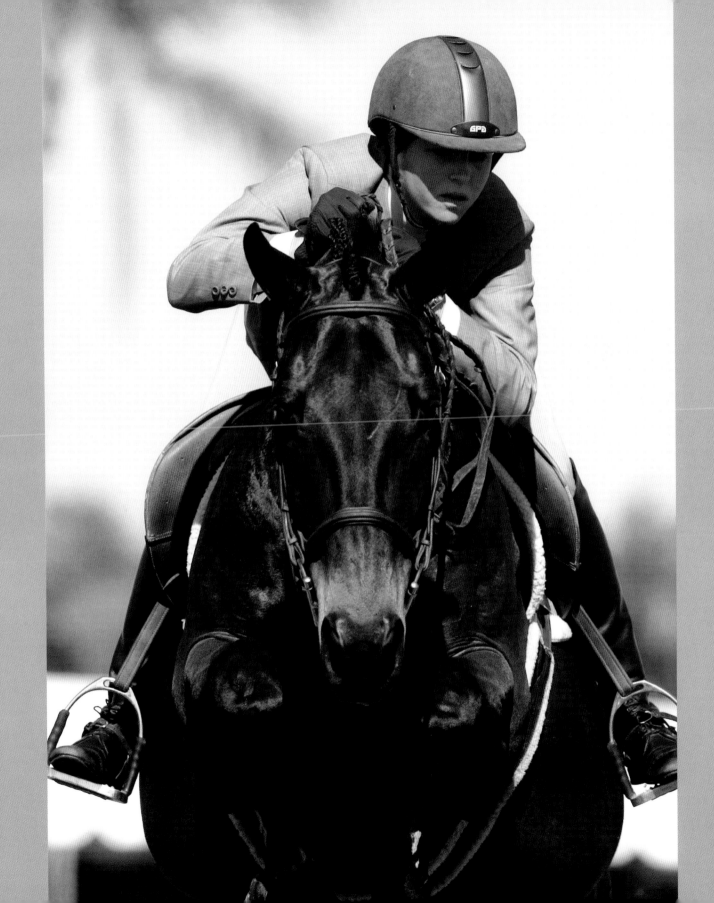

2

Seeing the Light

Photography is all about light. You need to make sure your camera receives the right amount and the right kind of light in order to make a good picture (Photo 2.1).

The word "photography" comes from two Greek words: "photo," meaning "light," and "graph," meaning "to draw." Photography literally means "drawing with light."

Drawing with light is not a new activity. In the late 1400s, Leonardo da Vinci utilized what was later called the *camera obscura*—a dark room with a hole in one wall that projected the scene from outside upside down onto the opposite inside wall—in order for him to make drawings from that image.

Without light, photography cannot exist. To make a good photograph, you need to have the right amount of light—or *exposure*—for that particular situation and media sensitivity (i.e., the film's ISO or the digital camera's ISO setting).

Exposure: The Right Amount of Light

Knowing the proper exposure for a particular situation is an important aspect of successfully taking an image (Photos 2.2 A – C). Determining how much light to let in is akin to knowing how much feed to give your horse: too much and he gets fat; too little and he gets skinny.

Without enough light, an image will be *underexposed*. It will be dark, with little or no detail in the darker or shadowed areas.

An *overexposed* image—one taken with too much light—will be too bright. Overexposed images are sometimes known as "washed out" photographs. They have no detail in the light or highlighted areas.

The *aperture* is a small hole enabling light to pass through the lens and enter the camera. Most cameras (except for very cheap disposables) allow for aperture adjustment.

The *f-stop* (sometimes called the *f-number* or *focal ratio*) is a way to express the aperture's diameter in terms relative to the lens' focal length.

The f-stop scale (f/0.7, f/1, f/1.4, f/2, f/2.8, f/4, f/5.6, f/8, f/11, f/16, f/22, f/32, f/45, f/64, f/90, f/128,...) is standardized on modern lenses. The slash indicates division, and numbers are rounded off for simplicity. For example, f/8 means that the aperture equals the focal length divided by eight. Therefore, if you are using an 80 mm lens, the light that reaches the film does so through an opening that is 10 mm (80 mm / 8) in diameter.

Shutter speed refers to the amount of time that the film plane or digital sensor is exposed to light. It is measured in fractions of a second. The higher the number, the shorter the amount of time that the shutter is open. Sixty means 1/60, or one sixtieth of a second. One thousand is 1/1000, or one thousandth of a second. (For a more complete explanation of shutter speed, see p. 25.)

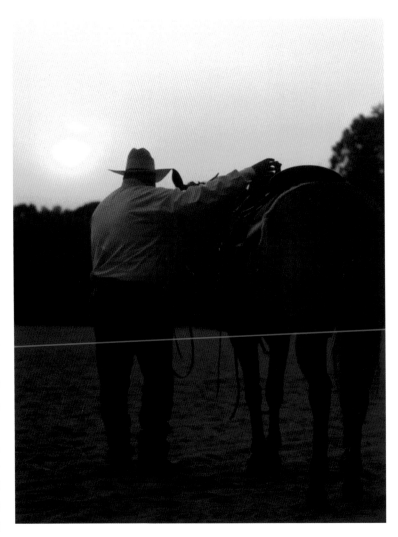

2.1 Knowing what light is available to you can make your photographs more interesting. Here, the setting sun illuminates this cowboy calling an end to his day.

One "step" in shutter speed corresponds to one f-stop. Increasing a lens opening by one f-stop means that twice as much light will fall on the film as before. In order to have the same exposure, you must allow the shutter to remain open only half as long, so you need a shutter speed that is twice as fast.

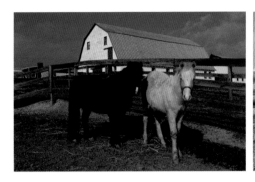

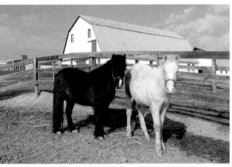

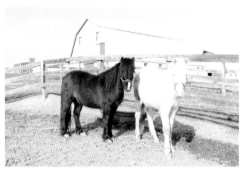

2.2 A An example of an underexposed image. Very little detail is visible in the shadows.

2.2 B This image is correctly exposed. Detail is apparent in both the shadows and the highlights.

2.2 C An example of the same scenario over-exposed. There is detail in the shadow areas but none in the highlights.

Photography is a balancing act. For every image you take, you will have to make decisions that require you to give up some things in order to gain others.

Any given situation has a specific light value, but a variety of exposures within that situation can produce a properly exposed photograph. To determine a correct exposure, you must take available light, f-stop, and film speed into consideration. Let's look at a common scenario:

Your horse is in a field, and the sun is behind you. Using ISO 200 film or an equivalent digital setting, you have all of the following exposure possibilities:

F-STOP	SHUTTER SPEED
f/2.8	1/4000
f/4	1/2000
f/5.6	1/1000
f/8	1/500
f/11	1/250
f/16	1/125
f/22	1/60
f/32	1/30

All eight of these exposures, though different, will give you a properly exposed image. In order to know the ideal exposure to use for that situation, however, you need to have some idea of how you want your final image to look (Photo 2.3).

Do you want to freeze the action? If so, then you might expose the image at f/4 at 1/2000—opening the aperture very wide for a very short time (.0005 seconds).

Or do you want to keep as much of the frame as possible in focus? That would require a greater depth of field (more on the subject on p. 30), so you would set the exposure at f/32 at 1/30. Such a setting allows a relatively small amount of light in, but the aperture remains open for .033 seconds—over 66 times longer than at 1/2000!

Photography is a balancing act. For every image you take, you will have to make decisions that require you to give up some things in order to gain others. Knowing the relationship between shutter speed and aperture and how they let in light, as well as understanding the effect of various shutter speeds and aperture settings on the final photograph, is an important part of your decision-making process.

Exposure Meters

No universal exposure will work all the time to give you a correctly exposed image. Whether you are outside in the daylight or in an indoor arena, your light values will change as the sun and clouds move, as you move, and as your subject moves.

Knowing how light affects your in-camera or hand-held exposure meter, in addition to knowing how your meter works, will help you determine the correct exposure for the image you are trying to create.

In-Camera Options

Your in-camera meter reads the light reflecting off your subject. In other words, it "sees" the brightness and darkness of the scene, and then determines the proper exposure based on averages and the settings you are using. In-camera meters typically have three settings from which you can select. They include *full frame* (sometimes known as *multi-segmented*), *center-weighted*, and *spot* meter settings (Photo 2.4).

The *full frame* or *multi-segmented* setting looks at the entire image to determine the correct exposure.

The meter divides the frame into a number of segments, and the camera then determines the brightness of each one. This allows the camera to look at each part of the scene so that no one segment will overly influence the overall exposure (Photo 2.5).

You can use this setting for most of your photographs, unless you have subjects that are extremely bright or dark, or are faced with tricky lighting situations. Then you need to use either the center-weighted or the spot meter setting.

The *center-weighted* setting looks at a predetermined area in the center of the frame (somewhere around 12mm) to determine the exposure (Photo 2.6). This center area

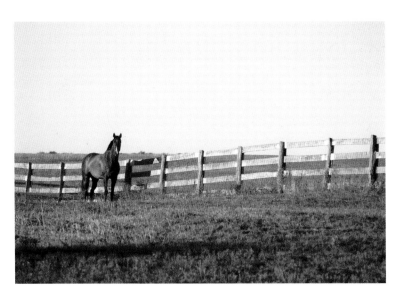

2.3 There are many exposure variations when photographing a scene such as this horse standing in a field. My final choice depends upon how I want the final image to appear, and how much of the fence I want in focus. I must also determine how fast a shutter speed I would need to freeze the horse's action, if he were moving, and take that into account.

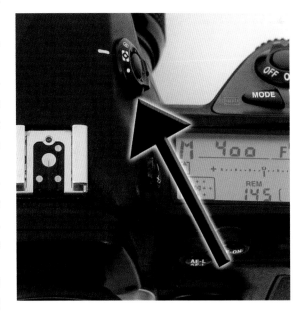

2.4 Light meter selection switch on a typical SLR camera.

ADVANCED TIP
SEEING SHADES OF GRAY

Older camera meters tried to make everything *18 percent gray*, which is neutral or middle gray in the photography world. When the camera detected the light reflecting off a gray horse, the camera wanted to make the horse darker. It would often automatically underexpose the image in order to make the horse that middle gray.

The reverse happened if a black horse filled the frame. Then, the meter wanted to lighten the entire photo in order to make the horse's color that middle gray.

When the frame was filled with a variety of light and dark tones that averaged to eighteen percent gray, you had a better chance of getting a properly exposed image.

Some higher-end SLR cameras now have smarter meters that read the color of a scene in addition to the brightness. These meters know the difference between the blue sky and the green grass. They know if your horse is gray or black or any other color. The camera manufacturers have taken the data from thousands of photographs and stored it in the camera's memory for it to refer to in any given situation.

Using the different program modes, the camera looks at only the data for that type of scene (landscape, portrait, night scene, or backlight, for example) to determine the proper exposure. Some cameras can get even more specific, and have program modes for situations such as snow scenes, close-ups, and even underwater photography.

Certain cameras also know what lens you are using and where in the frame you are focusing. This allows the meter to put more emphasis on that segment and properly expose your subject.

Though modern meters are more sophisticated, they are not always 100 percent correct. Consult your owner's manual to fully understand what type of metering system is in your camera, or ask the sales rep about the one you plan to buy.

can occasionally be made smaller or larger in the custom settings of some cameras.

This area determines 70 to 80 percent of the exposure. The remaining area outside the center-weighted pattern makes up the rest of the exposure. If, for instance, you have a large, white tent in the background or very bright sand footing, using this setting will keep your subject's exposure from being influenced, provided you keep most of your subject framed in the center-weighted pattern.

The *spot* meter setting looks at only one small area to determine the correct exposure. This allows you to have ultimate control, because you select the area of your subject that is most important, and the camera determines the ideal exposure for that small area (Photo 2.7).

Some cameras with *multi-focusing* sensors use these points for spot metering—thus, your focus point is your metering point. Some even have exposure and focusing lock buttons that let you lock in a spot meter exposure and focus point while you recompose your subject in the viewfinder.

A spot meter is very useful in difficult lighting situations, such as when your subject is strongly backlit, you are photographing a performer in a spotlight, or you have a scene with a lot of contrast (Photo 2.8).

Using an 18 percent gray card (readily available in any well-stocked camera store) and the spot meter will give you very accurate exposures.

Make sure the gray card is held vertically and is in the same light as your subject. This means that if you want to properly expose the shadow side of your subject, the card needs to be in the same shadow and not in the bright sun. With the card in place, take the meter reading and set the exposure. Then, remove the card and take your picture.

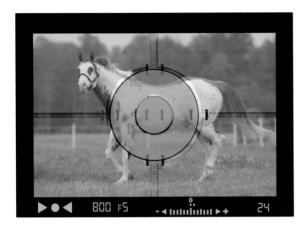

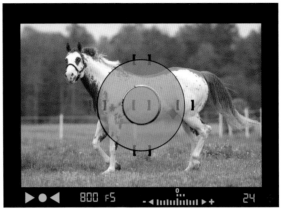

2.5 A sample of a *full frame* or *multi-segmented* meter and how it might look at a scene. Notice how the segments along the perimeter divide the frame into four equal parts, regardless of whether you hold the camera vertically or horizontally. The camera looks at the entire image to determine correct exposure.

2.6 When using the *center-weighted* meter, the camera bases 70 to 80 percent of the exposure upon the two circular segments in the middle of the frame.

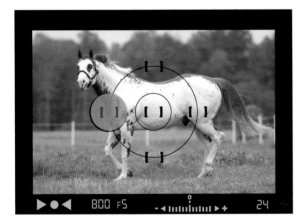

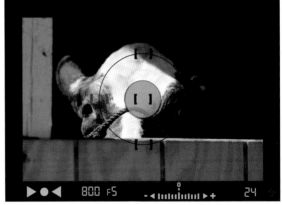

2.7 The *spot* meter pattern can be used to select the most critical area that you want properly exposed. Some cameras with multi-focusing sensors (red[ ]) use these same points for the spot metering (see p. 58).

2.8 An example of how the spot meter would come in handy. As this cow peers over the stall door, part of its head is in direct sunlight and the rest is in dark shadow. If I'd placed the spot meter in the middle of the frame, as it is here, my reading would be off. The cow's white blaze would have caused the image to be darker, and therefore underexposed. Instead, I placed the spot meter over a mid-tone to give me an accurate exposure for the area in the sunshine, then recomposed my subject.

ADVANCED TIP: THE F/16 RULE

When your light meter is not working (or you don't have one), you can always use the f/16 rule to estimate correct film exposure. To do this on a sunny day, simply set your camera's f-stop to f/16 and use the shutter speed closest to your film ISO speed. Less light requires a lower f-stop. If it is cloudy, use f/8. For heavy overcast conditions, use f/5.6.

For example, if you were using ISO 200 film on a clear day, you would set the f-stop at f/16 and choose a shutter speed of 1/250, since that is the number closest to 200.

You can change either your f-stop or your shutter speed, but remember to change the other to compensate (see chart below). Opening the f-stop to f/11, for instance, would require the shutter speed to be faster at 1/500th of a second.

F/16 RULE WITH ISO 200 ON A CLEAR SUNNY DAY

F-stop	22	16	11	8	5.6	4
Shutter speed	1/125	1/250	1/500	1/1000	1/2000	1/4000

Hand-Held Meters

Hand-held meters come in several different types and combinations. They include *reflected-light*, *spot*, *flash*, and *incident-light* meters.

The *reflected-light* meter reads the light that reflects off your subject, just as the built-in camera meters do. Like a full-frame camera meter, the reflected-light meter reads a wide area but can be influenced by a very bright or dark region.

The *hand-held spot* meter works in the same way as the spot meter on your camera. It looks at the light reflecting off a small area to determine the exposure.

The *incident-light* and *flash* meters read the light that is falling on the subject to determine the exposure. Incident-light meters measure the available light, while the flash meter reads the light from a flash or strobe and holds that exposure reading.

Both incident-light and flash meters use a 180-degree translucent white dome or flat disc and average the light falling on it. The dome is positioned to receive the same amount of light as the subject.

It helps to think of the dome as a person's face. If your subject is facing the sun and has little shadow, then the dome should have the same. If your subject is side lit, with half the face in the sun and half in shadow, the dome should have the same. You can also favor more or less light, depending on the look of your final image.

Incident-light and flash meters are not as influenced by bright or dark subjects as reflected-light meters are. You have to beware when taking the meter readings, however, that you are not affecting the light falling on the meter. If you are blocking any light or wearing bright clothing that reflects light onto the meter, you will skew the reading.

Every time you go out to take a picture, you must know what is most important about the image that you are about to take. Ask yourself these four questions:

1. *Do I need to stop any movement or action in the scene?*
2. *How much of the total framed image do I need in focus?*
3. *What am I willing to give up?*
4. *How much quality am I willing to sacrifice?*

As you can see, there are trade-offs to every picture. You can't have everything in focus and be able to stop the action unless you are prepared to sacrifice image quality by using high ISO film or comparable settings on digital cameras.

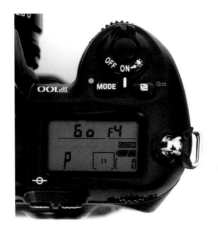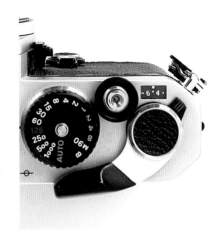

2.9 Examples of shutter speed dials. The new style digital readout (left) and the old-fashioned dial (right).

Shutter Speed

Remember, the length of time the camera's shutter is open to allow light to reach the film plane or digital sensor is known as the *shutter speed* (Photo 2.9).

A faster shutter speed is used to stop action. Speeds above 1/500th of a second will stop most horses' motion. Slower shutter speeds will not stop the action entirely. Use a shutter speed below 1/500th of a second and you will see some blurring of anything in motion. Once you start using speeds below 1/30th of a second, almost everything will start to get blurry, unless you use a tripod or other stabilizer (Photos 2.10 A & B). (For tips on shooting effective action shots, see p. 165.)

There are four primary factors to consider when selecting the proper shutter speed:

1. The speed at which your subject is moving.
2. The direction your subject is moving.
3. The focal length of your lens (more on this in chapter 3).
4. Your distance from your subject.

As you know, the speed of a horse at the walk is very different than that of a horse at full gallop. A slower shutter speed that stops a horse at the walk won't stop the motion of a galloping horse, but it may give you an interesting motion blur (Photos 2.11 A & B).

Because horses move at a variety of gaits and speeds, it is hard to say that a particular shutter speed will work for a particular gait. Only practice and experimenting will help you determine which shutter speed will produce what effects in your unique situation, using your particular camera, and the film or digital media of your choice.

As you consider shutter speed, realize that the direction in which the horse is traveling in relation to the camera is important. When a horse is moving across your field of view—from left to right or from right to left—it will appear to be moving faster than a horse heading directly toward or away from you.

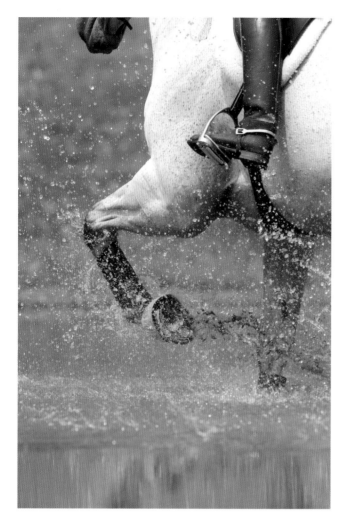

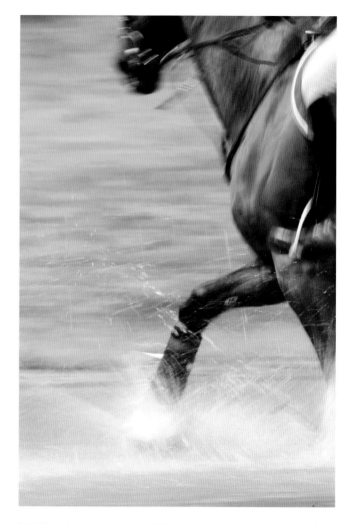

2.10 A A faster shutter speed will freeze the action, such as the water droplets seen here. This image was taken with a shutter speed of 1/1000th of a second.

2.10 B A slower shutter speed blurs the water drops as well as anything else in motion. *Panning*, or moving the camera to follow along with your subject, will keep the subject relatively sharp. Notice how the grass background shows more motion than the shoulder of the horse. This image was taken with a shutter speed of 1/25th of a second.

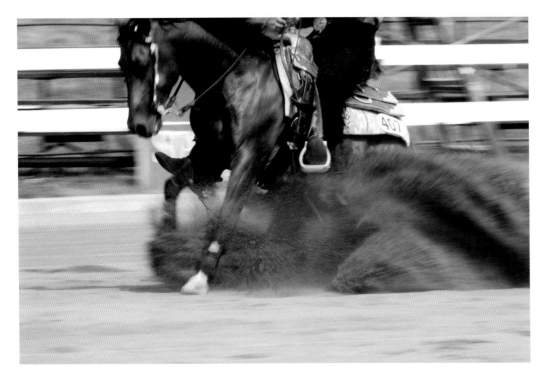

2.11 A The feeling of motion in this image was achieved with a shutter speed of 1/60th of a second.

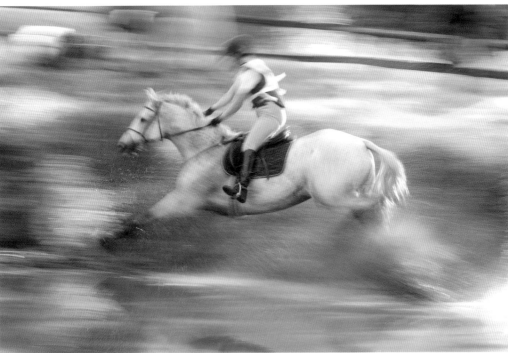

2.11 B A slower shutter speed can give you an interesting motion blur such as this horse going cross-country. This image was taken with a shutter speed of 1/15th of a second.

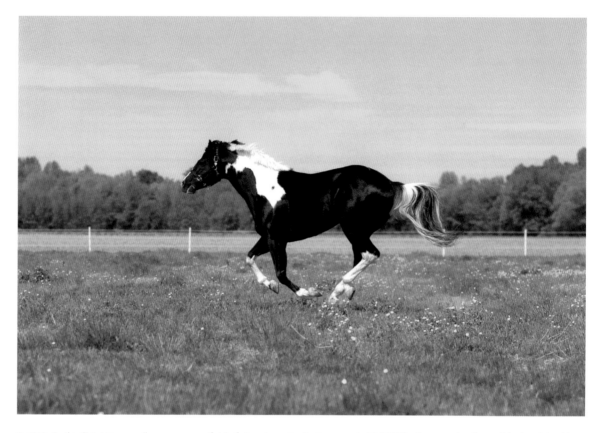

2.12 A As this Paint Horse gallops across my field of view, I need a shutter speed of 1/2500th of a second to freeze him in mid-stride.

A faster shutter speed is required in order to freeze the action as your subject moves across your field of view. However, a slower shutter speed can be used to stop the motion of a horse moving at the same speed heading directly toward or away from you (Photos 2.12 A & B).

You can use this principle to your advantage when you are in a situation that requires you to stop the action, but you don't have enough light to use a high shutter speed and you don't want to compromise the quality of the image with a higher speed film or a higher ISO setting on a digital camera.

Focal length plays a role in choosing your shutter speed. The longer the focal length of your lens, the larger your moving subject is on the film plane or digital sensor and the faster it moves across the film plane or sensor. Also, any movement when using longer focal lengths increases the chances of "camera shake" (Photo 2.13). Using a shorter focal length at the same distance makes the subject smaller so that it does not move across your film plane as quickly. To explore focal length more thoroughly, see chapter 3.

The distance between you and your subject has the same impact as the focal length. The closer you are to the subject, the larger the subject will appear and the quicker it will move across the film plane. The farther you are from the subject, the less motion will be detected.

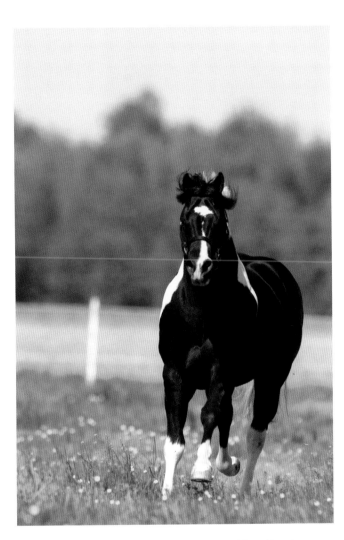

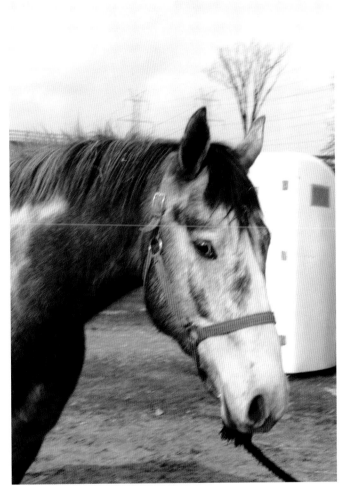

2.12 B As the horse comes toward me, I can stop him with a shutter speed of only 1/1000th of a second.

2.13 Be careful of camera shake when using low shutter speeds. Even at 1/90th of a second, camera shake is still a concern.

Depth of Field

Depth of field doesn't refer to how much acreage your pasture has or how tall the grass is in it! *Depth of field* refers to how much of the image in front of and behind your point of focus will be reasonably sharp.

A smaller aperture, or a higher f-stop number, equals greater depth of field and means that more of the scene will be in focus. The larger the aperture (or the lower the f-stop number), the smaller your depth of field, so less of the scene will be in focus (Photo 2.14).

In other words, a lens set at f/4 has a fairly wide opening, so less of the total image will be in focus. The same lens at f/32 will have a greater amount of the total image in focus (Photos 2.16 A & B).

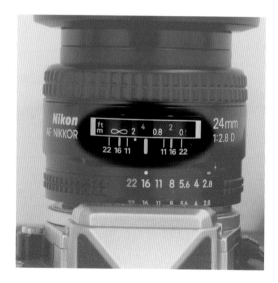

2.14 Camera lens showing aperture ring and depth of field scale. With this lens set for f/16, everything from a distance of 2 feet away, and extending out to infinity, should be in focus as indicated on the scale marked on the barrel of the lens.

UNDERSTANDING DEPTH OF FIELD

To understand how f-stop settings affect depth of field, perform the following exercise using a camera with aperture settings:

Stand next to a repeating object, like a fence row, or set up five evenly spaced cones or dressage letters along the length of an outdoor arena.

With your camera lens set to the largest opening (the lowest f-stop number), focus on the middle of your frame and take the photo.

Without changing your position (a tripod works best here) or focus point, change the aperture setting to the next smaller opening (higher f-stop number), change the shutter speed to the next slower speed and shoot the photo again.

Repeat, changing f-stops and shutter speeds, until you get to the smallest aperture setting.

When you look at the results of this exercise, you will see that the image taken at the lowest f-stop number will have only the object you focused on in focus. As the aperture gets smaller and smaller, and the f-stop number increases, more and more of the image will be in focus.

Your exercise should look something like this series of images (Photos 2.15 A – G).

In this series, I used a 200mm lens set at ISO 200 to illustrate how depth of field is affected by the different apertures. The smaller the aperture (the higher the f-stop number), the greater the depth of field. Notice how much more of the fence is in focus as the aperture gets smaller.

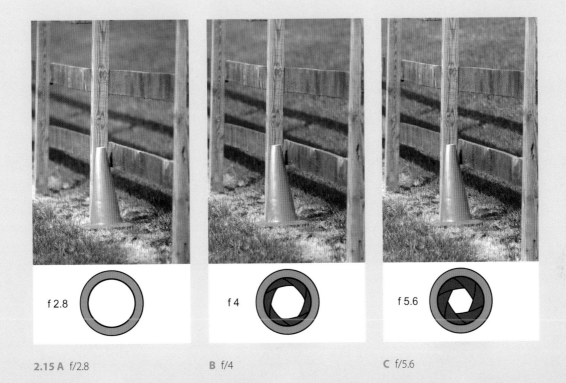

f 2.8

f 4

f 5.6

2.15 A f/2.8

B f/4

C f/5.6

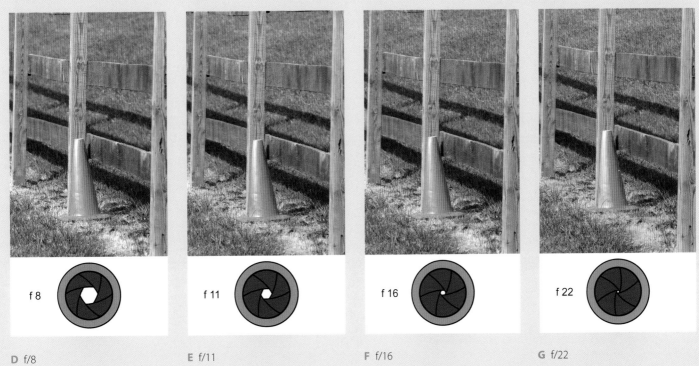

f 8

f 11

f 16

f 22

D f/8

E f/11

F f/16

G f/22

The smaller the aperture (the higher the f-stop number), the greater the depth of field.

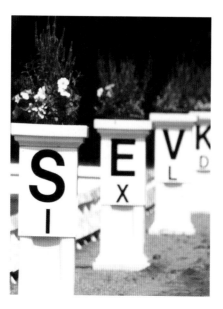

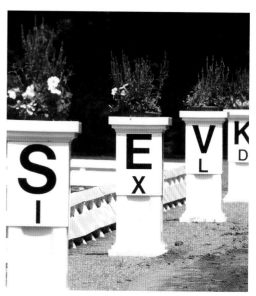

2.16 A A lens set at a larger aperture (lower f-stop number) will have less of the image in focus.

2.16 B A lens set at a smaller aperture (higher f-stop number) will have more of the image in focus.

A general rule of thumb is that one-third of the depth of field should be in front of the focal point (what you focused on) and two-thirds of the depth of field should be behind the focal point. To use that to your advantage when focusing on your subject, focus on the closest shoulder of the horse and rider in order to get both the horse's head and the rider's face in focus.

Qualities of Light

Understanding the different qualities of light is necessary in order to make sure you get the results you want in your photographs. When analyzing the characteristics of light, it helps to think in terms of "hard light" and "soft light."

Hard light—or direct light—brightly illuminates your subject and casts very defined shadows. A hard light is like the sun on a clear, sunny day. It is particularly useful for showing texture when the light is on the side of your subject (Photo 2.17).

A disadvantage of using a hard light is that it makes people squint. It also emphasizes wrinkles, blemishes, and minor imperfections.

Soft light, also called indirect light, is the type of light you get on an overcast or cloudy day. It casts less light on your subject and makes no clearly defined shadows. Soft light helps hide flaws. It "flattens" the subject because there are no defined shadows to show shape.

Soft light typically does not provide the same volume of light as hard light, so it requires slower shutter

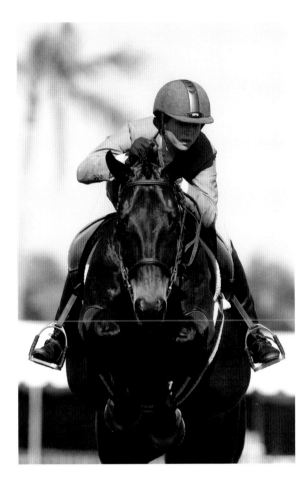

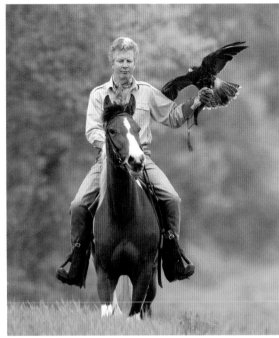

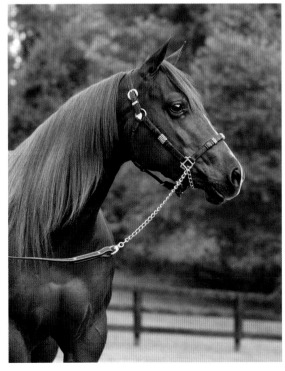

2.18 This image, taken on a cloudy day, shows the effects of a soft light source. There are no defined edges to the shadows, which produces a more even light on the subject and more detail in the shadowed areas.

2.17 An image taken in bright sunshine shows the effects of a hard light source. Shadows are well defined and there is a great deal of contrast.

2.19 This image was taken on a hazy day. There are some characteristics of both hard light and soft light. The shadows have a softer edge and are not as defined as they would be in hard light, but they are considerably more defined than in soft light.

speeds, wider apertures—or both—which may give a different look to your photos (Photo 2.18). In addition, soft light will not show the texture or definition of your subject, such as the muscles of your horse or the detail in the intricate tooling of a Western saddle.

When using terms such as "hard light" and "soft light," keep in mind that there are no absolutes. There are also many variations of light intensity. Your light source may be hard, soft, or a combination of the two (Photo 2.19).

Knowing the effects of hard and soft light on your subject will help you know which light to use to your advantage. Notice the difference in definition of the same horse photographed on both a cloudy day and a bright, sunny day (Photos 2.20 A & B).

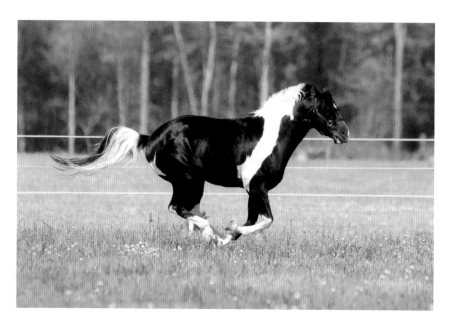

Hard light emphasizes wrinkles, blemishes, and minor imperfections. Soft light "flattens" the subject and helps hide flaws.

2.20 A The photo taken in hard light shows off the horse's muscle definition and makes his dark coat shine.

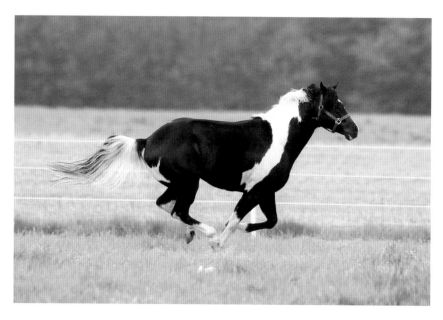

2.20 B The same horse photographed in soft light appears less defined and a little dull.

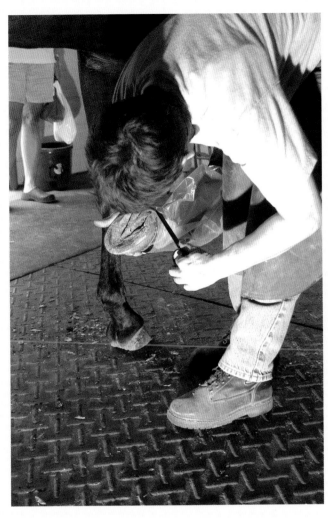

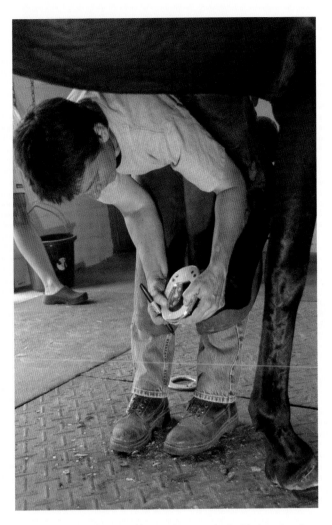

2.21 A This image of a farrier working on a horse shows what can happen when you leave the flash attached to your camera. You are limited to how you can orient the camera and flash.

2.21 B The same farrier and horse photographed with the extension cord attached to my flash. This allows me to place the flash in a better location to light the farrier as he works.

ADVANCED TIP: BOUNCING AND MOVING THE LIGHT

On some cameras, you can attach a separate flash unit that allows you to tilt the flash head up, to the side, or both. If you have a relatively normal ceiling or wall close to your subject, tilting your flash up or to the side enables you to bounce the light off that surface—creating a softer, more diffuse light. This reduces the shadows or covers a larger area with light. This technique is particularly useful if your subject is close to a wall and you don't want to see his shadow on the wall behind him.

You may wish to add attachments such as reflectors and diffusers to redirect or change the quality of the light. Doing so makes the flash an indirect source or a combination of both direct and indirect lighting.

On some higher-end SLR cameras, you have the option of controlling an off-camera flash, using either a wireless connection or a cord. This allows you to move the light to create a more unique image or to hide shadows in the background (Photos 2.21 A & B).

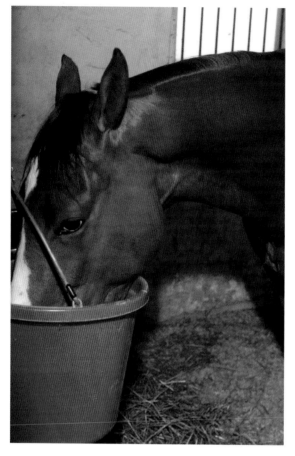

2.22 Sometimes you need to augment the available light with a flash, such as when shooting indoors or in a barn.

Using Flashes

When you do not have enough ambient light to get a properly exposed image, you need to add light (Photo 2.22). To do this you have several choices. You can do it with an on-camera flash made by your camera manufacturer or a third party. You can use an off-camera flash or strobes. Artificial lighting is another option.

Explaining the use of flashes, strobes, or other artificial lighting could fill several books. There are many good resources already on the market, if you want to read about these lighting options in more depth. Here, however, I will just touch on the basic features and settings.

The Inverse Square Law

The *Inverse Square Law* applies when adding a light from a point source such as a flash or strobe unit. The Inverse Square Law has to do with the intensity of light reaching your subject and what happens when your subject moves farther away.

Simply put, if you double the distance from the flash to your subject, the intensity of light that reaches your subject is not one-half, but one-quarter of the light's original intensity. Tripling the distance means that only one-ninth of the light's original intensity will get to your subject.

The Inverse Square Law is the reason why taking a picture with a flash often leaves the background dark.

For example, assume you have three horses: one 10 feet from you, another 20 feet away, and the third 30 feet away. If you take a flash photograph of the horse 10 feet away, only one fourth of the light will reach the horse 20 feet away. The horse 30 feet away will receive only one ninth of the light of the horse at 10 feet (photo 2.23).

Most of the point-and-shoot and consumer-grade cameras have a flash built into them. These flashes are typically not as powerful as those that are mounted on an SLR camera or those that are used off-camera. A practical application of the Inverse Square Law means that the distance a built-in flash effectively covers is much shorter than that of a larger flash unit.

Flash Position

Your on-camera flash is considered a hard light source. When used in normal situations, the flash casts direct

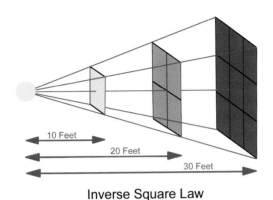

Inverse Square Law

2.23 This illustration of the Inverse Square Law shows how the light from your flash loses intensity as it travels.

light on your subject, causing hard shadows. This can be pleasing for some subjects, but it can be very unflattering for others.

Be aware of the location of your camera's built-in flash when taking a vertical picture. When the camera is held with the built-in flash at the bottom of the frame, you increase the possibility of casting unpleasant shadows upward behind your subject.

Always make sure the flash is at the top or at its highest point of the frame when shooting vertically. This way you minimize the possibilities of unflattering shadows behind and on your subjects—unless, of course, that is the look you're going for.

Flash Features

Most of the newer flashes, even those on some point-and-shoot cameras, have automatic settings to allow ease of use. Red-eye reduction and TTL ("through-the-

lens") settings are quite common (see below). More specialized settings and options for advanced work are readily available.

Some flash units have a prism/diffuser that needs to be placed over the flash head when used with a wide-angle lens. This spreads the light in a wider arc to cover the wider angle of view of the lens. Other flashes allow you to adjust them in order to govern the amount and quality of light output.

Red-Eye Reduction Mode

When set for *red-eye reduction,* the flash gives off several short bursts of light prior to the exposure. This causes the person's pupils to constrict, thus reducing the chance that the light from the flash reflects off of the subject's retina and causes "red-eye."

While this mode works effectively with human subjects, I have not seen it work very well on horses.

One of the drawbacks of using the red-eye reduction mode is the lag time between when you push the shutter button and the time the camera records the image (see p. 15 for more on shutter lag). If timing is critical, you can turn off the red-eye setting to decrease shutter lag.

One way to reduce the chances of red-eye is to move the flash as far away from the axis of the lens as possible. A cord that attaches to your camera at one end and your flash at the other will allow you to move the flash farther away from the lens (Photos 2.24 A – C).

Through-the-Lens (TTL) Mode

The *Through-the-Lens,* or *TTL,* setting means the camera reads the light that comes through the lens to reach the film plane or digital sensor. The camera then governs the output of the flash to create a correct exposure.

2.24 A A camera equipped with an extension cord for the flash. Such a set-up allows you to move the flash off the camera and place the light where you want it.

The TTL setting is fine when photographing people, but not for horses. Because horses are generally much darker—or much lighter—than people, you can't always rely on the automatic TTL program setting to properly gauge the exposure for your horse.

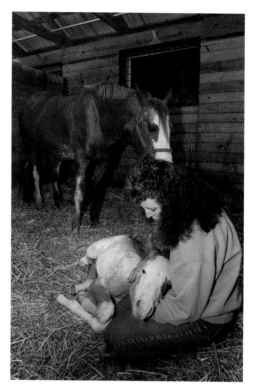

2.24 B Notice the red-eye in the mare.

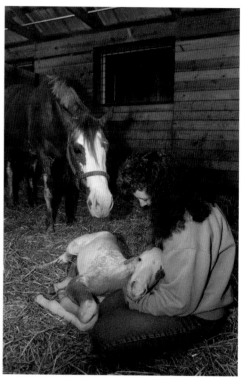

2.24 C Moving the flash a little off the camera lens axis reduces the red-eye effect.

In TTL mode the camera "knows" the distance to your subject. It knows where you are focusing, what lens you are using, and whether or not the flash head is tilted. Using TTL will produce good images most of the time, because the camera knows how much light should be required to properly expose the image.

The TTL setting is fine when photographing people, but not for horses. Because horses are generally much darker—or in the case of a gray horse, much lighter— than people, you can't always rely on the automatic TTL program setting to properly gauge the exposure for your horse.

Ideally, your camera will give you the option of overriding the flash to get a properly exposed image. This option is particularly useful when taking a picture of a gray

horse. Without an override, the flash might put out too much light and overexpose the horse, washing it out, and leaving little or no detail. With a flash you can override yourself, and you might want to *reduce* the amount of light by one stop or more. When photographing a darker horse, the TTL override allows you to set the flash to *increase* the output of light in much the same way.

Most flashes will tell you their optimum range, in distance of feet or meters, for certain settings. It is difficult to get the right amount of light on a subject that is 30 feet away if your settings will allow the flash to only produce the proper amount of light up to10 feet (Photos 2.25 A & B).

To increase the distance the flash will work, you may either use a faster speed film (or increase the ISO of your digital camera) or open the f-stop. Increasing the ISO makes the media more sensitive to light. Opening the f-stop lets more light in.

Advanced and Specialty Flash Settings

For those of you who remember the old days, when all you had were flash bulbs or flash cubes, you know how easy flash photography has become.

Lighting technology has progressed to a point where even amateur photographers can use fairly advanced flash features with great success. Some of these features include *aperture priority*, *manual*, *high-speed sync*, *rear curtain sync*, and *multiple*—or *repeating*—flash modes.

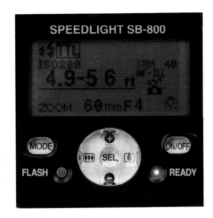
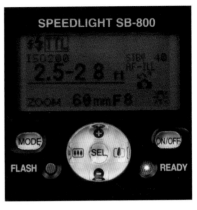

2.25 A This flash set on TTL, with the aperture set at f/4, has a range of 4.9 feet to 56 feet at ISO 200.

2.25 B With the aperture stopped down to f/8, the range of the flash is reduced. Now it will only reach from 2.5 feet to 28 feet.

Aperture Priority Mode

The *aperture priority* setting allows you to set the f-stop so you control the range of the flash output. This setting is ideal if you are taking a series of photographs within a controlled distance. To use the aperture priority setting, use the scale located either on the back of your flash unit or in the owner's manual to set the aperture and the flash to output only enough light to cover a narrowly defined range.

The flash typically does not fully discharge in this mode, so you have a faster recycling time. This, in turn, allows you to take multiple pictures more quickly.

Manual Mode

The *manual* setting is just as it sounds. It allows you to set the flash manually—telling it how much power you want it to produce.

The manual mode can be used for creative lighting situations. You can use it as a fill flash to eliminate dark, shadowed, or shaded areas on bright, sunny days. You can

also set it to output only 1/16th of its power to add just a little light onto your subject when doing close-ups.

High-Speed Sync Mode

The *high-speed sync,* if available on your camera, allows the flash to synchronize with the film at much higher shutter speeds than normal. This is very useful when shooting action at high shutter speeds. It is also useful when using fill flash on bright, sunny days and your exposure requires a high shutter speed in order to control the depth of field with a wider aperture.

Not all cameras allow for this mode. High-speed sync also requires certain camera and flash combinations. Check your owner's manual, or ask the store's salesperson, to see if this feature is available to you.

Rear Curtain Sync Mode

The *rear curtain sync* mode allows the camera to fire the flash right before the shutter curtain closes, instead of when it first opens.

If you have a fair amount of light on your subject, but not enough for a full proper exposure, using the rear curtain sync can give the illusion of movement. When you press the shutter release button and the shutter is open, the available light produces a streaking effect. The flash fires just before the curtain closes and properly exposes the subject. Freezing your subject while showing a streak of light behind it can be a creative and effective way to show motion.

Multiple (Repeating) Flash Mode

The *multiple*—or *repeating*—flash acts like a disco light. Remember the bouncing ball images from physics class, where you see the path of a ball in motion? You can achieve this look using the multiple flash setting (Photo 2.26).

In this mode, you set the flash to fire a certain amount of times during a given period. In addition, you can control the light output much as you can in manual mode.

Strobes and Other Off-Camera Lighting

Strobes and off-camera lights are used to illuminate a larger area, such as indoor arenas or barn aisles. Using them gives you the freedom to move around and be more creative with the lighting of your subject.

Strobes include a *head*, which contains the actual light source, and a power supply. They come in many styles, including a standard power pack with separate head (Photo 2.27) or a mono unit in which the power pack and head are combined. Strobes are available in a variety of physical sizes and power outputs. Most styles of strobe allow for attaching accessories to modify or direct the light output.

Off-camera light sources are available in a variety of sizes, as are the many accessories that can modify the light (Photo 2.28). Some models of off-camera flashes and strobes run on batteries. Others need a heavy-duty AC power source. Almost without exception, off-camera lights get very hot, so if you use them, be careful where you place them.

The main advantage of off-camera lighting options is the quantity of light these systems produce. They also allow you to use different add-on accessories—reflectors, gels, softboxes, and grid spots—to modify the light in order to get the final look you are trying to achieve.

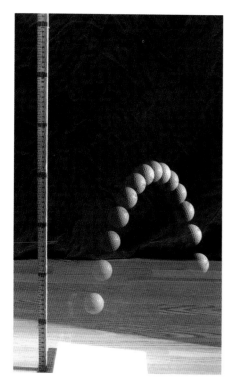

2.26 Using a multiple flash for your science experiment.

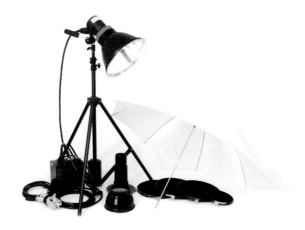

2.27 Strobes can be a very useful tool if you plan on doing a lot of indoor photography.

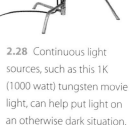

2.28 Continuous light sources, such as this 1K (1000 watt) tungsten movie light, can help put light on an otherwise dark situation.

I have found that using off-camera lighting, like strobes, produces a much better photograph than using an on-camera flash. The entire image is better lit, and I can typically use a slower ISO film or digital setting, which gives me a higher quality image.

In addition, despite what you might think, strobes are less distracting to the horse and rider than on-camera flashes. Since the strobe light typically comes from overhead, and lasts for a much shorter duration than an on-camera flash, I have found that most horses and riders are not spooked or distracted as easily by this type of setup.

For many years, I have photographed riders at the Washington International Horse Show—including the World Cup U.S. League Dressage Finals. The event takes place at the MCI Center in Washington, DC.

At this show, I rent the arena strobes and use the same setups that they use for professional basketball and hockey games (Photos 2.29 A & B). They have six 4,800 watt packs, with each pack powering one head. These heads are specially designed for a very short flash duration, so they give out a lot of light in a very short time.

The strobes have given great results and got little reaction from the horses and riders. In fact, I have only had one rider ever ask me not to use strobes when she was competing.

Off-camera lighting is definitely not a quick and simple method. Nor is it a cheap investment, unless you plan on using the lights often. These systems can be rented, but you must be sure you know how to operate them before you use them around animals or people. High voltage can be dangerous—even deadly—if not used or set up correctly.

You can light an entire arena with as few as four power packs and heads, but—depending on the system you purchase—they can be very expensive. Rigging the lights can also be a chore. In some cases, it takes several hours just to rig and position the lights to get the right effect.

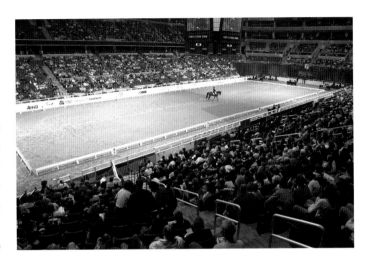

2.29 A An overall view of the MCI Center in Washington, DC, during the Washington International Horse Show. Note the shadows of the jumbo screen being cast on either side of the horse and rider.

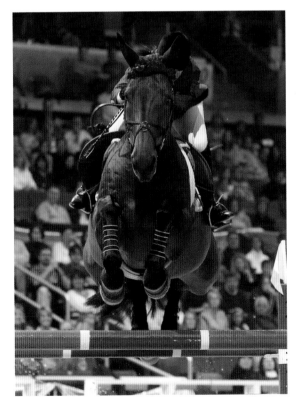

2.29 B Using strobes placed overhead gives the image a more natural look. It is also less distracting to the horse and rider than an on-camera flash pointed directly at their faces.

2.30 A An indoor arena without strobes or other off-camera lighting.

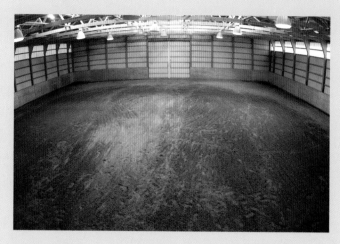

2.30 B The same view with the strobes in place.

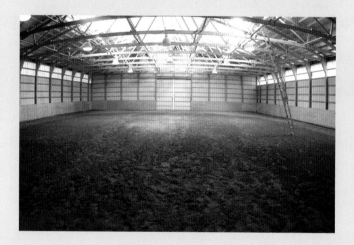

2.30 C From this angle, you can see how aiming the heads into the silver insulation of the roof diffuses the light falling on the arena floor.

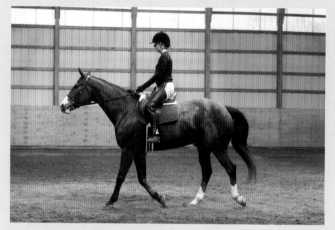

2.30 D One of the images from the shoot. The strobes give the same effect as arena lights, lending a more natural look to the images than an on-camera flash would provide.

INDOOR EXERCISES

EQUUS magazine once asked me to do a shoot to show indoor exercises that people could do in the winter. That meant shooting the photographs in an indoor arena, which can be a problem because the light levels are not adequate and the color temperature (see p. 43) of the light source does not render accurate color.

In this series of shots, note the difference that placing and positioning strobe lights can make to the overall lighting (Photos 2.30 A – D).

Artificial Lighting

Artificial lighting ranges from the available light in regular incandescent, halogen, or fluorescent light bulbs, to the sodium or mercury discharge lighting used in many indoor arenas.

The advantage of artificial lighting is that you can see the effect of light on your subject with the naked eye. Shadows, contrast, highlights, and other details are immediately and consistently visible under artificial lighting. To see the effects of strobes, on the other hand, you need to do test Polaroid shots with film, or view the images when shooting digitally.

The problem with artificial light is that it typically does not have the volume (or brightness) of strobes and, in turn, requires you to use higher speed films or ISO settings. Furthermore, the color temperature of artificial light sources is not the same as that required for daylight film.

KELVIN COLOR TEMPERATURE OF VARIOUS LIGHT SOURCES

(From warmer (redder) to cooler (bluer) values)

ARTIFICIAL AND NATURAL LIGHTING		COLOR TEMPERATURE IN DEGREES KELVIN (approximate values)
Candle flame	1,500	
100 watt light tungsten bulb	2,850	
Sunrise / sunset	2,000 – 3,000	
500 watt photo flood	3,200	
Warm white fluorescent	3,700	
Daylight fluorescent	4,800	
Noon sun	5,800	
Electronic flash / strobe	6,500	
Cloudy sky	7,000	
Northern sky	10,000	

Color Temperature

All light has a *color temperature*. Color temperature is the reason that artificial lights appear different colors when you view them from different locations or light sources. To illustrate this, leave the lights on in your house while you go outside right after sunset. Look at the colors of the lights in your house. Incandescent or tungsten lights will have a reddish-orange cast. Fluorescents have a greenish cast. High-intensity discharge lights are more orange-yellow in hue. (In most cases, discharge lights aren't very flattering to your subject because of the color of light they emit.)

Color temperature is measured in degrees Kelvin. Film color temperature is determined in relation to the *Kelvin Color Temperature Scale* (named after Lord Kelvin who, in the 19th century, discovered that when a carbon rod was heated it glowed with different colors at different temperatures).

All visible light has color. When determining color temperature, the higher the number, the "cooler," or more blue, the source of light. Strong daylight, for instance, has a high Kelvin number. The warm, red tones of candlelight, on the other hand, have a very low number on the Color Temperature Scale.

The chart above gives some examples of the Kelvin Color Temperature ranges from warm (candle flame) to cool (blue of the northern sky).

The human eye is great at adjusting to compensate for these color differences, but *film* isn't. (For *digital* see "White Balance," p. 45.) Furthermore, different films are

44

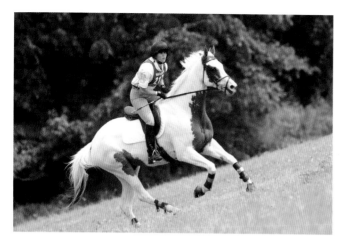

2.31 A The original image shot with a "daylight" white balance.

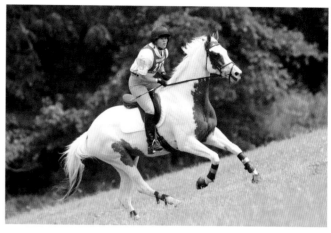

2.31 B Using a "cloudy" white balance setting yields this result.

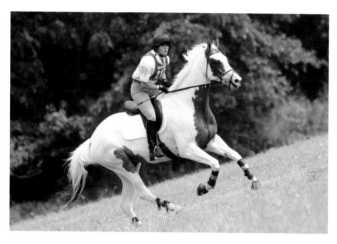

2.31 C This was shot with "shade" white balance.

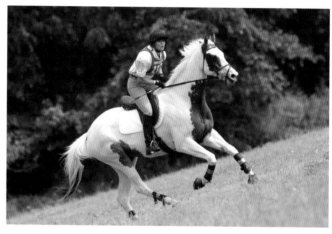

2.31 D Here, the white balance is on "tungsten," giving the same effect as using Tungsten film.

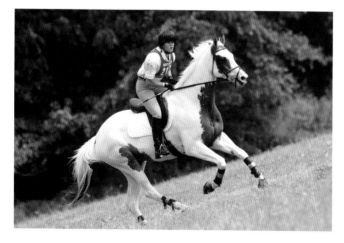

2.31 E This shot was set for "fluorescent" white balance.

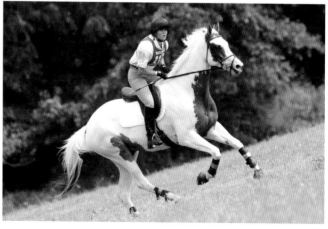

2.31 F Here, the white balance is set to "flash."

designed for certain types of light. Knowing the origin of your light source allows you to choose a film that is made for that light source.

Most film is *daylight balanced*, which means that it should be used outside during daylight hours, or with an electronic flash.

Some films have different types of emulsion for use under different lighting sources. *Tungsten film* is designed for use when your light source is a tungsten or incandescent light, such as a regular household light bulb. Some filtering may still be required to produce a neutral, naturally colored image.

In addition to capturing visible light, *infrared film* uses an additional layer to capture infrared light. Using infrared film can give an interesting and unusual look to your images.

If you are shooting in lighting conditions that do not match your film's color balance, you will need to use filters to correct the color. Some higher speed films have special layers within them to help correct for outdoor or stage lighting. Even these films might need additional filtering to correct for some situations where you are shooting under high-pressure discharge lamps.

White Balance

Digital cameras are especially sensitive to variety in color temperature. Fortunately, they are capable of correcting the color balance of an image electronically. You simply select the "white balance" setting for a given situation.

This feature allows you to tell the camera under what type of light you are shooting. The camera then automatically adjusts the color of your image to make it more natural.

If, for example, you are shooting under tungsten lights, setting the white balance for "Tungsten" instructs

the camera to adjust the color temperature to render the image correctly.

The series of images to the left shows the different color cast to an image if the white balance is not set correctly on your digital camera, or if you used the wrong type of film (Photos 2.31 A – F).

Filters

Filters are used to correct the difference between the film type and the light source, or to enhance or change the colors in a photograph. In addition, they help protect the front lens element from being scratched or damaged. It is much cheaper to replace a filter than have the lens repaired or replaced (Photo 2.32).

Do not use filters to correct for color when shooting digitally. Filters can negatively affect your digital camera's autofocus ability. Instead, change the color temperature in the camera or do it during postproduction.

Some of the most common filters are the *ultraviolet (UV)* and *skylight* filters. Both are designed to absorb UV radiation that the sun produces. Even though UV rays aren't visible to the naked eye, film and digital cameras

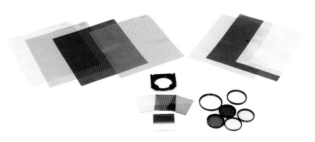

2.32 Filters come in a variety of shapes and sizes. Some fit on the front of your camera lens (front row). Others fit on your light source (back row).

can detect them. The skylight filter also has a slight amber cast that "warms up" the image and reduces the bluish cast that is often noticeable in open shade and on overcast days.

The *polarizing* filter is useful for removing reflections from nonmetallic surfaces, such as glass. Another benefit of using a polarizing filter is that it intensifies the colors in a scene, particularly the colors of blue sky and water.

Color correcting and *color enhancing* filters are popular choices.

The most common of the color correcting filters are special yellow- and blue-tinted filters used to correct between daylight balanced films and tungsten light, and vice versa (see sidebar).

Color enhancing filters enhance or exaggerate the colors in a scene. Some color filters are used to increase the contrast in black-and-white images.

In addition, there are filters to correct for various fluorescent light sources, filters to improve the contrast in black-and-white images, and filters to create special effects. These special effects filters can add drama to the image or add elements that are not there naturally.

ADVANCED TIP
CORRECTING FOR COLOR WITH FILM

When daylight-balanced *film* is used under a tungsten light source, the images appear yellowish. To correct for this, use a No. 80A filter that has a bluish tint.

On the other hand, if you take a tungsten-balanced film and shoot outside under bright sun, your images will have a bluish cast. The filter to correct for this is a No. 85B filter with a yellowish cast.

While the 80A and the 85B are the two most common color correcting filters, there are many other slight variations of these filters that will allow you to make minor corrections to the color of the final image.

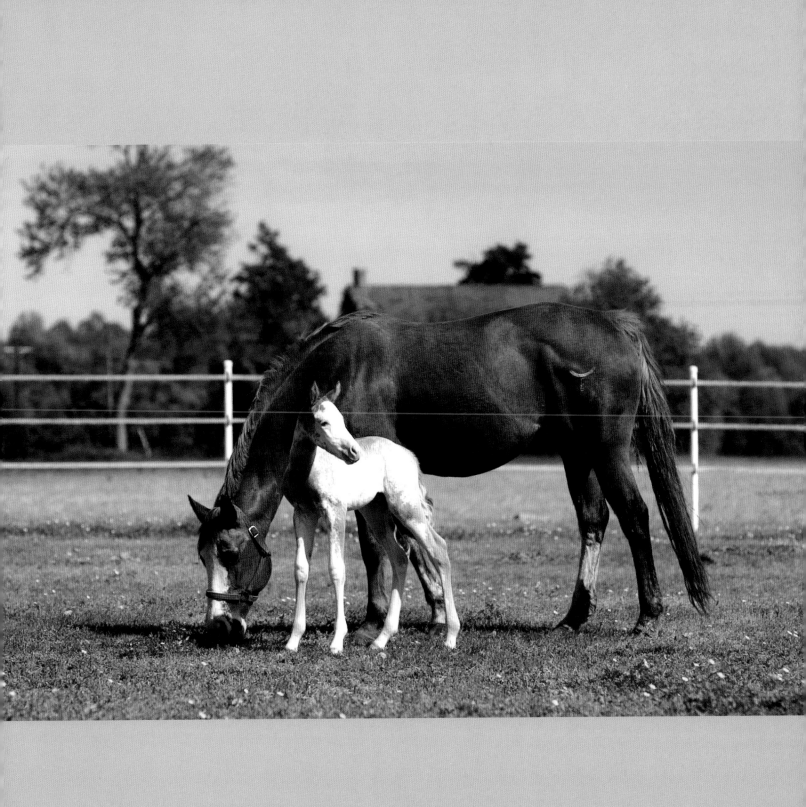

3

The Language of Lenses:
Getting Up Close and Personal

Choosing the right lens can mean the difference between a good picture and a great photograph. It is all too common to shoot a bucolic pasture scene, only to discover that after developing the film, you can barely recognize that the dark dot is a horse—let alone *your* horse (Photo 3.1).

Lens selection on today's cameras makes it easy to get closer to your subjects, whether they are out in the middle of a field or in the middle of a competition arena (Photo 3.2). In this chapter, you will see how different focal lengths can affect the look of your subject. You will also discover other factors to take into consideration when choosing and using different lenses.

Lens Basics

As I noted earlier (see p. 11), there is a wide variety of lenses and an even wider variety of features to choose from. Focal lengths range from the short 8mm fish-eyes at one end of the scale to the 1200mm telephotos at the other. You can even purchase adapters for telescopes!

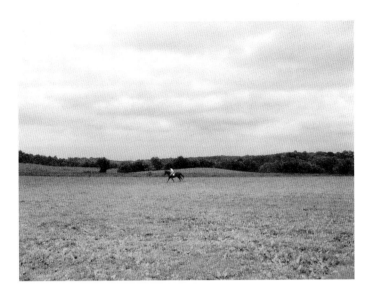

3.1 *Do I even know who that is? Is that my horse?* Choosing the correct camera lens combination will help prevent you from taking this kind of photograph.

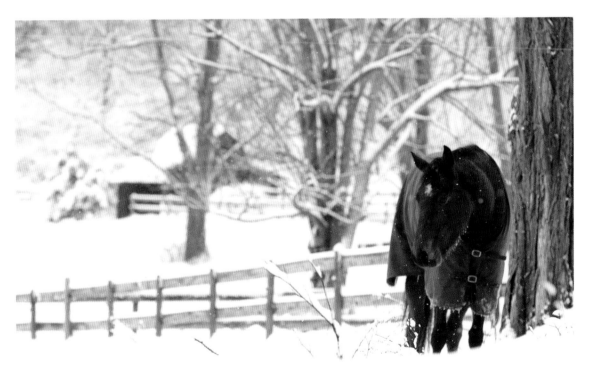

3.2 A combination of the right lens and cropping can help when you cannot fill the frame with your subject.

> A 50mm lens sees images in about the same way as our normal field of view. Therefore, if you use a 50mm lens and fill the frame with your horse, the horse should look proportionally correct.

ADVANCED TIP
THE F-STOP TRADE-OFF

An all-in-one zoom lens might sound like the perfect accessory, but remember that most of these lenses have a variable f-stop. While often less expensive than their fixed f-stop counterparts, they typically have a slower f-stop.

Take, for example, a 28~200mm zoom lens with a variable aperture of f/3.5 to f/5.6. At 28mm, this lens has a maximum aperture of f/3.5. At 200mm, its maximum aperture is f/5.6. The aperture varies as you zoom between the two.

When using an all-in-one zoom, keep in mind that the image in the viewfinder will appear darker at 200mm than it does at 28mm. Also, be aware that you will lose 1 1/3 stops of light in your exposure when shooting at 200mm.

Zoom vs. Fixed

To add to the choices, the range of *zoom* lenses is continuously increasing. Options include *super wide-angle, wide-angle, normal, telephoto,* and *super telephoto.* Some zoom lenses even combine several options in one. Zoom lenses—especially those in the last category—can be very convenient and compact, and can eliminate the need to carry a whole camera bag full of lenses.

Fixed focal length lenses are sometimes faster than zoom lenses. Faster lenses allow you to shoot in lower light situations. In addition, you might find fixed sizes that are not available in a zoom, like a fish-eye or super telephoto. If you have some of these specialty lenses available to you, don't hesitate to experiment with them. Though they may seem to have limitations, they can actually help you be more creative in your photography.

Effect of Focal Length

Remember, *focal length* is the distance from a lens to its focus. Your choice of focal length will affect the way a horse looks in the final photograph. In 35mm photography, a 50mm lens is typically considered "normal." This is because it sees images in about the same way as our normal field of view. Therefore, if you use a 50mm lens and fill the frame with your horse, the horse should look proportionally correct.

You can change the look of your horse dramatically, depending on the focal length of your lens and the angle to your subject.

If you use a wider-angle lens with a focal length shorter than a normal lens, and fill the frame with your subject, then whatever part of the horse that is closest to the lens will look larger than the rest of the horse (Photo 3.3).

Lenses that have longer focal lengths will give you a sort of reverse distortion. Therefore, whatever part of the horse is farthest from the lens will look compressed, or larger than it does in real life (Photo 3.4).

As a general rule, if you are doing conformation photographs, keep your lens selection between 50mm and 85mm to achieve an accurate representation of the horse. You can use a longer focal length lens for your conformation images as long as the horse is parallel to the film plane. This will also help you avoid distracting backgrounds. Moving from the parallel position, however, increases your chances of distortion.

If exact conformation is not important, a wide-angle lens is often a good choice to show the horse in its environment.

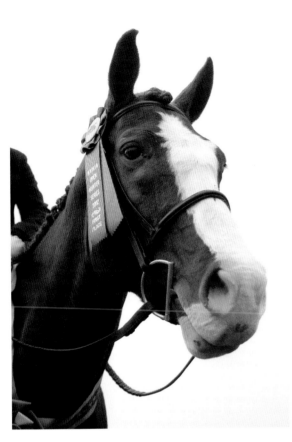

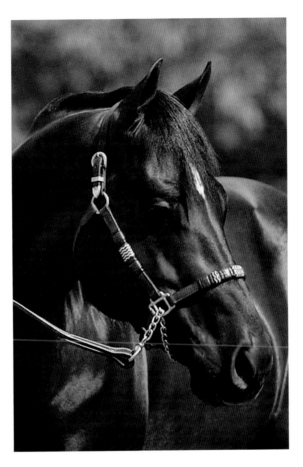

3.3 When using a wide-angle lens, be aware of the distortion that will happen when you get close to your subject. Notice how big the horse's nose is, compared to the rest of his face.

3.4 When using a long telephoto lens, compression can distort the horse. In this case the hindquarters look much bigger than they really are.

Angle of View

The angle of view differs for each lens. Knowing the angle of view of your lenses will help you decide which lens will be the best option for capturing the image you want. You can capture a pasture or landscape scene with a wide-angle lens, for instance. Or you can use a lens with a longer focal length to isolate your subject from the background.

The images on pp. 52 and 53 show what happens when you photograph the same horse with a variety of focal lengths (Photos 3.5 A – L). In each image, I tried to keep the horse's head roughly the same size in the camera's viewfinder.

Notice how the nose gets smaller and the hind end gets bigger as the focal length increases. In addition, note how the background gets closer and less defined as the focal length increases.

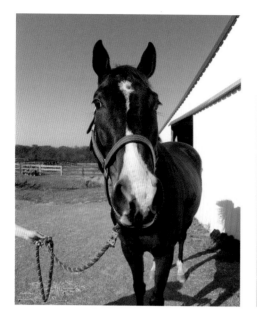

3.5 A A 15mm lens has an angle of view of approximately 180 degrees.

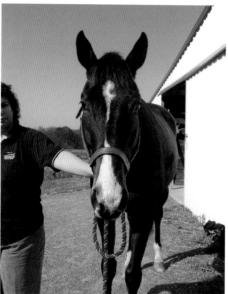

B 20mm ≈ 94 degrees.

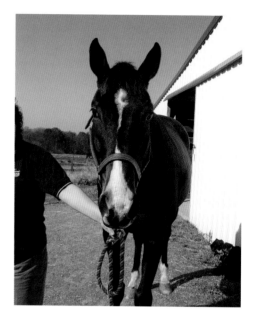

C 24 mm ≈ 84 degrees.

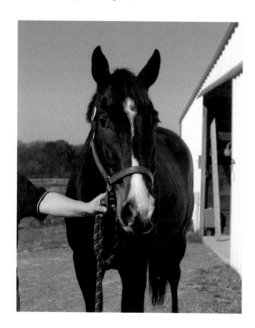

D 35 mm ≈ 62 degrees.

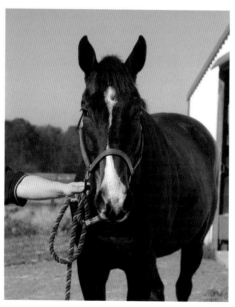

E 50mm ≈ 46 degrees.

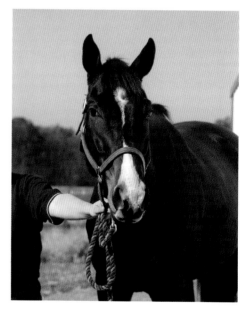

F 70mm ≈ 34 degrees.

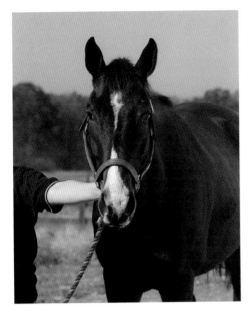

G 80mm ≈ 28 degrees.

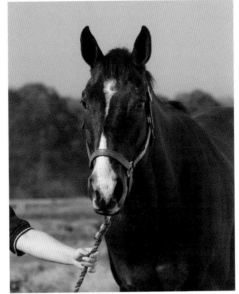

H 105mm ≈ 23 degrees.

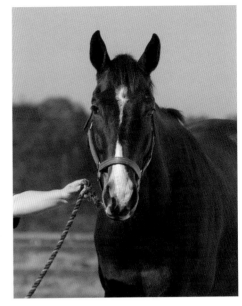

I 135mm ≈ 18 degrees.

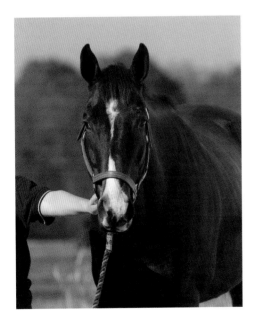

J 200mm ≈ 12 degrees.

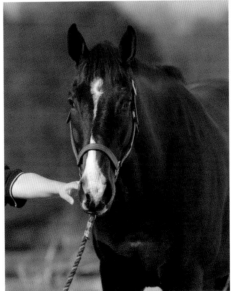

K 300mm ≈ 8 degrees.

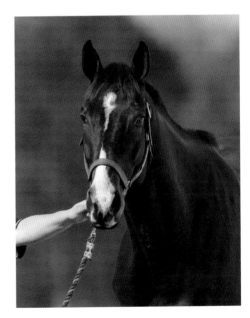

L 400mm ≈ 4 degrees.

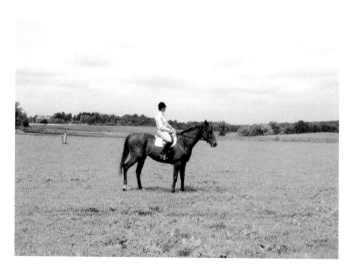

3.6 A This image shows the extent of the optical zoom of a point-and-shoot digital camera.

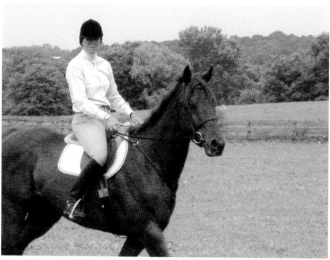

3.6 B This image shows the effects of digital zooming. Notice the "noise" or digital grain.

Understanding Optical and Digital Zoom

Many digital cameras feature both optical and digital zoom options.

The *optical zoom* is the actual zooming capabilities of the lens optics (Photo 3.6 A). Using the *digital zoom*, however, isolates a smaller area of the picture—and then stretches it to the full size of the sensor. Using a digital zoom requires the camera to interpolate, or make up, some of the pixels in order to produce an image. Such interpolation inevitably results in an image of lesser quality (Photo 3.6 B).

Let's say you have a 4 megapixel camera with a 2X digital zoom. Using the 2X digital zoom means that the camera will zoom in on a small portion of the image already captured on the image sensor and digitally enlarge it. The gaps in the image are digitally "filled in" to bring the image up to the 4 megapixel sensor size. This essentially turns your camera into a 2 megapixel camera (or one with half the resolution).

Just imagine what happens to an image with a 10X or greater digital zoom!

Zooming vs. Moving

The range of today's zoom lenses allows you to cover a lot of ground with one or two lenses (Photo 3.7). But zoom lenses are much more than just a means of getting closer to your subject.

You can use your zoom lens in many ways to give a different look to your photographs. For example, if you snap the image *while zooming in* tightly with a longer focal length lens, you can blur a busy background so that your subject gets all of the attention. You can also zoom out to the widest angle that your lens will go and then *physically move in closer* so your subject fills most of the frame. This technique is great for showing a horse and its surroundings.

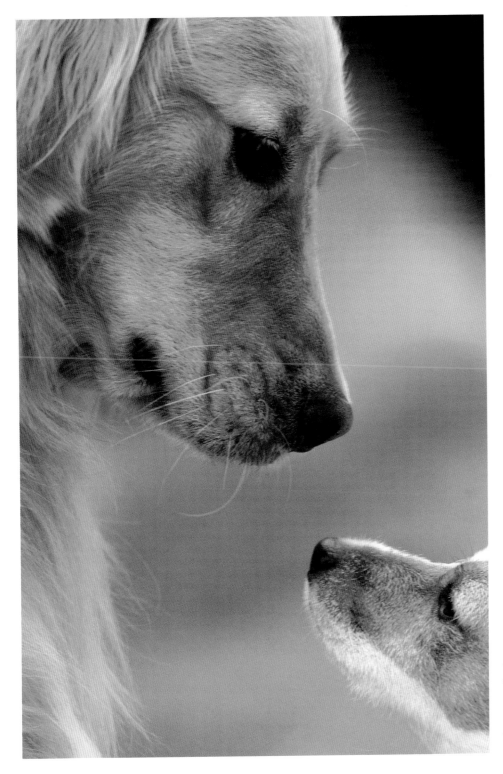

Zoom out to the widest angle that your lens will go and then physically move in closer so your subject fills most of the frame. This technique is great for showing a horse and its surroundings.

3.7 Using a longer telephoto lens allowed me to capture this moment between a Golden Retriever and Jack Russell Terrier. If I had used a shorter lens and tried to get closer, I might have distracted the dogs.

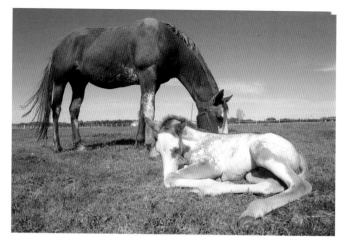

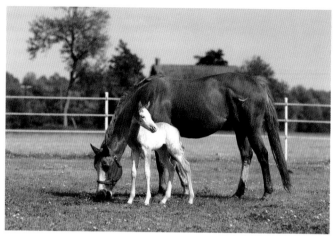

3.8 A Using a 15mm wide-angle lens makes it feel like you are sitting next to the sleeping foal. The fence line and buildings in the background are almost non-existent. The distortion from the wide-angle lens makes the foal seems much larger than the mare.

3.8 B With a 150mm lens, the mare and foal almost fill the frame. The fence line and buildings are more noticeable. Yet the proportions of the mare and foal are more accurate.

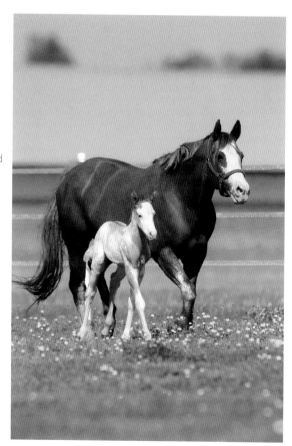

3.8 C Moving up to a 400mm lens isolates the mare and foal from almost everything else in the frame except for the yellow flowers immediately around the horses. The fence line and buildings, though bigger, are out of focus and do not distract from the subjects. The long telephoto lens compresses the image, making the hind ends of the mare and foal look larger than in the other images.

Various zooming techniques will produce a unique look, so experiment to see how moving and zooming will affect your final image.

The images on this page show how filling the frame using lenses with three different focal lengths gives three totally different looks to the same mare and foal (Photos 3.8 A – C).

Autofocus vs. Manual Focus

As technology advances, the newer generation of *auto-focus* cameras makes taking pictures of horses in motion relatively easy, because the continuous autofocus setting of the camera will track the movement of your subject. This is achieved with an internal computer that can calculate the direction and speed of a moving object and then anticipate where that object is going—thus keeping up with its movement.

Autofocus can encounter some problems, however, with subjects that move erratically or change directions quickly, as with horses performing in cutting or gymkha-

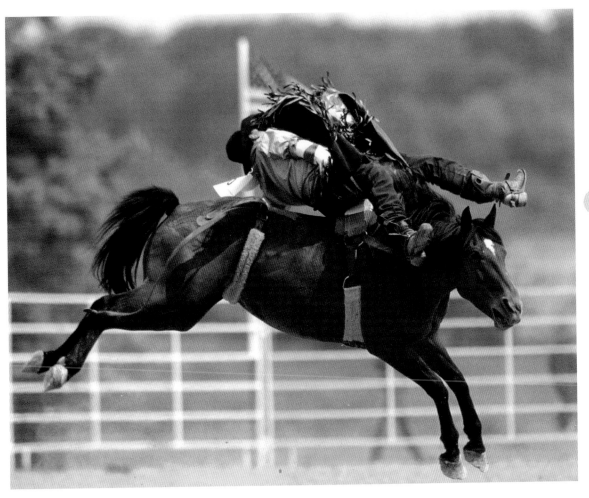

3.9 When photographing a subject that does not move in a predictable manner, you may have to switch from autofocus to manual focus.

Autofocus can encounter problems with subjects that move erratically or change directions quickly, like in cutting or gymkhana. Any type of radical direction change makes it difficult for the autofocus to keep up.

na. Any type of radical direction change makes it difficult for the autofocus to keep up (Photo 3.9). For this reason, you will need to manually focus your images from time to time. Knowing whether you should focus *manually* or trust your autofocus can be a difficult decision.

Most autofocus SLR cameras have three focus settings: *manual, single,* and *continuous* (Photo 3.10).

The viewfinder provides a number of different focusing indicators that the camera uses to select a point

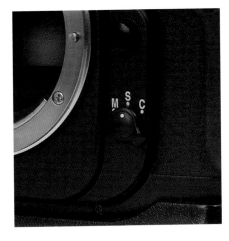

3.10 Autofocus selector switch.

of focus. If more than one indicator shows up, you can tell the camera which one you want to use. Some cameras even have custom settings for both the autofocus and the indicators to give you more options (Photos 3.11 A – D).

The manual focus setting allows you to manually adjust the point of focus of your subject. This can be useful if you are doing some creative work or framing and the autofocus does not focus where you want it (Photo 3.12).

Pre-Focusing

Whenever you have an obstacle that blocks the line of sight to your subject, yet you know where the subject will appear, you can *pre-focus,* either manually or using the focus lock in autofocus, at the point where you know the subject will be when you want to take the photo.

Pre-focusing is extremely useful when photographing a hunter/jumper show or cross-country events, where the horse is often blocked from view until he is over the obstacle. You can pre-focus on the jump and wait until the horse is jumping over it to take the picture (Photo 3.13).

You generally have two *autofocus* settings to choose from—*single* and *continuous.*

Single autofocus allows you to focus at a point on a stationary subject. Depressing the shutter release button halfway (and keeping it depressed) holds the focus. In some cameras, pressing the AF button, then locking the focus, activates the single autofocus (Photo 3.14). Consult your owner's manual to see if your camera has this option.

Single autofocus is similar to manual focus, but the camera does the focusing. Sometimes when using single autofocus, the focus might change to where the focus indicator is pointing, instead of remaining on your subject after you take the picture. Keep this in mind, as you might have to refocus for each exposure.

Continuous autofocus means the camera is constantly focusing as you hold the shutter release halfway down, or after you have pressed the AF button to activate the autofocus. This allows you to focus on a moving subject without losing focus.

Some cameras have multiple autofocus points that you may select. They tell the camera what part of the viewfinder you want to remain in focus.

In addition, some cameras have smart technology that can actually track your moving subject even if it leaves the indicated autofocus area—which is very useful when photographing any type of action. Your camera's owner's manual will tell you whether your camera has this ability and, if so, how these settings work.

Using Tripods and Monopods

Camera shake causes a blurry photo due to any small movement of the camera or lens at a shutter speed too slow to freeze the movement. When holding the camera by hand, a general rule is that your shutter speed should be equal to or greater than the focal length of your lens. For example, a 200mm lens should have a shutter speed of no longer than 1/250 to prevent camera shake.

Tripods and *monopods* are designed to help stabilize your camera and lens to prevent camera shake when using very long lenses or shooting at slower shutter speeds.

A *tripod* is a three-legged stand that can support the camera without being held. It helps steady a camera, particularly when using slower shutter speeds. Cameras with long lenses can also benefit from the use of tripods, because the long lens magnifies any movement of the lens, no matter how slight.

A *monopod*—a one-legged camera stand that the user supports—is commonly used with long lenses. A monopod essentially does the same thing as a tripod, but allows the user more portability and is not self-standing.

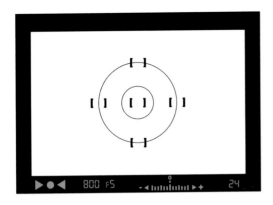

3.11 A This sample viewfinder shows five focusing sensors ([ ]) positioned around the center of the frame.

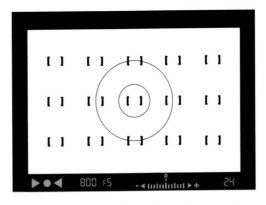

3.11 B This sample viewfinder shows fifteen focusing sensors ([ ]) spread around the frame, allowing more options for composing your images.

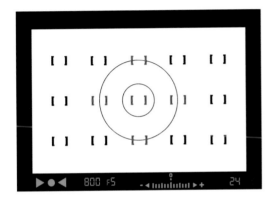

3.11 C The higher end SLR cameras have custom settings that allow you to select a cluster of focusing sensors (red [ ]). This tells the camera to shift the focusing point automatically so that it follows your moving subject.

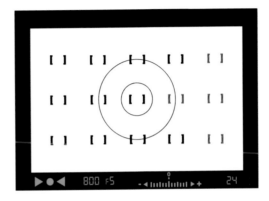

3.11 D Another example of a cluster of sensors that might be selected (red [ ]).

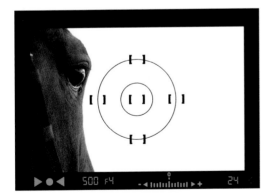

3.12 In this example, none of the focus sensors ([ ]) is over the horse. The autofocus would then try to focus on the sky. To avoid this, you may want to switch to manual focus.

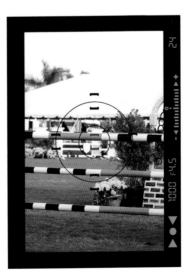

3.13 This sample viewfinder shows how I would pre-focus on the center of the top rail.

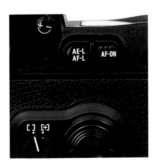

3.14 The Autofocus button (AF-ON) on the right, and the Autofocus and Auto-Exposure Lock button (AE-L AF-L) on the left.

When using longer lenses, you can use either a tripod or a monopod. Some people only use a tripod. For my photography work, however, I prefer a monopod because it allows me the freedom to quickly move to set up my next shot. Try both and see what you feel most comfortable using.

To eliminate camera shake when holding the camera by hand, a general rule is that your shutter speed should be equal to or greater than the focal length of your lens.

STOP THE SHAKE
THE CABLE RELEASE

Some SLR cameras have a mirror lock up feature, which moves the mirror to the "up" position before you take the exposure to eliminate its movement from shaking the camera.

Even without this feature, an accessory that is helpful when using long exposures is a *cable* or *remote release*. The cable release eliminates the need to touch the shutter release button and removes a potential source of camera shake.

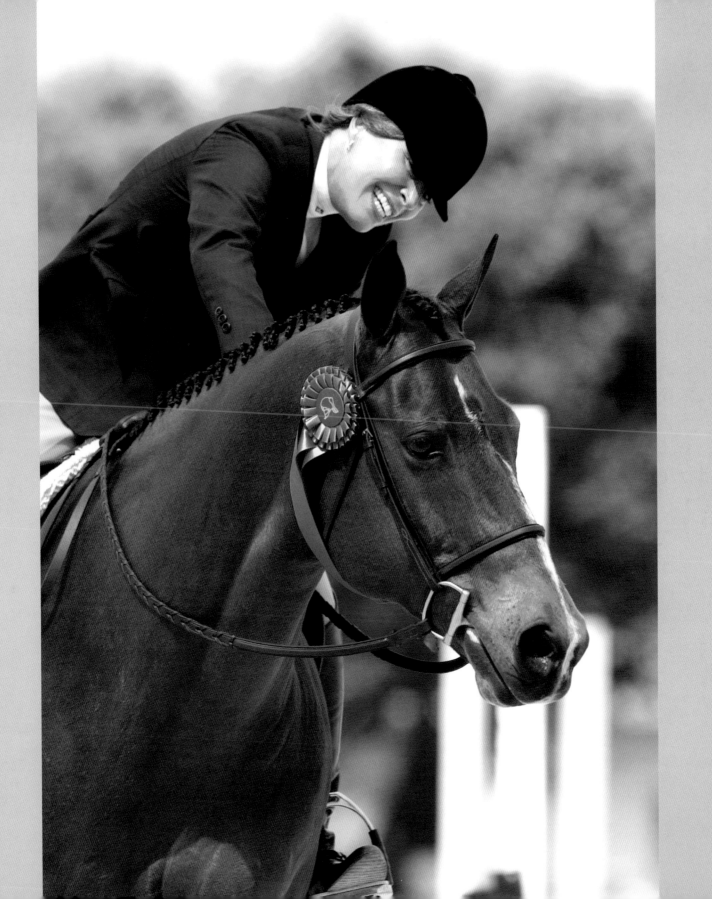

4

Planning the Perfect Shoot

Carrots Anyone? Getting Your Subject's Attention

Though humans decide when a photo shoot will happen, the horses involved have no say in the matter. Fortunately, it is amazing what you can get a horse to do with a little bribery.

Have plenty of carrots, apples, grain, sugar cubes, or other treats on hand to get and keep your horse's attention (Photo 4.1). When doing posed photos, there isn't much worse than having your horse pin his ears back and ruin an otherwise beautiful shot.

While treats are invaluable, be careful about the amount you give a horse. I find that some horses get fixated on the treats and will do nothing but try to get them, making photographing them tricky. So use treats sparingly.

If you give the horse anything to eat, make sure your assistant wipes off the horse's mouth. You wouldn't want to have your portrait taken with spinach in your teeth (Photo 4.2)!

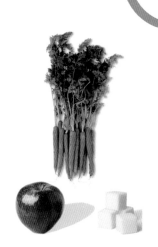

4.1 Carrots, apples, sugar cubes, and other treats will work to keep your horse's attention. Just don't overdo it with the treats, or the horse will be thinking only about them.

Other items to have on hand to help get your horse's ears up are things like training clickers, party noise makers, plastic bags, pompoms, small flags, squeaky toys, film canisters filled with gravel, a handful of grass, small stones or hay, reflectors, dogs, cats, other horses, whips, and mirrors. Keep in mind, however, that some of these items may spook the horse, so always start out small and work your way up. It's important to have several different things with you, because a horse—just as a child—can get bored very quickly.

Details, Details!

Before you pull out the camera, check the details. Make sure you take the time to clean the horse and any tack you plan to use. If you are going through the trouble of a photo shoot, you might as well make sure everything looks nice (Photos 4.3 A & B). The only thing worse than a beautiful photo with the horse's ears back is an otherwise beautiful portrait of a dirty horse with hay in his forelock and a big, green manure spot on his cheek!

If a human will be in the image, make sure he or she is wearing a clean, pressed shirt, his hair combed, and her makeup done. Also pay attention to small things, like making sure the handler doesn't have dirt under his nails or hay in her hair.

It helps to have someone in addition to the handler available to assist you. Having an extra set of hands to

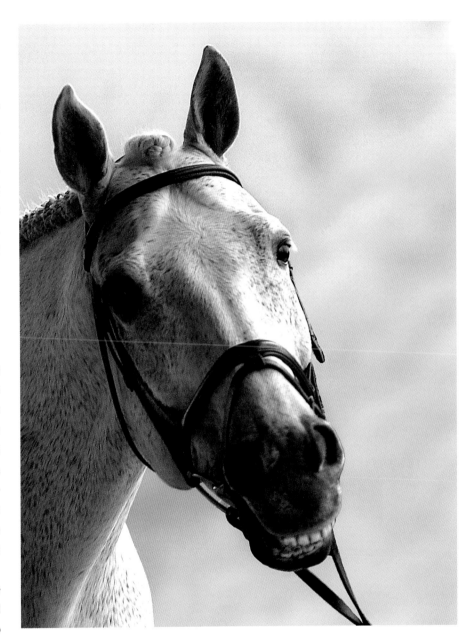

4.2 Even "Foot" agrees with the whole idea of working for treats and food.

Make sure to wipe off the horse's mouth. You wouldn't want to have your portrait taken with spinach in your teeth!

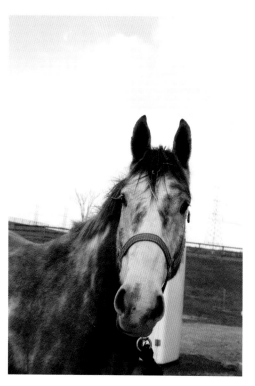

4.3 A   Taking a little time to clean up your horse before you take his picture will make a world of difference. In this photo, the horse is dirty, the halter is old, grass is hanging in his mane, and the background is cluttered.

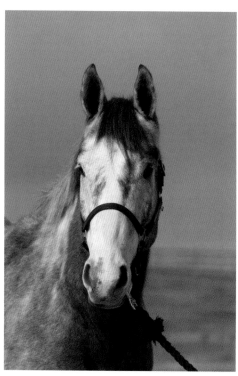

4.3 B   This image, taken about 15 minutes later and about 30 feet to the left, shows how a little cleaning, a new halter, and being aware of your background can make a big difference in your photographs.

work on keeping the horse's ears up, and another set of eyes to look for anything out of place, is invaluable. Your assistant can be anyone—a friend, spouse, child, groom, owner, or rider.

The person who assists you plays a key role in getting the horse's attention and directing—to a point— where the horse stands or looks. Your assistant should also be comfortable handling and moving the horse around for you. You need to be free to observe the horse as he moves, in order to find other flattering or interesting ways to photograph him.

Background Checks, Port-a-Potties, and Power Lines

"Location, location, location!" doesn't just apply to buying real estate. Placing your subjects in the proper environment can make or break a photograph.

Try to find a location that is most natural to the horse and rider. See if you need to pick up any manure, trash, or anything else that will take away from the image. Taking a couple of extra minutes to look around and find a nice location will make a significant difference in your photographs.

MAKING THE MOST OF LOCATION

I was asked by a tack manufacturer to photograph Laura Kraut and her horse Anthem during the Washington International Horse Show. The client wanted the shot to look like a country setting. The event takes place in early fall, downtown, in the middle of nothing but concrete, glass, steel, and tents. Furthermore, I could not take either horse or rider too far from the show grounds.

I went outside to scout a location, and the only thing I could find was one lone tree along the sidewalk next to the MCI Center (Photo 4.4 A). So I grabbed my 300mm lens, Anthem, Laura, and her groom, and we headed outside.

I made sure that the groom had carrots, treats, a brush, and a towel. I lined up Laura and Anthem about 20 to 30 feet from the tree. Then I lay on the ground to hide the street traffic behind them. We had to stop every couple of frames to let people and horses pass by, because we were in the middle of the sidewalk (Photo 4.4 B).

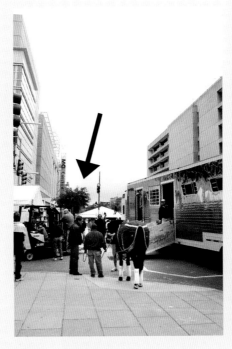

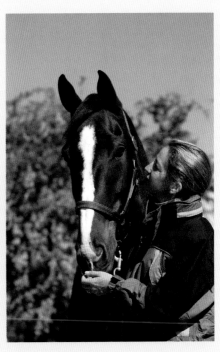

4.4 A Outside the MCI Center during the Washington International Horse Show is a hub of activity. Horses are constantly coming in and leaving. This, coupled with the regular street traffic, not to mention the concrete, glass, and steel buildings all around, made it difficult to find a spot to shoot this image request. The arrow is pointing to the lone tree that I had to work with.

4.4 B One of the images from the shoot. The horse was constantly distracted by everything going on outside. Here, he is looking at the groom who was standing just off to my left with treats.

Examine your background as well, looking for things that could distract from your subject. Be aware of things like telephone poles, light posts, or power lines that appear to be coming out of the horse's or rider's head. Also, be on the lookout for trailers or other farm equipment, port-a-potties, buildings, and the like. You don't want stray items in the photograph to steal the attention away from the horse—unless, of course, there is a reason for them to be there (Photos 4.5 A & B).

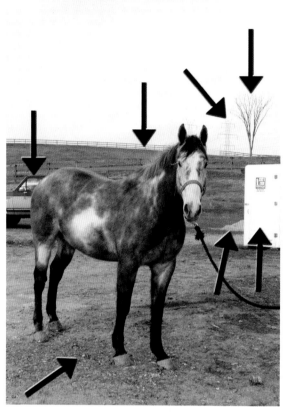

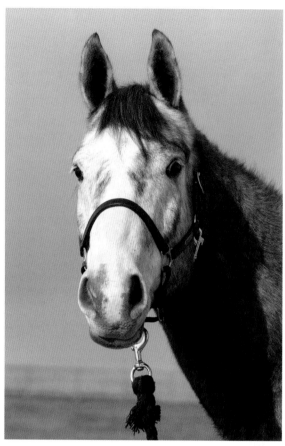

4.5 A Take a minute to examine the surroundings before you spend a lot of time photographing your subject. In this image, I have indicated seven things that distract from the main subject: the horse. Beginning with the pickup truck and moving clockwise, notice the fence line through the horse's head, power lines, a tree, a port-a-potty, a manure pile, and the gravel and dirt area along the barn.

4.5 B Because this was taken during early winter, there were no good grass areas to use. So I decide to crop in on the horse's head and neck. I moved over about 30 feet, and that eliminated most of the other distracting items. Using a longer lens also helped soften the fence line in the background.

Another aspect of your environment to take into account is the color of your background. You want a background color that complements or contrasts with the color of your horse. A gray horse against a darker background will make the horse stand out more. A dark horse placed against that same dark background will get lost. Look for colors, textures, and patterns that will help make your horse stand out, but will not be so busy that the background distracts from your horse (Photos 4.6 A & B).

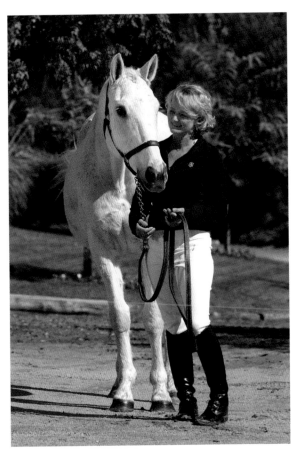

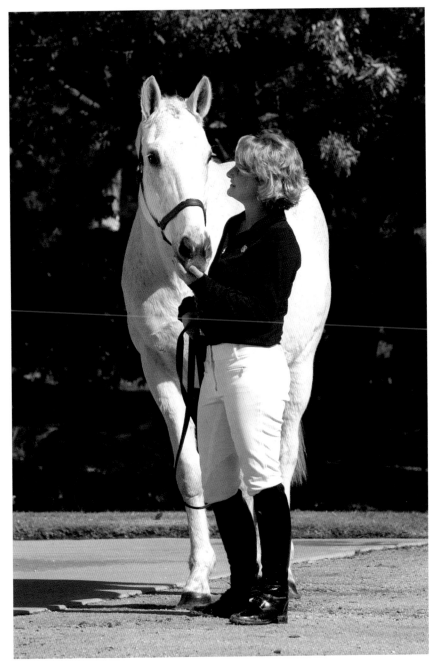

4.6 A When choosing your background, try to use a color that complements or contrasts with both the color of your horse and the handler's attire. In this image, the gray horse looked fine against the green foliage, but the girl's top started blending into the shadow areas.

4.6 B In this image, I moved the subjects over to make the horse "pop" from a darker background. I then placed the girl against the horse as her own background. This did two things. First, it separated the girl from the darker background. She also blocked the left side of the horse's body that was in direct sun and getting overexposed.

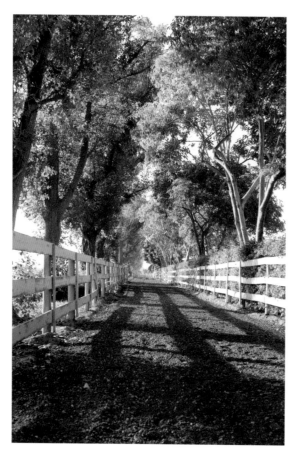 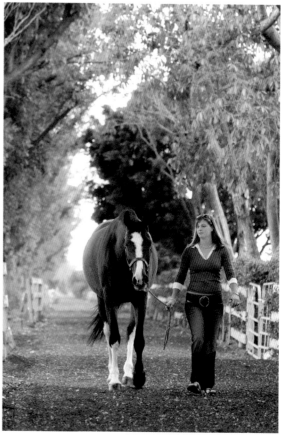

4.7 A Walk around a couple of days before shooting and try to visualize your subjects in different places. Take a few pictures of the location to refer to later. Here, for instance, I noted that this was looking south and was taken early in the morning. I should get the same effect later in the day as the sun sets.

4.7 B The same location later that day. The only change was that it got overcast and cut down on the amount of light. This actually worked out better because the contrast was not as extreme as it would have been if the sun were out.

Take pictures of the location without your subjects in the photograph. This will give you a reference of what the backgrounds might look like. It will also give you a chance to carefully look over the location to see if you need to make any changes.

If you are really serious about capturing a perfect photograph, looking for a location should be done a couple of days in advance and at several different times during the day. This allows you to see how the light changes the look of the place and will help you plan your shot list (Photos 4.7 A & B).

Preparing and Planning a Shot List

It is good practice to prepare a shot list before you head for an important shoot. The time you spend on the details beforehand can be an invaluable aid in assuring that the actual photo session runs as smoothly as possible.

A *shot list* outlines what you plan to shoot. It itemizes the various shots that you and the horse's handler feel will best illustrate the subject. It notes the horse's tack, handler's clothing, and any special "props" that each shot will require. It also provides an estimated time frame for preparing the horse, handler, and lighting for each shot.

If at all possible, take the time to talk to the rider, handler, or owner well before a formal photography session. Asking a few general questions about a horse's talents and strengths can yield a great deal of usable information. It can help you transform a routine session into one that yields extraordinary images.

Ask what specific attributes of a particular horse the images should highlight. The people involved with the horse may not know exactly what they want from the photo shoot. But they do know what they love about their horses. For instance:

▶ If the horse has an unusually long, full, flowing mane and forelock, you might wish to plan some shots that emphasize his head and neck.
▶ If the horse performs advanced maneuvers or works well at liberty, find out what types of action he does best. Plan to capture some of that action on film.
▶ If the horse is used for breeding, ask if any offspring are available for photographing. Many potential breeders would welcome the opportunity to see a multi-generational image.

Write out a sample shot list before you begin filming. Then, during the session, look for the chance to cross things off the list. When an opportunity presents itself, make the most of it even if it is out of sequence with what you had planned. You never know when—or if—the situation will arise again.

Smooth Sailing

Your preparation and attention to detail will help shots of formal, standing poses go smoothly. Advance preparation will also pay off when shooting "posed" action shots (as opposed to shots that happen during an event or competition), regardless of whether you are shooting a hunter/jumper or a barrel racer.

Take the time to scout out your location. Move any jumps or barrels that you need into the light and make sure they are away from any distracting backgrounds. Have the arena dragged before and during the shoot, depending on the amount of traffic.

Also, don't forget to clean up the jumps or barrels. Tell the owners and handlers that a fresh coat of paint on any obstacles to be photographed is best. At the very least, they should have the benefit of a good scrubbing with water and a stiff brush.

If you are shooting a camera on anything but automatic settings, before bringing your subjects in and beginning the shoot, take some exposure readings of your situation so you can determine the required shutter speed and f-stop.

Earlier, we discussed what you are willing to give up in your photograph (see p. 25). Now is the time to envision how you want your final image to look. Ask yourself:
▶ *How much depth of field do I want?*
▶ *What is the safest shutter speed to use to prevent movement of the horse or to counter camera shake?*
▶ *What lens am I going use?*

Be prepared. If you plan on using more than one lens, make sure all your camera accessories are close by.

4.8 When checking over the horse, try to have someone present who is not always around that horse. Fresh eyes might notice problems with things that the regular handler has grown used to seeing—like the halter being too big, as it is here.

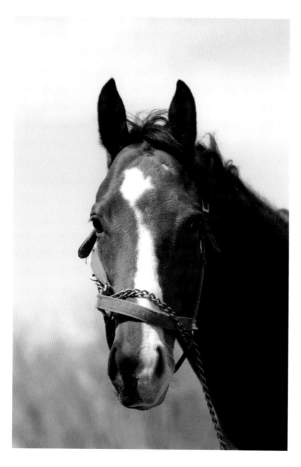

Be prepared. If you plan on using more than one lens, make sure all of your camera accessories are close by. If your subjects plan to change tack or change clothes, have everything handy and readily available before you begin. (Also, don't forget those treats and attention-getters.)

When you have everything ready, set up the shot. First, give your subject(s) a very close once-over. Do one more wipe of the horse's mouth and nose. Check the hooves, tail, mane, and tack. Everything should be clean, groomed, and ready for the shoot (Photo 4.8).

"Just Relax"

Whether you are doing award presentations, conformation shots, casual photographs, or formal portraits, a naturally posed subject looks best on film.

When you're behind the lens, try to keep the shoot as simple as possible, depending on the horse and the rider. Talk to the horse's owner to see what the horse likes or dislikes. Find out what the handler likes or dislikes. Chit chat about anything from the horse's breeding and accomplishments, to a favorite horse, to the weather.

The point is to try to make the subjects look relaxed. Be open to gaining new information that will help you get a great image.

If possible, when working with a horse and rider on the ground, start out photographing the rider without a hat or helmet on so "helmet hair" isn't an issue. This also keeps the subject from getting too sweaty. Another advantage is that you won't have to worry about the hat casting a shadow over the person's eyes. These images typically require a tighter crop on the face and provide a more intimate portrait.

You'll find that even the most relaxed person stiffens up once a camera is around. Interacting with the horse is an easy way to get the handler to relax, which makes the horse relax, too.

Ask the handler to pat the horse, talk to the horse, or interact in some way. Once you see that both horse and human are comfortable, ask them to look at the camera for the testimonial shot.

If you notice the person or horse getting stale, encourage the two of them to connect again. Repeat this process several times until you are reasonably certain that you have the image you want (Photos 4.9 A & B).

The same approach holds true if the person is mounted. Having the rider play with the horse in an af-

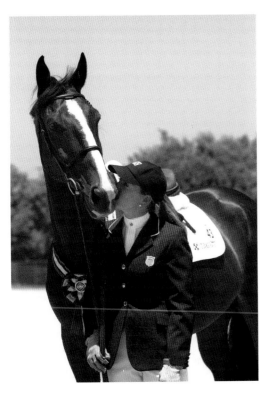

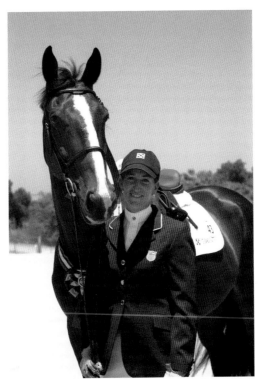

4.9 A Interacting with her horse Anthem allows Laura Kraut to loosen up and look more relaxed.

4.9 B After giving her horse a kiss, Laura is more comfortable for a few more frames.

fectionate way makes for some very nice casual portraits. To accomplish this, ask the rider to give the horse a big hug, rub on his neck, or play with the ears or any other "sweet spot" (Photo 4.10).

As the shoot progresses, have the horse and person move around so you capture them from different angles. This also encourages the person to drop his guard and you might catch a nice moment. You don't want to always have your subjects facing straight at the camera. It can make for a nice change to have the horse or rider looking off into the distance.

Again, once both subjects are comfortable, ask them to look at the camera for the formal shots.

Sweet Serendipity

Try to be aware of everything that goes on during a shoot, because some of the best moments are those that aren't planned. As the handler is circling the horse or moving to a new location, be ready to take pictures of unscripted moments. Both horses and humans typically loosen up when they aren't focused on the camera (Photos 4.11 A – C).

Running the Show

The shot list you prepared earlier (see p. 69) comes in

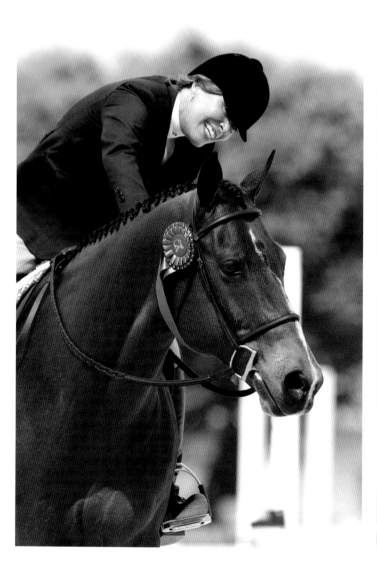

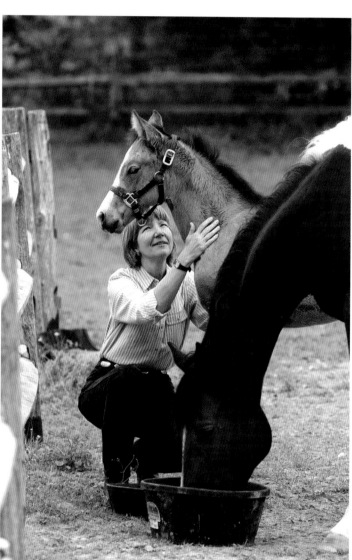

4.10 People love their horses. When I asked Kelly to praise her horse, she had no problem filling my request.

4.11 A As we finished a shoot for the *American Paint Horse Journal*, Anne stopped to spend a moment alone with her new foal.

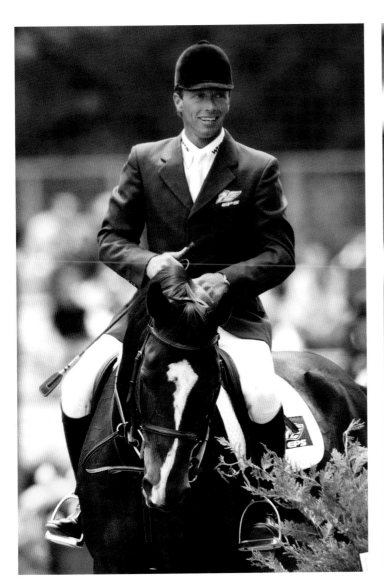

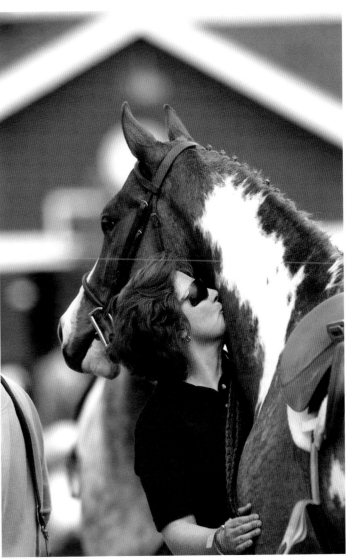

4.11 B You would not know from this image of show jumper Todd Minikus that he was just disqualified for going off course.

4.11 C Using a long lens allowed me to remain unnoticed as I captured this owner showing her horse how much she loved her.

4.12 A While doing a shoot for Horseware of Ireland and their Signature Series of blankets, I had to photograph David O'Connor's Olympic Gold Medal horse Custom Made. David helped out in the beginning and gave "Taylor" verbal commands as you would a dog (i.e. "Stay," and "Walk." I was waiting for "Sit.") Then, after David left, it was up to the groom and me to get the horse's attention.

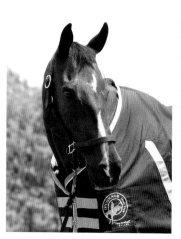

4.12 B After about 3 hours, "Taylor" had seen everything we had and nothing would get his ears up. Here, he shows his opinion of wearing a heavy blanket in early summer.

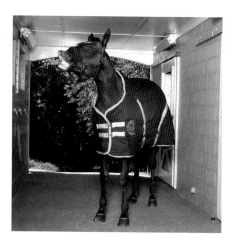

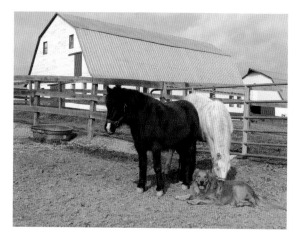

4.13 A While doing the photos for this book, my dog, Buddy, decided he would sit in on one of the shoots.

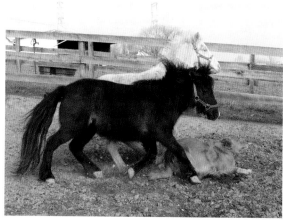

4.13 B After a while, Buddy decided to leave. Suddenly, the two ponies charged and almost trampled him. Luckily, nobody was hurt.

handy as you direct the subjects to a new location or scenario. It will be up to you to decide whether or not to give them a five-minute break between set ups. And when you do, use the time to change film or memory cards and double-check your exposure.

Working with just a horse can be a little more difficult because you cannot tell the horse what to do. (I suppose you can, but I doubt he will listen very well!) Here is where

the preplanning really comes into play (Photos 4.12 A & B).

Always keep safety in mind as you work around horses. Use the "attention getters" sparingly and cautiously. Accidents can happen quickly. Take a few extra seconds to think things through before having somebody do something that could be dangerous.

Be alert. You never know what might happen (Photos 4.13 A & B).

4.14 A When applying the "rule of thirds," divide your frame into thirds both horizontally and vertically, then place your point of interest on one of the intersections. Here, the racehorse's nose that is in focus falls on one of those intersecting lines.

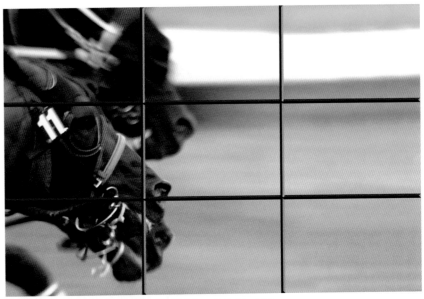

Composition Basics

Composing and cropping your images in the camera will save you a lot of time in postproduction—whether in a computer graphics program or at the photo lab.

The Rule of Thirds

Most photography classes will teach you the "rule of thirds," which was used for many years in fine art before it was adopted for photography composition. To utilize the rule of thirds, mentally divide your frame into thirds both vertically and horizontally, for nine equal sections. Your point of interest should fall at one of the intersections (Photos 4.14 A & B).

You will find that most images composed following the rule of thirds are more visually compelling. They seem balanced and are generally pleasing to the eye.

Layering for Depth

Adding depth to a photograph is another way to make your images more compelling. Layering objects adds depth.

When layering, think in terms of foreground, middle, and background. In the foreground, you might add such things as a tree branch or shrub, part of a fence line, or a dressage letter. The subject is in the middle layer. Background elements include such things as fence lines, tree lines, mountains, or other items of note (Photos 4.15 A & B).

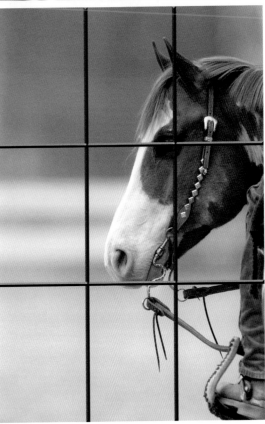

4.14 B Here, I placed the horse's eye on one of the intersecting lines.

4.15 During the cross-country phase of the 2000 Sydney Olympic Games, there were very large crowds of spectators. To illustrate this, I found a spot where the crowd was visible both behind and in front of an obstacle. With the layering of the crowd in relation to the obstacle, it looks like Andrew Hoy is jumping into the crowds of people.

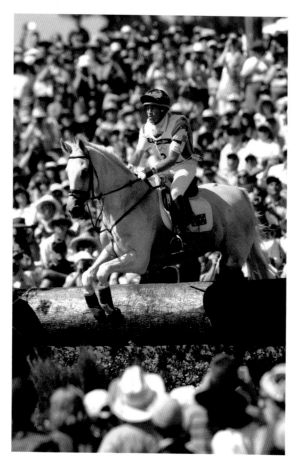

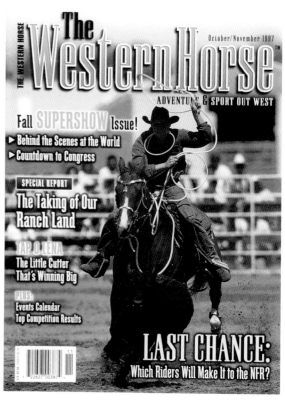

4.15 B This calf roping shot, featured on the cover of *The Western Horse* magazine, is a good example of a layered photograph. The singled-out calf is in the foreground, the horse is in the middle, and the audience serves as a backdrop.

Going Vertical

One final note regarding composition: turn your camera and take some vertical pictures as well as horizontal ones. People naturally hold their cameras in the horizontal position when taking pictures (Photo 6.16 A). The vertical format often works well when you are head-on to your subject. Your subject ends up being larger in the frame and you don't have a lot of dead area to worry about (Photo 6.16 B).

Get Down, Up or Over: Finding New Angles

Once you have mastered the basics of the formal, posed shot, don't limit yourself to shooting on the same plane or from the same vantage point.

Experiment. Shooting from different angles can add enormous interest and keep things from getting too boring.

One of the biggest mistakes I see photographers make is shooting pictures only from their own eye level.

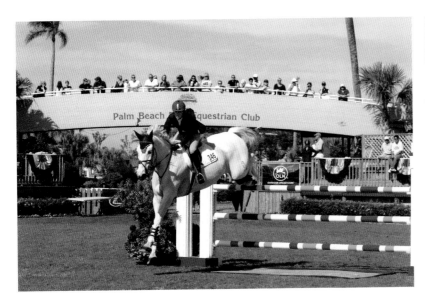

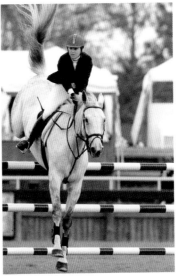

4.16 B Here, I turned the camera 90 degrees because the image of a show jumper landing from this angle is more vertical than horizontal. Shooting vertically allows me to fill the frame with the horse and rider.

4.16 A Horses can be long, as demonstrated in this image of a show jumper. I wanted the bridge in the background to illustrate the location of the show, so I shot it horizontally.

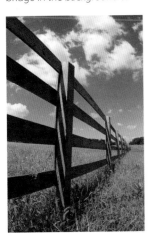

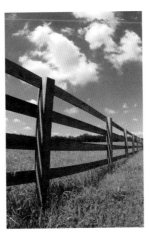

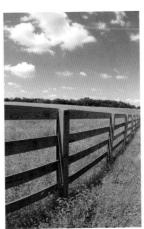

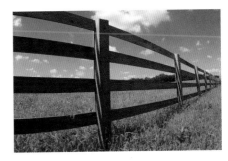

4.17 A – D Experiment. Shoot from different angles.

I am usually the dirtiest one to leave a show or a photo shoot because I am always kneeling in the dirt—or even lying on my stomach—shooting up at my subjects.

Spend some time looking at your subject from different angles. Get down on your knees or lie on your back to *look up*. Get a higher perspective up on a hill, or on the top rail of a fence or balcony, and *look down*. You will be surprised what a difference even a couple of feet can make in a photograph.

These four images of the same fence line help to illustrate how moving just a couple of feet in any direction can change the look of a scene (Photos 4.17 A – D). Whether you kneel, stand, or turn the camera 90 degrees, it will change the way things look.

When you look up, it typically makes your subject look more heroic and larger than life. I am always trying to make the horse into a heroic subject.

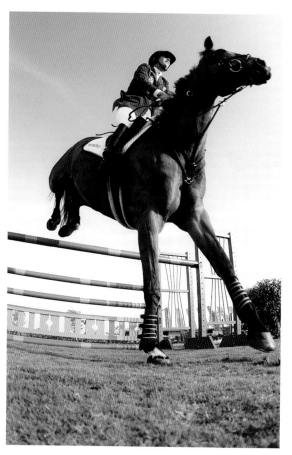

4.18 An ad agency requested an image with the feeling of "the photographer in mortal danger." I came up with this scenario because I had not seen a jumping shot done like this before.

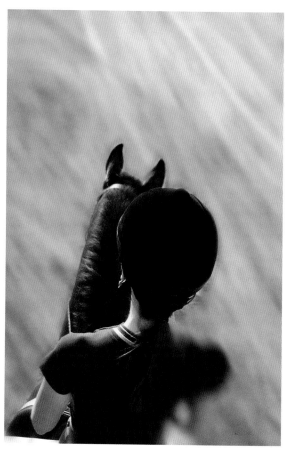

4.19 A Looking down on your subject can give an interesting twist to your everyday photographs. Here, I perched on some stands next to the arena, while the rider rode below.

When you look up, it typically makes your subject look more heroic and larger than life. During photo shoots for advertising clients—and especially during award ceremonies at horse shows—I am always trying to make the horse into a heroic subject.

Shooting while looking up is also useful when photographing any type of jumping. It makes the fences look bigger than they really are (Photo 4.18).

Looking down on your subject can yield some interesting shots as well. You have to be careful, however, not to make your subject look too submissive or cowering. Remember, a couple of feet can make a big difference (Photos 4.19 A & B).

Experiment. If something does not look right from 8 feet high, try shooting it from 10 feet or even 6 feet. Try new angles and new vantage points (Photos 4.20 A & B).

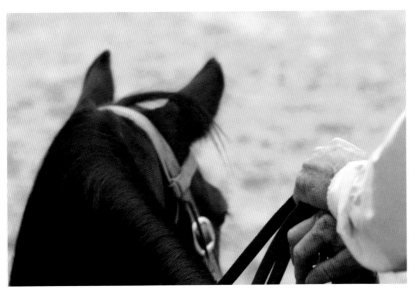

4.19 B This image from a slightly elevated position behind the horse provides for an interesting composition of the rider's hands and the horse's ears.

One of the biggest mistakes I see photographers make is shooting pictures only from their own eye level.

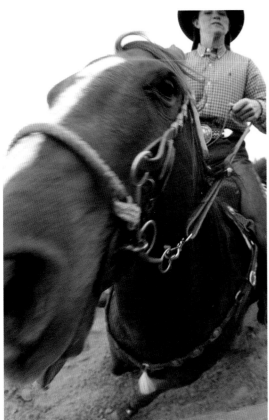

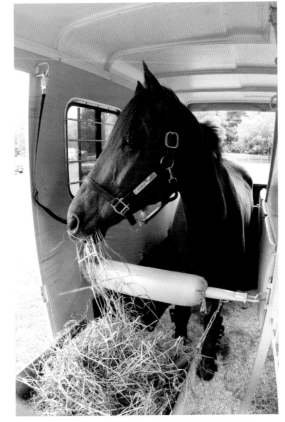

4.20 A For years, I wanted to photograph a barrel racer while standing inside the barrel. This image gives a whole new meaning to "up close and personal."

4.20 B While waiting for my girlfriend to sign up for her classes, I started to play with different angles for shooting the horse in the trailer. I climbed in the tack area, opened the window to the horse, and photographed him from there with a wide-angle lens.

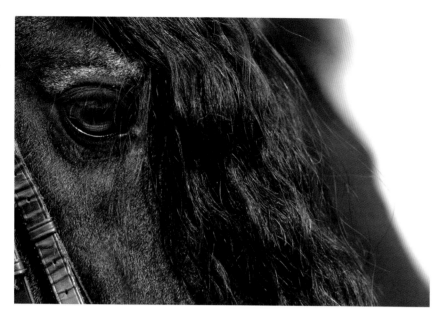

4.21 A Close-up of a Friesian's eye.

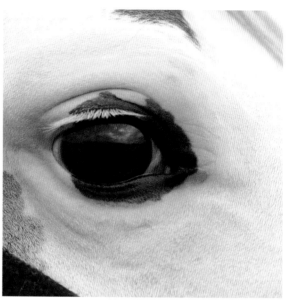

4.21 B Close-up of a Paint Horse's eye.

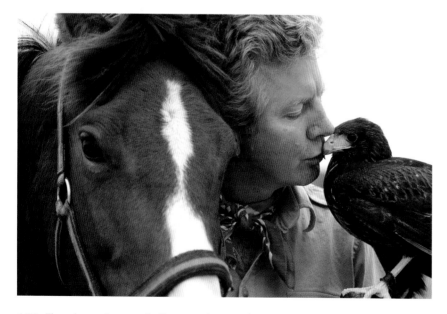

4.22 Though people generally like to see the entire horse in a photograph, there are times—such as in this shot of Jonathan Shaw with his Paint Horse and falcon—when seeing the entire horse is not necessary.

Get Closer

As I have refined my photography, I have discovered that the closer I get to my subjects, the more interesting the photographs become.

The equine face and body can be very beautiful. The adage, "The eyes are windows to the soul," holds true for horses as well as humans. I find focusing on the horse's eye very interesting (Photos 4.21 A & B).

Many of the people I know in the horse world like photos showing the entire horse. I, myself, like to be a little tighter so I can see the horse's expression or other small details (Photo 4.22). I try to mix things up, depending on the show or what I have been asked to illustrate. I will usually shoot what clients ask for, but if something along the way catches my eye, I will shoot it as well.

An idea of what the images are for and how they are going to be used is important when deciding how you

ADVANCED TIP
QUALITY SELLS

When putting together an ad to sell a horse or an equine service, make sure you use a good quality photograph to showcase the product you are selling. It's no secret that big companies spend millions of dollars on advertising campaigns. They know they will get more return on high quality photographs of their product or services.

You must first make the customer stop to look at the image in order to get him to read about your product or service. In today's fast-paced world, getting someone's attention is getting harder and harder to do. Big companies are spending more and more trying to figure out how to make people stop and look at their ads.

My girlfriend used her digital video recorder to capture some images of a horse she was trying to sell. She reduced his price considerably, since she had tried to sell him online for a long time and had not gotten much response to her internet ads. She eventually asked if I would come out and do some "professional" photographs for some print ads.

One afternoon, I photographed her horse in various situations. We narrowed down the shots and chose three images to use in her print ad. She placed the ad in three separate publications and the response was enormous. She quickly sold the horse at the *original* asking price (Photo 4.23).

Before

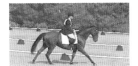
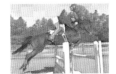
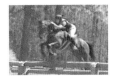

After

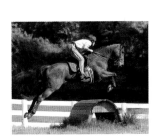
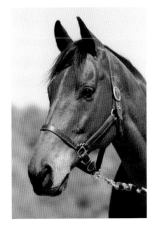
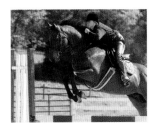

4.23 In the top row of pictures that were used as ads on the internet, you can (barely) see a series of images of a horse going over a cross-country obstacle. In the next row, also online, the images are shown a little better, but they are still too small to see how well this horse can perform. The images in the bottom row are the result of the shoot for the print ads that sold the horse.

The moral of the story is that quality photography can make the difference in how fast—and for how much—your product or service will sell. If you want to get somebody to pay attention to an ad, you need to make it look as appealing as possible.

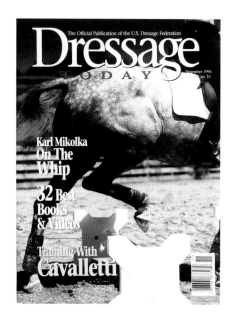

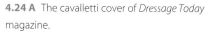

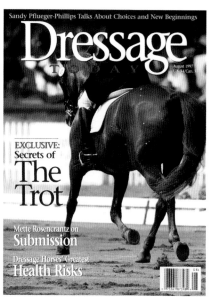

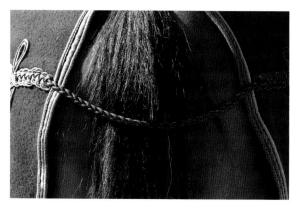

4.24 A The cavalletti cover of *Dressage Today* magazine.

4.24 B Less then a year later, another *Dressage Today* cover featured a horse's butt.

4.24 C: The detail in the blanket made this shot visually interesting.

The closer I get to my subjects, the more interesting the photographs become.

will shoot your subject. If you are putting together a sale ad and want to show great conformation or how good a mover a horse is, then a full body shot is a must. But a nice head shot portrait to show off his cute face can also be very compelling.

Getting in tighter and not shooting the entire horse has helped move my business forward in a rather humorous way.

I have been known to do lots of photos of horses' butts. This all started during a 1996 photo shoot for *Dressage Today* magazine. I was asked to illustrate the proper use of cavalletti. At the time, I had no idea what they were.

The magazine's technical advisor equated the cavalletti with a line of tires that football players run through

in practice to teach them to pick up their legs. As the horse passed over the cavalletti, I got in close and shot the hindquarters as the horse picked up his hind leg. This was the first of many "butt shots" (Photos 4.24 A – C)!

The bottom line is: go experiment. Go out and *play*! Try something different.

If you own a digital camera, your experiments are almost free. You also have the instant gratification of seeing your image immediately.

Of course, if you are shooting film, experimenting can be a little expensive. But it is still very rewarding when you pick up your film.

Now, let's take a look at what happens once you have finished your shoot.

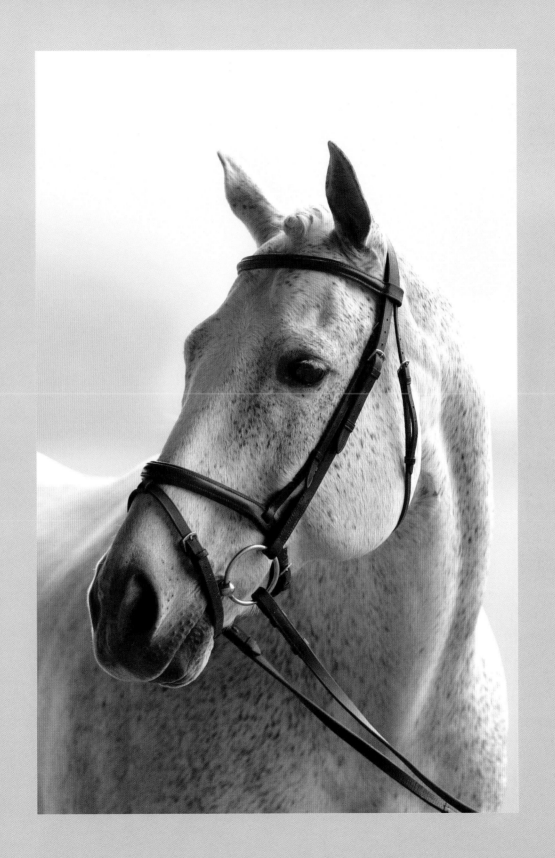

5

The Photo Lab

Once you have captured the images, you need to "head back to the barn" to get your photos ready for viewing. Just as you have a way to manage things like cleaning, feeding, checking equipment, first aid, and training when taking care of your horse, you need to manage your final shots, too.

Whether you are shooting with film or digitally, it is important to have a system in place to get your images printed, made into enlargements, or posted on your computer or Web site, so you and others can see them.

Get to Know Your Photofinisher

Having a good relationship with your photofinisher is essential if you shoot slides or negatives. Just as you would communicate with your farrier, trainer, or vet and listen to their recommendations to improve the performance and health of your horse, a similar relationship with your photofinisher can make a big difference in the quality of your images.

As we discussed in chapter 1, most of the photofin-ishing machines are calibrated to print images of people and places (see p. 13). When you drop off your negative film to be developed and printed, there is nothing on it to tell the processing machine operator how the colors should look. The operator must rely on averages for that film type and on the test strip he did when he started up the machine that morning. The color and hue of your pictures is purely a subjective call on the operator's part.

This is where having a personal relationship with the people who work at the lab can be very beneficial to you. Talk to them. Let them know what is important to you. They can tweak the processing so your bay horse doesn't look like a chestnut and your palomino doesn't look like a dun in the prints.

Discount department stores prices might be very attractive, but remember that the quality of the final result probably won't be.

Keep in mind, though, that the color in your final prints can vary from day to day, from lab to lab, and even from operator to operator.

When you pick up your prints, try to look at them in the lab the day they are done. That way, if they are not right, you can explain the problem to the lab technician and have the photos reprinted to more closely match your horse's color. If done the same day, the settings, pa-per batch, and (possibly) the operator will be the same, eliminating a lot of variables that can cause variations in the printing process (Photo 5.1).

When I was shooting film, I would ask the lab to keep a couple of my correctly printed photos on file as a refer-ence for the operator to use when printing my images. You can also have your lab scan your negatives to be put on a photo CD. Most lab managers appreciate this, be-cause not having to reprint your photos will save them both time and money.

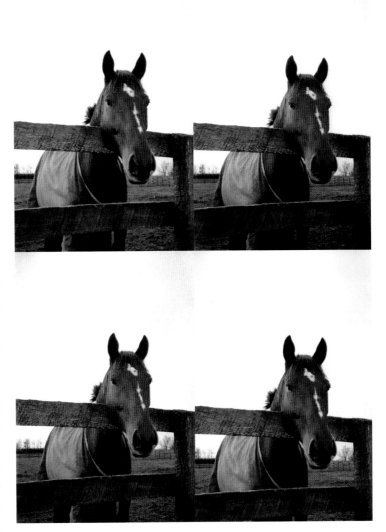

5.1 These four versions of the same image are from a disposable camera. The image in the upper left is the closest to the original scene after I had the lab reprint it on the same day as the original processing. The image in the upper right, I made on a do-it-yourself kiosk at the camera store. It looks a little red. The image in the lower left I printed on my inkjet printer at home from the CD the photo lab furnished at the time of processing. The image in the lower right was the first print from the lab—it looks a little green.

Photo labs now imprint data on the back of every print done on a machine. This information tells the technician the image's frame number and what settings were used to make that print (Photo 5.2).

If you have a problem with the colors of your prints and you also have a photograph that was printed correctly at the same lab, take both sets of negatives and prints in with you so they can compare the two.

This is also a good practice when you are having enlargements made—even if the print you have is off. At the very least, the machine operator will know how *not* to print the enlargement.

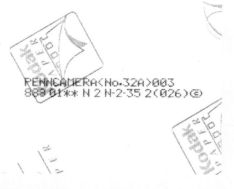

5.2 Photo lab information recorded on the back of a print. This information can help the lab technician correctly reprint or make enlargements of your photographs.

When shooting slide or transparency film, it is important to work with a lab that has good quality control. For example, if your lab does not have the temperatures set right, or if the chemicals are not replenished at the required intervals, the images may look flat, the colors may be muddy, or there may be dirt or roller marks on your film. Unlike negative film, which has greater latitude in the printing process to correct for these things, slides don't have this luxury. The lab has only one chance to get your transparency film right when it is processed.

Using Home Computers for Viewing and Printing Photos

The digital age has made it very easy to be your own photofinisher at home. With software becoming cheaper and easier to use, and the quality of ink-jet printers improving (some don't even need to be hooked up to a computer!), you can make photo-quality prints and enlargements at home. But remember, you must have a system for producing good quality prints time after time.

Monitor Matters

When you begin to print out digital images, your computer monitor is the first place where things can go wrong. How do you know that the colors you see on your monitor are accurate? How can you determine whether or not the brightness and the contrast are correct (Photo 5.3)?

Monitors vary widely in their color quality. For a good example of this, walk into any electronics store and examine the wall of televisions. Take a close look and notice how rarely any two TVs have the exact same color, brightness, and contrast. Even televisions from the same manufacturer

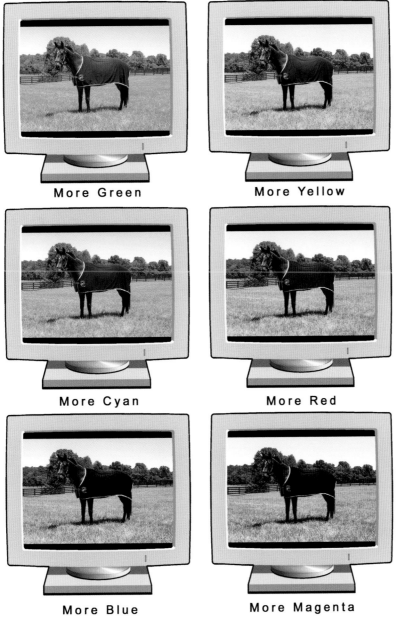

More Green

More Yellow

More Cyan

More Red

More Blue

More Magenta

When you begin to print out digital images, your computer monitor is the first place where things can go wrong.

5.3 These six images show the variations of a slight color shift to green, yellow, cyan, red, blue, and magenta.

The first step toward producing consistent, predictable color prints is setting up and profiling your monitor.

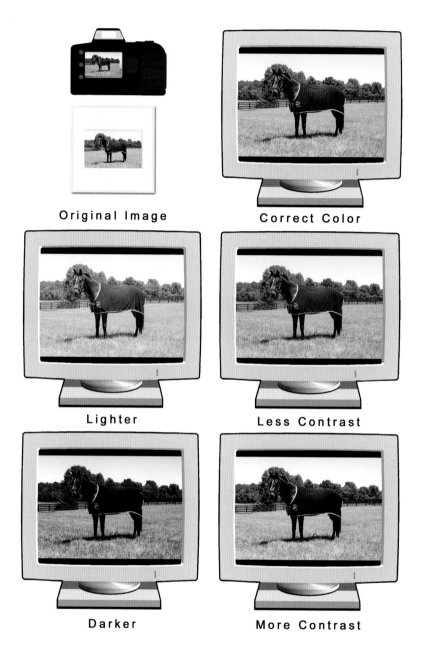

Original Image

Correct Color

Lighter

Less Contrast

Darker

More Contrast

5.4 This series illustrates an original image from a digital camera or film displayed correctly on a computer monitor. The monitors on the left show how more or less brightness can affect the photo. The monitors on the right show the effects of too little or too much contrast.

will be slightly different. This is true with computer monitors as well, whether you are using an LCD (liquid-crystal display, or flat-screen) or an older CRT (cathode-ray tube, or traditional style) monitor (Photo 5.4).

Color Management

The most important issue to consider when printing your own digital images is color management. In plain English, *color management* is a system to reproduce color in a consistent predictable manner.

All photographic hardware has a particular color space. *Color space* refers to the range of colors that your camera, printer, or monitor can recognize and accurately reproduce.

In addition, your software will have a variety of *color space profiles* available. These profiles stipulate the color ranges available to you. They provide a consistent medium for you to edit your images. Profiles include RGB, sRGB, Adobe RGB, CMYK, Lab Color, Index Color, and no color Grayscale (which is used for pure black and white images).

All color spaces produce color in varying degrees, but if you send a file with the wrong embedded color space profile to a device, such as a printer, you will not get the results you are expecting.

Think of it like this: riding your horse is like an embedded color space profile. Let's say you take your horse to an English show in Western tack and apparel. You might be able to compete, but you would probably look strange or out of place. The same concept applies if you send an embedded RGB file to be printed on a CMYK printer. You will get a print, but the colors won't look the way they should.

If you want to score high with the English judges, then you want to follow the rules and traditions of the English show world and use English riding apparel and tack. The same is true when working with digital images

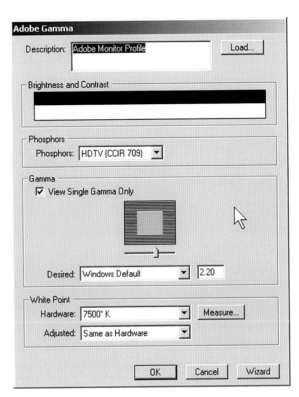

5.5 Adobe Gamma utility control panel.

at home. You must know the color space of both the files you are working with and the output device you are going to use to print your photos.

The first step toward producing consistent, predictable color prints is setting up and profiling your monitor. Most photo manipulation software allows you to set the *gamma*—the brightness, contrast, and color of your monitor—without buying any additional hardware or software.

To calibrate and profile your monitor, you can use visual calibrators like Adobe Gamma (Windows) and Monitor Calibrator (Mac OS) (Photo 5.5). If you want even more precision, you should look into a calibration hardware and software package, like Color Vision, Gretag Macbeth, or Monaco EZ Color, to produce more accurate results.

A thorough explanation of the various nuances of color management and profiling would fill several books. But, as I promised earlier, this is not a technical manual. Many Web sites and books that go into great detail about this subject are available.

The best advice I can give you is: read the instructions that came with your digital camera, software, monitor, video card, and printer. You can also seek advice from your photo lab personnel. When you take in digital files or e-mail them to the lab, see what color profiles they recommend that you use to produce consistent, predictable color.

Monitor Resolution

The resolution of your monitor is another consideration. Just as the *color* of a printed photograph can differ from how it looked on a computer screen, the *quality* of the same file often does not look the same in print as it does on the monitor. Here's why:

Most computer monitors display at 72 dpi, which means that there are 72 "dots" or *pixels* in every linear square inch. An image will measure 72 pixels high by 72 pixels wide. It will therefore contain 5184 pixels in a square inch. Increasing the dpi display increases the number of pixels in a square inch of standard resolution.

Your computer's video card may have several screen resolution options to choose from, such as 800 x 600, 960 x 720, 1024 x 768, or 1280 x 1024, for example. Increasing the resolution does not change your dpi display rate. It only changes how compressed, or close together, the pixels are onscreen (Photos 5.6 A – C).

Increasing your monitor's resolution will allow you to gain more desktop area and may sharpen your images. Because of the compression, however, text and other objects may be smaller and more difficult to read. Be sure to choose a resolution that is comfortable for you to view.

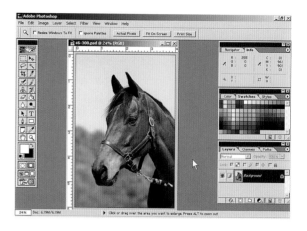

5.6 A An image on your monitor might look like this at a resolution of 800 x 600.

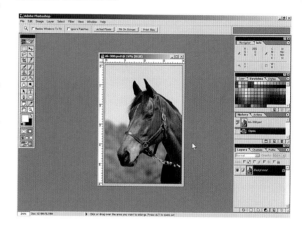

5.6 B The same image at a resolution of 1024 x 768.

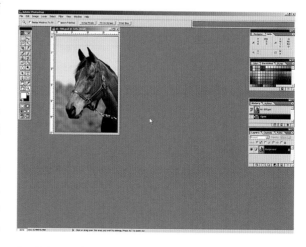

5.6 C At a resolution of 1280 x 1024, your monitor might look like this.

Photo Browsers

Browsers are software that easily allow you to view and access the digital images from a photo CD, camera, or scanner. Think of browsers as a sort of digital filing system.

Many browser programs are available on the Internet. Some are free. Others are under $50, depending on the features they offer.

One of the Windows-compatible programs I have found to be very good for the money is ACDSee® (see Photo 5.7). A more basic version of the program is available for Macintosh users.

This program allows you to create and view *thumbnails* (very small images to use as an organizational aid) and to scroll through larger images. It includes several tools to help you edit your images and offers several printing options. With it, you can organize your photos, adding keywords to each photo's file so you can quickly search your archives and find what you are looking for. You can use it to easily create Web pages. It also has optional plug-ins—additional, compatible programs—available that allow you to do even more.

Whether you use a PC or a Mac, most software companies have free demos of their programs that you may try out for a short period of time before you buy. Do a little research and try a few browser demos to see which program will work best for you.

Bundled Software

Many digital cameras have basic software programs bundled with them that allow you to view, print, and make minor adjustments to your images. These are generally easy to use and don't require a lot of time to master.

Bundled software allows you to make prints without having to do much more than select the image and hit the "print" button.

Bundled software is also available for upgrading

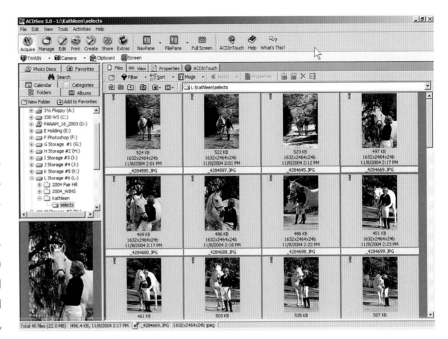

5.7 An ACDSee® Browser window.

printers, or adding after-market options. For instance, Epson's Film Factory® software allows me the aftermarket option of using long rolls of photo paper with my Epson 1270 inkjet printer. I can select the images I want to print, choose the quantity of prints, and the software tells my printer how to print them on a long piece of paper that I then trim to length.

Photo Manipulation Options

For more advanced and creative work, you can choose from many programs that will allow you to display, print, and manipulate your images.

Photo manipulation software gives you nearly limitless flexibility and creativity with your photos. Some software, such as Adobe PhotoShop®, has several levels of

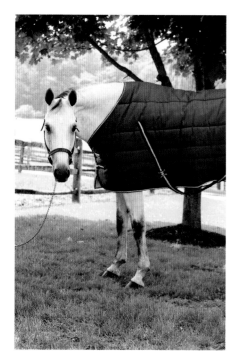

5.8 A The original shot, with a green blanket.

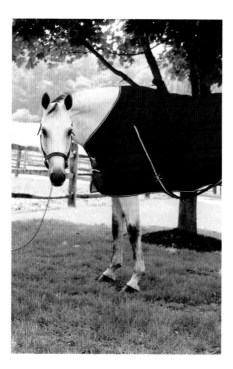

5.8 B Photo manipulation software allowed me to change the green blanket to blue without reshooting the image.

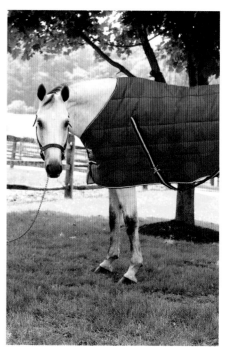

5.8 C Be careful what you wish for…

programs, ranging from Adobe Photoshop Elements for novices to Photoshop Creative Suite for advanced users and professionals.

Photo manipulation software literally allows you to create images that never happened. For instance, after I had completed a shoot for Horseware of Ireland, I received a call from my contact, asking if we had shot one particular blanket style in blue.

I told her that I shot everything the rep had brought to the shoot, but I only shot the green version of that blanket (Photo 5.8 A).

She asked if there was any way to get the blue one shot within a couple of days.

I told her I could make the green one blue, digitally. She was skeptical until I sent her the file (Photo 5.8 B).

Then she replied, "I am glad I did not ask for pink with purple polka dots" (Photo 5.8 C).

Furthermore, photo manipulation software allows you to combine existing images in new and interesting ways. The possibilities are endless—all that is required is a little imagination (Photos 5.9 and 5.10 A & B).

Printing: DPI and Image Quality

Color inkjet printers are commonly found in most do-it-

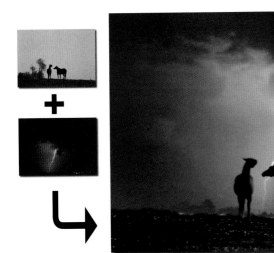

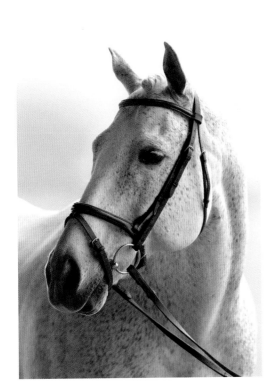

5.9 Photo manipulation enables you to combine elements of various images. An intern at the *Chronicle of the Horse* once asked if I had an image of horses in a field with a lightning bolt in the same frame. I found some old slides of lightning that I had taken while in high school. I also found some images of horses from a shoot in Kentucky. With the magic of Adobe PhotoShopCS ®, I combined the two photos to create a new image.

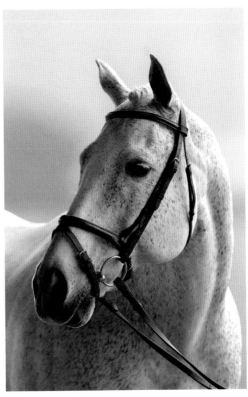

5.10 A Photo manipulation software allows you to easily convert a color photograph…

5.10 B …into black and white at the touch of a button.

ADVANCED TIP
MAKE COPIES

When doing any work with digital files, it is very important that you work from copies of your original files.

The original files are, in a sense, your negatives or transparencies. There is only one version of the image you take. If you make the wrong changes to it and save it, then you have altered that file forever. This is especially true when working with JPG (or JPEG) files, because the JPG file is a *lossy compression* type of file. Every time you save a JPG file, the computer compresses the file size and throws away the unused information. This makes the file's size smaller, but makes it impossible to retrieve older versions.

Always copy the images you want to work on into a separate folder on your hard drive, or make a back-up CD or DVD of your images before doing any work on them. This way, you have your originals in a safe place and can go back and retrieve them in the future, if necessary.

An exception to this working rule of thumb is the RAW files that some camera manufacturers have created, enabling users to make changes to the final image without changing the original.

Changes are made using *macros* (a means of automating computer functions and executing instructions within a program) that adjust such factors as color, contrast, and size on the image when it is viewed with the specified software. The macros tell the software to make adjustments to the original image when it is viewed, without actually changing the values of the original image.

To permanently change a RAW file, you must save the image as a different format (such as JPEG, TIFF, PDF, or PSD).

yourself photofinishing "labs." These printers are rated according to such things as dots per linear inch (dpi), the number of inks, ink longevity, nozzle size, printing speed, and maximum paper size. In addition to inkjet printers, color laser, dye sublimation, and regular photo printers are also available.

Before making a decision on what printer to buy, ask yourself the following questions:

▶ *How high-quality a printer do I need?*
▶ *How long do I want the prints to last?*
▶ *How much money am I willing to spend?*
▶ *Will this handle my other computer printing needs?*

Most inkjet printers will produce good quality prints from files of most resolutions, but if you want more detail in your photos, the higher the resolution, the better. The image will be sharper and cleaner at a higher resolution.

Be careful that you don't overdo it, however. You can get to the point where you have an image's resolution so high that the printer cannot reproduce all that detail, and you just end up with very large files taking up room on your hard drive.

As a general rule, I size my files to 300 dpi as a standard resolution when making prints or when sending images to be printed in magazines. At 300 dpi, a 4 x 6-inch print becomes an image with the dimensions of 1200 x 1800 pixels (4 inches x 300 dpi = 1200 pixels and 6 inches x 300 dpi = 1800 pixels). In contrast, the same size print at the standard 72 dpi resolution would result in an image with only 288 x 432 pixels (Photo 5.11).

Resizing

Depending on the printer and the software, you may be able to resize your images. This will allow you to make larger or smaller prints from your files. If you are making larger prints, like 5 x 7 inches or 8 x 10 inches, you could use a slightly lower dpi resolution. A larger photo is more

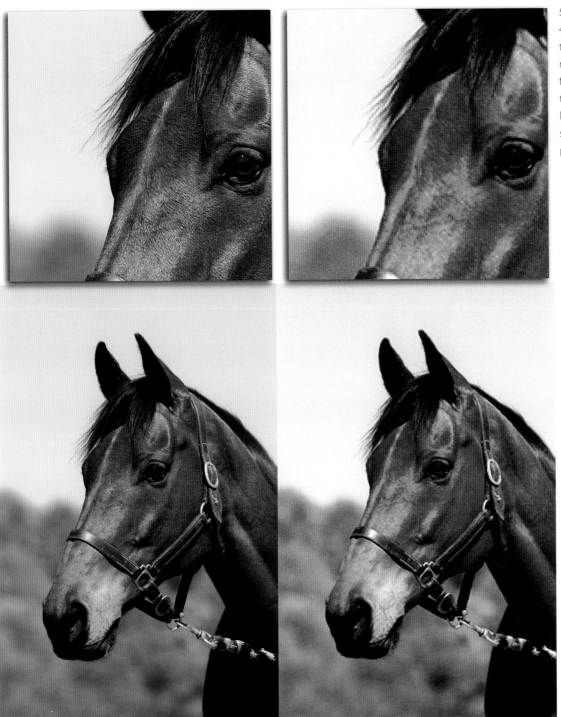

5.11 Both of these prints are 4 x 6 inches in size. The one on the left is at 300 dpi. The on the right is at 72 dpi. As you can see from the magnified images of the horse's eye, the 72 dpi image lacks detail and you can start to see the jagged edges of the pixels.

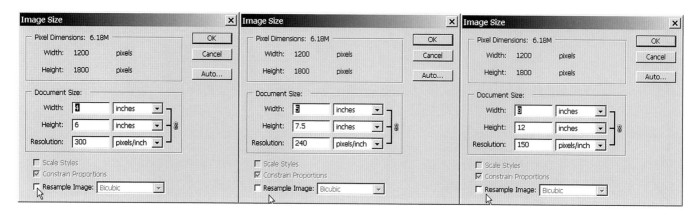

5.12 These three Adobe PhotoShopCS ® "Image Size" windows show how changing the "Document Size"—but not checking the "Resample Image" box at the bottom left—affects the image. The "Pixel Dimensions" do not change from 1200 x 1800 pixels per image. As the image grows larger, note how the dpi changes, going from 300 dpi at 4 x 6 inches, to 240 dpi at 5 x 7.5 inches, to 150 dpi at 8 x 12 inches.

likely to be viewed from a distance and, once framed, most people will not notice the difference in resolution.

The larger the final print, the less resolution is required. For example, the next time you are walking down a city street, take a close look at a large ad on a billboard or on the side of a bus stop shelter. You will be able to easily count the number of dots per inch. However, these images are intended for viewing from a distance, not up close. Therefore, once you step back, you see the whole image and not the individual dots.

As a practical illustration, let's enlarge that 4 x 6-inch file at 300 dpi, and make it into both a 5 x 7 inch, and an 8 x 12-inch print. If you use a program like Adobe Photo-ShopCS ® and edit the image size without checking the "Resample Image" box, the image will enlarge, but no new pixels will be added to it. The image will now be 5 x 7.5 inches at 240 dpi, but the pixel dimensions (still 1200 x 1800) will have not changed. If you continue enlarging the image to make an 8 x 12-inch print, the resolution drops to 150 dpi at the same pixel dimensions. Each

of these enlargements will produce acceptable prints (Photo 5.12).

Another option, when making enlargements, is to maintain the dpi and resample the image at each new size. *Resampling* an image means that you permanently change the pixel dimensions.

When you make an image smaller than the original file and you check the "Resample Image" box check, you are throwing away information from the image. On the other hand, if you make a larger image, the software adds new pixels to fill in the gaps. The number of pixels will increase in proportion to each enlargement. It also means that the computer will have to interpolate its existing data and make its best guess about how the added pixels will appear.

Going from a 4 x 6-inch image to an 8 x 12-inch image at the same dpi forces the computer to interpolate and create 6,480,000 additional pixels. This increases the total number of pixels from 2,160,000 in the 4 x 6-inch image to 8,640,000 in the 8 x 12-inch image (Photo 5.13).

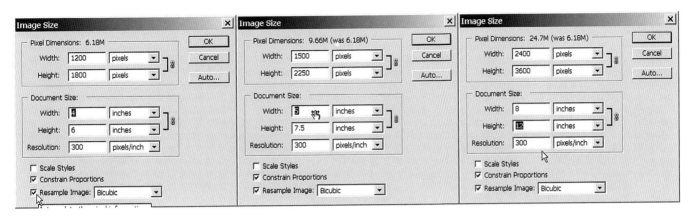

5.13 These three Adobe PhotoShopCS ® "Image Size" windows show how changing the "Document Size" and resampling the image while maintaining the resolution at 300 dpi causes the "Pixel Dimensions" to change as the image enlarges. At 4 x 6 inches, the file has 1200 x 1800 pixels. At 5 x 7.5 inches, it has 1500 x 2250 pixels. An 8 x 12-inch print has 2400 x 3600 pixels.

ADVANCED TIP
PLAN FOR PROPORTION

When sizing your images for enlargements, keep in mind that the proportions of a 4 x 6, 5 x 7, and 8 x 10-inch print are not the same. A photo printed at 3.5 x 5 inches or 4 x 6 inches has roughly the same proportions as a negative frame of 35mm film or the dimensions of the image sensor of your digital camera (Photo 5.14).

Most labs will print an 8 x 12-inch print that will show the entire frame. They may also do an 8 x 10-inch "full frame" print that actually reduces the image to fit on an 8 x 10-inch piece of paper with borders along the long sides.

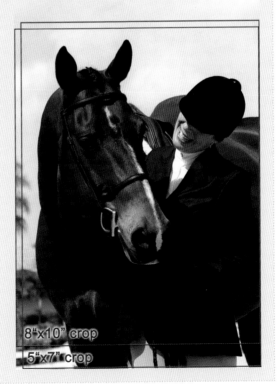

5.14 Notice how much of the frame is lost in an enlargement. The full photo shows 4 x 6-inch image size. The blue lines show a 5 x 7-inch cropping of the image. The red lines show an 8 x 10-inch cropping.

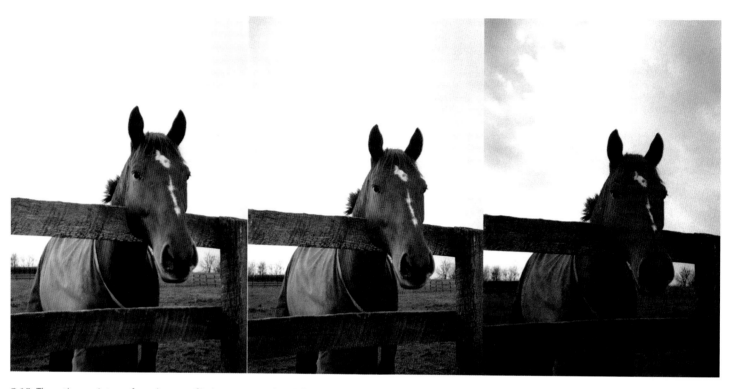

5.15 These three prints are from the same file, but are printed on different papers. From left to right: glossy inkjet paper, matte photo paper, and plain copier paper.

Printer Paper and Inks

Choosing the right paper and inks for printing is another important factor to consider, because all printer paper and inks are not made equal.

A wide variety of photo printer papers available, and the choices can be confusing. Printer manufacturers typically say they only recommend using their brand of inks and paper in their printers. This is because they have tested their inks with their papers to produce consistent, accurate results.

However, there are many other paper manufacturers that have everything from the standard glossy, luster, and matte finishes to canvas, metallic, and watercolor—and everything in between (Photo 5.15). Make sure that whatever paper you use is compatible with the inks in your printer and the thickness tolerance of your printer.

A personal preference is Ilford's inkjet paper—especially the luster finish, which looks and feels just like the luster paper from a photo lab. Higher-end photo papers like this can be found at your local camera and arts-and-crafts stores, and online.

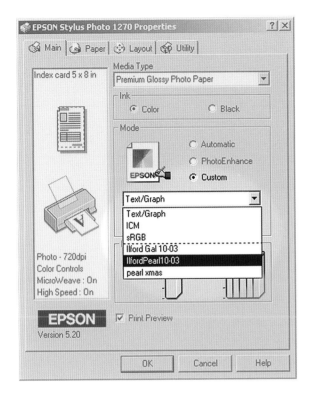

5.16 The Epson Stylus Photo 1270 ® Properties window allows you to save different settings for different papers.

Most paper manufacturers make sample packs that contain several sheets of the company's different offerings. Don't hesitate to try a variety of these sample packs until you find a paper you like.

Remember that each paper might require a different printer profile in order to print correctly (Photo 5.16). This is because each paper has a different brightness value. The way each absorbs ink can also vary. Check your printer or software owner's manual for more information on creating profiles for each individual paper.

Inkjet printer ink can be expensive—and most

PAPER PRIMER

When it comes to choosing the right paper stock for printing your photographs, the options can seem limitless.

▸ Paper weight (or basis weight) is measured in pounds. As a frame of reference, common copier paper has a basis weight of 20 lbs. The higher the weight, the thicker each individual sheet of paper. Higher weight paper is more durable, heftier, and feels more substantial. It also higher in opacity—it allows less light to pass through.

▸ The *brightness*, or whiteness of a piece of paper is typically expressed on a scale of 1 to 100. The higher the number, the brighter the paper. One hundred is the brightest, whitest paper available. Most copier and printer paper has a brightness rating in the 80s. Photo-quality paper usually has a brightness of 90 or more.

Trust your eyes. Don't allow labels such as "UltraBright" or "Bright White" to mislead you. If in doubt about the whiteness of one paper or another, place them side by side and see for yourself which is brighter. If an in-store printer of the same make and model as yours is available, it is not unreasonable to ask to print an image or two on it. Some paper supply stores are happy to provide you with paper samples to try at home.

Experiment with a variety of papers until you find the weight and feel that you prefer.

▸ *Printer paper* refers to any kind of paper manufactured for use in computer printers. Some paper is specially developed for optimum use in laser printers, while other paper is better suited for inkjet printers.

▸ Paper with a *matte finish* features a bright white coating that dries quickly. The finished print has a rather flat aspect and does not readily reflect light.

▸ Paper with a *glossy finish* has a shiny coating. The finished print has a shiny surface that readily reflects light. Most photo paper has a glossy finish specially manufactured to produce sharp, crisp, high-definition prints.

▸ *Luster Paper* dries instantly and produces vivid images. Print quality is said to rival that of traditional silver halide prints.

manufacturers suggest that you only use their inks. In my experience, the manufacturer's inks tend to be more reliable, more fade-resistant, and faster drying. For consistent, reliable results, it's probably best if you stick with the manufacturer's brand of ink.

Be careful of claims by some ink companies that say you can refill your ink cartridges to save money. Some of these refills can clog the nozzles of your print head. They can also void the warranty of your printer, and they may not be as fade-resistant as the manufacturer's inks.

Having compatible inks and papers is important if your prints are going to last for a long time. You will find that certain paper-and-ink combinations will have better archival quality then others. The best combination will make your prints able to last for 100 years or more! Other combinations may only last a couple of years before they start to fade. You can check the longevity of inks and papers at Wilhelm Imaging Research, online at www.wilhelm-research.com.

Manipulating, editing, and saving or printing out your images is an important part of every photographer's business. If done well, your images will be readily accessible for many years to come.

The original digital files are, in a sense, your negatives or transparencies. There is only one version of the image you take. If you make the wrong changes to it and save it, then you have altered that file forever.

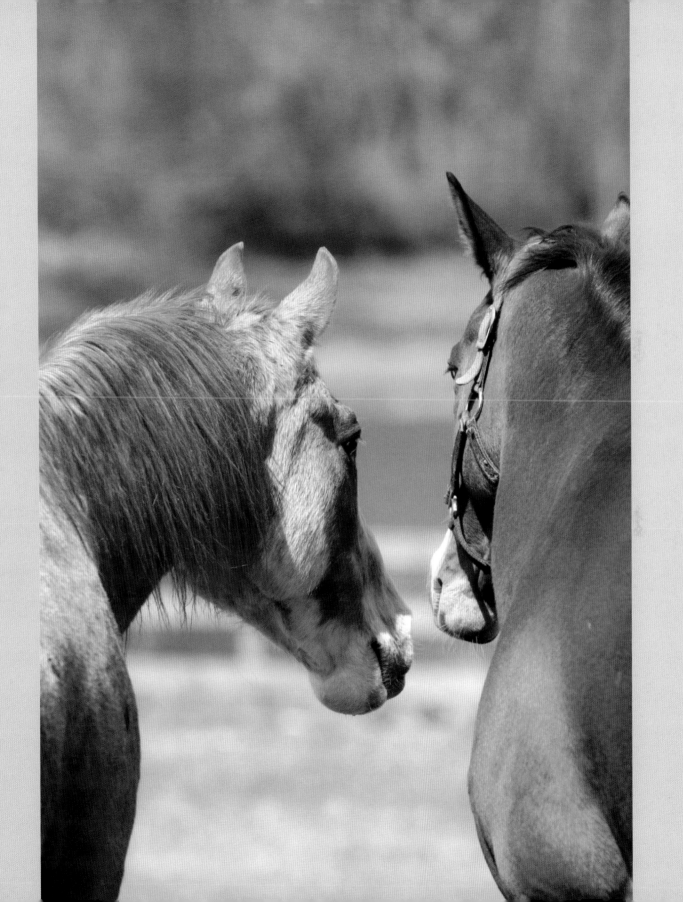

6

Storing and Managing Your Images

Once the images are out of your camera, you must have a plan for handling and storing them.

Whether you shoot with film or digitally, keeping track of negatives, slides, or digital files, as well as sorting and storing your images, can be a daunting task—if not a full-time job. Keeping all your old negatives in a shoebox on the shelf of your closet is *not* the recommended storage method.

Film and Prints

Archival pages that fit into loose-leaf binders are a good way to store negative or slide films. You spent a lot of time and energy creating your negatives. Storing them properly will keep the images they hold viable for years to come.

Pages are available in a variety of layouts to hold your slides and negatives safely and securely. This keeps them safe and makes looking for a particular image relatively easy. In addition, the pages have an area at the top or along the side where you can make notes about the subject and record the dates the images were taken.

Keeping the binders in a cool, dark, dry place is essential in order to preserve the negatives or slides. Above all, make sure that your negatives are not susceptible to the high temperatures of attics or the humidity of basements. Excessive heat, fluctuating temperatures, and moisture will destroy your negatives.

The same companies that make pages for storing negatives and slides also manufacture pages to store your prints and enlargements. These, too, come in several different configurations and album sizes. All these choices make it easy to organize your photos according to the year, month, horse, show, or whatever makes it easy for you to find them when you need them.

In order to help your photos last as long as possible, make yourself follow good basic handling and storage procedures. For instance, never handle film with your bare hands. If you have to, then be sure you touch only the edges. The oils in your skin can leave marks on the film that will reproduce when printed or scanned. It is best to keep the film in its sleeves or file pages until you get to the photo lab to have reprints made.

Film and prints should always be protected from direct sunlight. The ultraviolet rays from the sun can break down film and fade prints.

Avoid storing negatives or slides in pages made from PVC or polypropylene. These materials can create a static charge. They may attract dirt and dust that can damage the film. It is wise to spend a few extra dollars on archival quality storage products so you can view or make additional prints in the future.

No matter what type of storage device you choose, check to make sure it passes the *Photographic Activity Test (PAT)*. There is no standard or legal definition for using the word "archival" in advertising, but the PAT is a worldwide standard of archival quality.

Storing Digital Files

Archiving your digital images so you can find them later may be even more important than storing negatives and slides.

Digital images are nothing more than a bunch of electrons on your hard drive, CD, or DVD. What happens if your hard drive gets full or—even worse—crashes? What if you accidentally set your tape backup next to a strong magnet? Or what if you accidentally scratch your CD or DVD? Since you are not dealing with a physical image that can be recreated if something happens to it, a plan to create long-term digital archival storage is essential.

Have a Backup Plan
Backups, or duplicate copies of your digital files, are the key to digital storage. I break out in a cold sweat when I am about to hit the "delete" button on any of my digital images—even after making multiple backups of those images. I often copy the images I take at a photo shoot or competition from my laptop to my workstation before I delete them from the laptop, even if I have made backups of them on CDs or DVDs from the laptop files.

Unfortunately, I learned my lesson on the importance of backups the hard way. During the 2000 Olympic Games in Sydney, I had an external hard drive crash with all of my images on it from the first ten days—over 14,350—including one-of-a-kind photos of David O'Connor's victory lap with the American flag after he won the individual

Archiving your digital images so you can find them later may be even more important than storing negatives and slides.

gold medal in eventing. Fortunately, after sweating it out for two weeks, I was able to recover all but five or ten images that were irreparably corrupted.

I place a set of backups in my office's fire safe. Another set goes into a storage library that is networked to the office computers. A third set goes into a safe deposit box at the bank.

Even with files copied in triplicate, I still have problems hitting the "delete" button! You never can be too safe—or have too many backups!

Bear in mind that all digital and electronic media can deteriorate over the years, rendering the information stored on it unusable. So how do you archive digital files forever? The person who comes up with an answer to that question will have found the "brass ring"—and we photographers will be eternally indebted.

Quality Counts

As you consider how to best store your digital images, choose a device that will cover most of the formats currently available. Make your backups on high-quality media and store them in a proper location, in accordance with the manufacturer's recommendations.

You may be tempted to cut corners when choosing media for storing your digital files. Don't.

I once bought 100 of the no-name CDs for less than ten dollars. I reasoned that if the CDs lasted long enough to send to a client to use within a month, they would be worth buying. Once the client had made his own copies, it wouldn't matter if the CD decided to self-destruct (like tapes in the old *Mission Impossible* TV show).

The discs never even made it out of my office. A Mac computer would not recognize them, and I had all kinds of problems trying to "burn" them on my PC. Like the adage says, "You get what you pay for."

Buy high-quality CDs or DVDs for storing your digital

files. These discs have a more stable data layer material (like gold and silver alloy) than discs of lower quality. Try to stay away from DVDs with a silicon data layer because they can crack and cause loss of data.

"Burn" your CDs or DVDs in a format that both PC and Macintosh computers can read. For years, the most widely used format for CDs was ISO 9660. Currently, UDF (Universal Disk Format) and MPV are *file systems* (a means of organizing many files on a storage medium) that are popular with DVD and CD users.

Keep in mind that technology is constantly changing and new formats are being developed all the time. What is common now may not be in five to ten years. Everything that you have backed up now may have to be transferred to a new type of media in the future.

Managing Your Digital Images

Once you have backed up and archived your digital files, you need a way to recall particular images quickly and easily.

Several software programs are available that can assist you in managing your digital files. In addition to the browser programs mentioned earlier (see p. 91), *digital asset management programs* such as Extensis Portfolio® or Cumulus® provide more tools and options for managing your images. They also allow you to make digital catalogs of your images and digital files.

Digital asset management programs offer keywording and cataloging capabilities. This means that you can include a list of descriptive words with each file and can then sort the files according to the descriptors.

For example, let's say that you take a series of photographs at a local schooling show. The final pictures include a short stirrup rider on a gray pony going over cross-rails. Keywording the file would allow you to type the word "cross-rails," "short stirrup," or "gray" months later, and the jumping pony would be one of the images that appeared in response. When used correctly, descriptive keywords can save a lot of time that would have been wasted poring over prints or negatives.

Digital asset management programs allow you to make slide shows that you can send via e-mail, CD, or DVD to family and friends. You can also create animated books to e-mail or place on a Web site.

Digital asset management programs create thumb-nails of your images that are separate from the original files. You can also add searchable keywords and descriptions to the thumbnail images. This enables you to store your backed-up CDs and DVDs in a safe location—like a fire safe or safe deposit box—and only pull them out when you need the original file or a high-resolution file.

A reminder: just as you regularly make backups of your images, so you must also make backup copies of your catalog and database files. Then, if you have a problem with your computer, hard drive, or files, you can easily restore all of the information.

Bear in mind that all digital and electronic media can deteriorate over the years, rendering the stored information unusable.

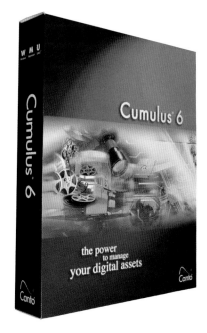

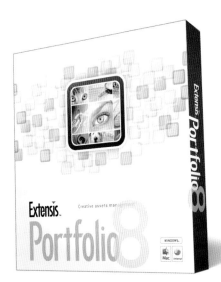

6.1 Digital asset management programs.

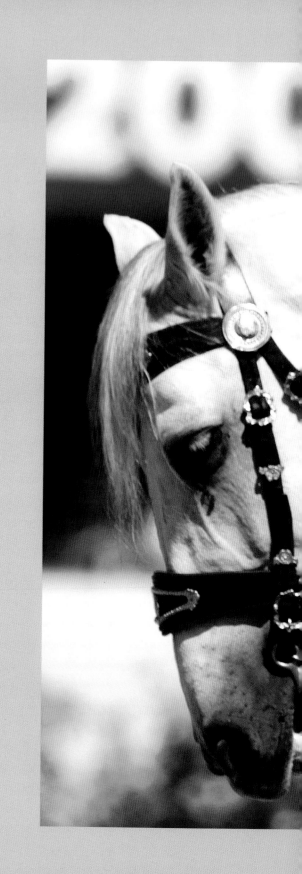

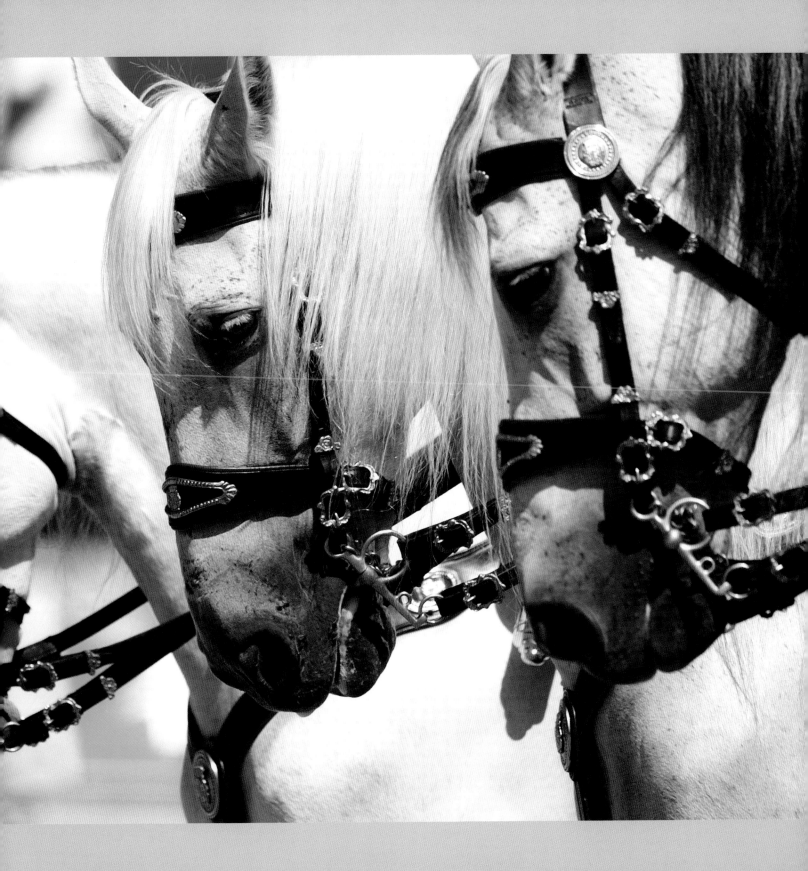

7

Troubleshooting Clinic:
25 Common Problems Solved

Just as you would attend clinics to improve different aspects of your horsemanship, the same holds true with your photography. You can find photography classes and seminars at local bookstores, camera stores, camera clubs, colleges, community centers, and online. Many of these places will have classes to help you in nearly every aspect of your photography, from Photography 101 to Advanced Photoshop®.

Finding the Right Solution to Your Problem

Identifying what went wrong and learning how to fix it is an ongoing aspect of photography. Often, understanding the cause can help you resolve the problem.

The next few pages will focus on the most common problems in everyday photography, both with film and digital cameras. Each problem will include some reasons why the trouble occurred and offer some tips for how to fix it in the future.

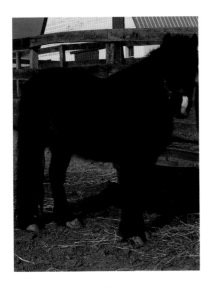 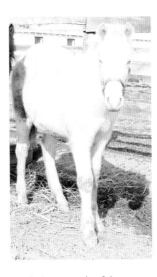 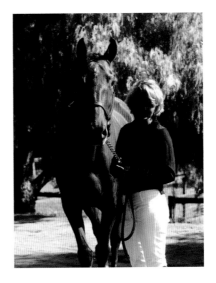

7.1 A An example of an underexposed image. Very little detail is visible in the shadows.

7.1 B An example of the same scenario over-exposed. There is detail in the shadow areas but none in the highlights.

7.2 Backlit situation where the light source (the sun, in this case) is behind the subject.

Exposure Problems

Exposure issues are common. Not only is every situation unique, but it may also contain elements that complicate the matter of taking a good photo.

Problem 1: Very Light or Very Dark Subjects

One exposure issue arises when you try to photograph either a very light gray or a black horse in bright sunshine (Photos 7.1 A & B). Most camera meters want to make both the gray horse and the black horse 18 percent gray, which is "middle gray." (For more information on this, see p. 22.) The exposure will vary depending on how much of the horse is filling the frame.

FIX: Take a meter reading on a grassy spot that is lit the same as your subject. Lock the exposure (or manually set the camera for that exposure) and take the picture. On some cameras, the exposure compensation feature can be used to make the meter believe that a scene is brighter or darker than it appears.

Problem 2: Backlighting

Another situation that can be tricky occurs when the light behind the subject is much brighter than the light in front of it. Backlighting tends to occur when you are standing outside on a sunny day and the sun is behind your subject (Photo 7.2). It is also a common problem when photographing while standing in a barn, with a brightly sunlit scene outside the door behind your horse.

FIX: Backlighting problems happen because the photographic media (the film or digital sensor) has a limited *latitude range*, or range of tones that it can record at a given exposure. This means that it cannot record all of the tones in a situation that has both very bright and very dark elements.

The meter takes all available information and averages the exposure. This is why movie sets have so many lights—to bring all the light levels on each element in the scene to within the latitude of the film they are using. Reflectors, fill-flash, or *scrims* (netting-like fabric used in lighting effects) can add or subtract light and even out the exposure in a scene (Photo 7.3).

Backlighting problems happen because the photographic media (the film or digital sensor) cannot record all the tones in a situation that has both very bright and very dark elements.

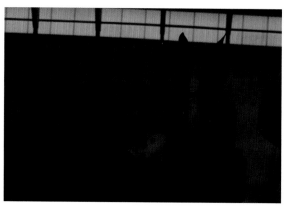

7.4 Finding adequate light can be especially difficult when photographing inside a barn or indoor arena. Even when using all the available overhead lighting, your chances of having adequate light on your subject are very small.

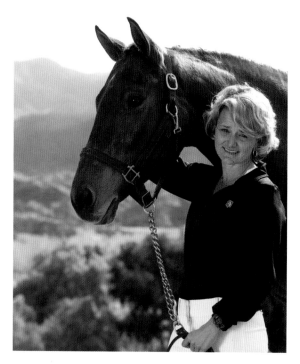

7.3 Adding a fill flash enabled me to light the subjects' faces while still keeping the background exposed properly.

If you don't have additional light sources available, and you are not worried about keeping the background as an integral part of the shot, you can use the center-weighted or spot metering patterns to calculate the exposure of your subject (see "Exposure Meters" on p. 21 for more information).

Problem 3: Not Enough Light

A particularly difficult lighting situation is one where there isn't enough light. This can happen inside a barn or

indoor arena (Photo 7.4), or occur very early or late in the day, and on very overcast days.

FIX: To add light to a situation, you can use a flash or photographic reflectors. You can also find a makeshift *windshield sun blocker*. This can be anything with white, silver, or gray sides, such as a sheet, trailer, barn, or any other bright object or structure (Photos 7.5 B & C).

Did you ever wonder why gray horses have a green cast on their bellies in some pictures? It is because the light reflecting off the green grass lights the belly of the horse. As you try to add light to a situation, beware of anything that has color, because the color will reflect onto your subject (Photos 7.6 A & B).

Problem 4: Too Much Light

Just as you may not have enough light, there are times where there is too much light. A good example of this is when you want to photograph a very light colored gray horse that is almost white with another horse that is darker, or in a setting with a lot of dark elements.

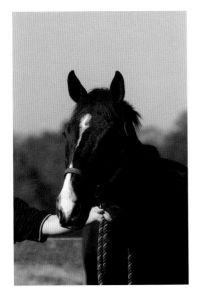

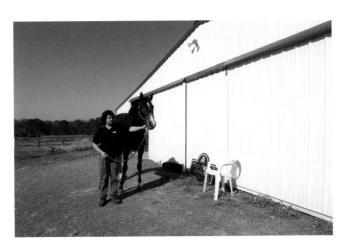

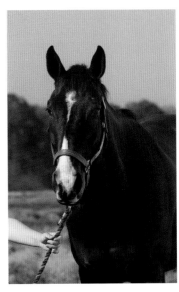

7.5 A On bright sunny days you can have a situation like this, where the shadow side area is too dark.

7.5 B Positioning the horse next to a white barn, trailer, or shed…

7.5 C …can help fill in the shadow side with light.

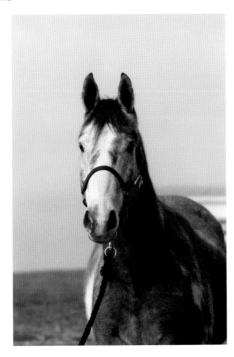

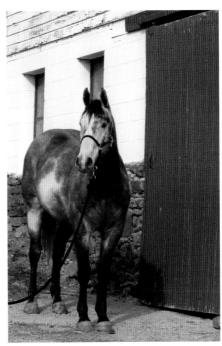

7.6 A Any colored surface will reflect color onto your subject. Notice the red on the horse's left side.

7.6 B Standing next to a red barn caused the color of the door to be cast back on to the horse.

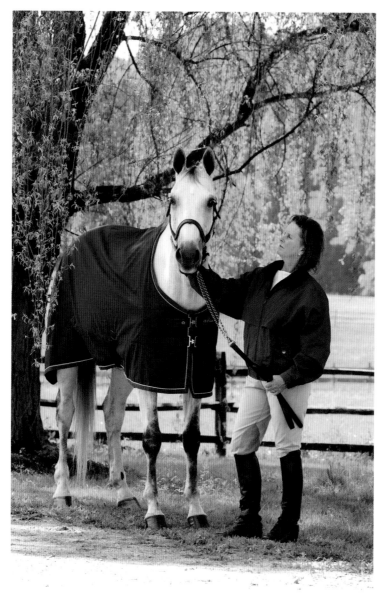

7.7 Placing this gray horse under a tree allowed for a correct exposure of both horse and blanket, while making the background look like early fall.

FIX: Things that can be used to subtract or block light include photographic scrims, darker windshield sun blockers, white or black sheets, trailers, buildings, trees, and other barriers (Photo 7.7). Just remember that nearby objects will reflect their color onto your subjects.

Focus Problems

A number of things can contribute to focusing issues. When assessing focusing problems, first be sure that your image is not suffering from camera shake (see Problem 5 below). Then examine the camera and lens you are using.

Problem 5: Blurry Photos— Camera Shake

Images taken with a longer lens may appear soft or out of focus because of "camera shake." This happens when the camera shakes or moves while the exposure is being taken at a slow shutter speed. Because the longer lens has increased the size of the image on the film plane, any movement is also magnified (for more on this subject, see "Using Tripods and Monopods," on p. 58).

FIX: A general rule of thumb is to have your shutter speed the same as, or greater than, your focal length. For example, a 200mm lens should have a shutter speed of 1/250 or greater.

You may wish to use a tripod or monopod to help steady your camera and lens if you cannot use a higher shutter speed. Keep in mind, however, that if your subject is moving, then it still might look blurred.

Some high-end zoom or telephoto lenses come with optical image stabilization technology. (Canon lenses will have an IS suffix. Nikon labels their optically stabilized lenses with a VR, for "vibration reduction.") When using lenses with very long focal lengths, optical image stabilization can help compensate for camera shake, and can allow you to take handheld shots up to two f-stops slower.

Problem 6: Blurry Photos—Incorrect Focusing Range

For my high school graduation, my mother put her camera on the "closeup" setting, thinking it would make me look closer. Instead, I ended up looking like a blob in all of those pictures.

All lenses have a focusing range, which is indicated on the focusing ring or stated in the owner's manual. Some disposable cameras and point-and-shoot cameras have a limited focusing range. They might only focus from 5 feet to infinity, so anything closer than 5 feet will not be in focus.

FIX: Make sure that your subject is in an acceptable range for your camera and lens.

Problem 7: Blurry Photos—Autofocus Error

The autofocus technology in today's cameras is far better than in previous generations. No doubt, it will improve in the years to come. But is it not foolproof.

Many situations can cause the autofocus not to perform as well as you would like. Problem areas can include objects moving erratically, subjects with little detail, something passing between you and your subject, lenses with slow apertures, and low light.

FIX: When shooting in situations where your subject will be moving at high speeds, erratically, or in various directions, use the continuous autofocus setting (if available) to allow the camera to track your subject.

You can also "fool" the autofocus if you anticipate where your subject is going and manually pre-focus or use the focus lock button on that area.

Always try to place your focus indicator on an area with some texture or pattern to help the camera discern a difference in contrast, such as the edge between the saddle pad and the saddle, the eye and the face, or the edge of the horse against the sky. Avoid focusing on large areas of the same color or tone, like the body of a solid color horse.

An object that passes between you and your subject can trick the autofocus into thinking that it should focus on the new object. Some cameras have a custom setting to help prevent this from happening. Check your owner's manual to see what options you might have with your particular camera.

Problem 8: Shallow Depth of Field

The depth of field can play a role in whether an entire image looks in focus or not. When you have a shallow depth of field, especially with longer lenses, your image may seem soft and not all of the elements in your photograph will be in focus.

FIX: Check to see what is in focus in the picture. If a point is in focus—if, for instance, the horse's nose is sharply defined but the rider is "fuzzy"—you did not have enough depth of field to keep your whole subject in focus.

On SLR cameras, use the depth of field preview button or use the depth of field scale on your lens to determine what will be in focus before taking the photo.

Remember that nearby objects will reflect their color onto your subjects.

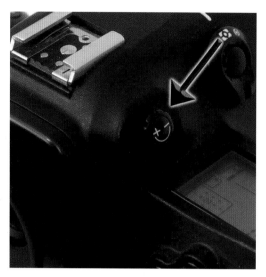

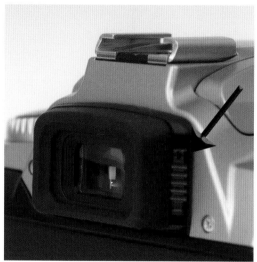

7.8 A Higher end SLRs and some mid-range cameras have a diopter adjustment…

7.8 B …that allows you to set the viewfinder for your eyesight.

Problem 9: Corrective Lens Interference

Wearing eyeglasses can be an issue for photographers—especially for those who require a high level of vision correction. You may need to remove your glasses to see things correctly in the viewfinder.

FIX: A fellow photographer once asked me why her images looked out of focus in the camera but OK on her laptop. We discovered that the diopter that adjusts the viewfinder to compensate for vision problems had been moved. Resetting it to neutral solved the problem.

Most SLR cameras have either corrective eyepiece lenses for the viewfinder or a diopter control (Photos 7.8 A & B). Check your owner's manual for more details.

Lens Problems

Problem 10: Dirt on Your Images

Every time I send my equipment in for cleaning and service, the technicians always ask me, "Where has this stuff been?"

Dirt and smudges on the lens or eyepiece can cause the same sort of trouble as wearing a pair of dirty glasses or sunglasses. Images just don't look clear and sharp through dirty lenses.

Dirt can also get on to the sensor of your digital camera (Photo 7.9).

FIX: Keeping all of your optics clean will help the camera work better, longer. Your images will look clearer and sharper.

Always use the proper lens cleaning solutions approved for camera optics and the appropriate lens cleaning cloths or tissues. Canned air can be effective for cleaning dirt and dust from film cameras and lenses.

Make sure you follow the manufacturer's instructions for cleaning digital equipment. Using the wrong solutions and even using canned air can irreparably damage the sensor.

Problem 11: Lens Flare

Any time you shoot toward a bright light source, you run the risk of the light reflecting off the lens elements and producing what is called *lens flare* (Photo 7.10 A & B).

Using too many filters can also cause this problem, because the light bounces back and forth between the filters.

Furthermore, while you can generally count on the quality of name-brand manufacturer's lenses, some third-party lenses may have poor quality coatings on them and contribute to flare.

FIX: To minimize lens flare, purchase high quality multicoated optics and use the proper lens shade for that lens. You can also use a lens hood or *flag*, which can be your hand or a piece of paper, in front of the lens to shade it from the light hitting the lens. Just make sure that the flag does not show in the picture.

Problem 12: Dark Images in the Viewfinder

Lenses with a slow aperture—typically those with a minimum f-stop of 5.6 or greater—can cause a number of problems. One of the most obvious is that the image in the viewfinder is dark, making it hard to see if the image is in focus.

Sometimes the autofocus may not work correctly in dark situations because it does not have enough light to see the subject.

In addition, some zoom lenses with variable apertures can cause exposure problems if the camera cannot detect the changing aperture.

FIX: To avoid these issues, consider purchasing lenses with a minimum aperture of f/2.8 or f/4. Select lenses with a fixed aperture, ones that have the same aperture throughout the zoom range.

When buying any lens, remember to check whether or not any third-party lens will function fully with your

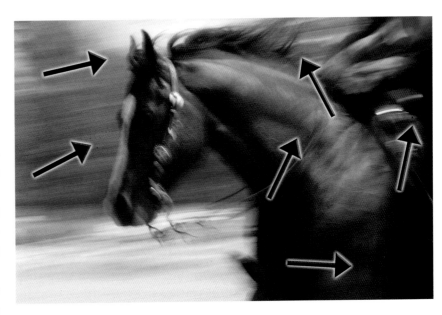

7.9 The arrows are pointing to dust on the sensor of my digital camera. If this was a print from a negative, the spots would have been white and the dirt would have been on the negative.

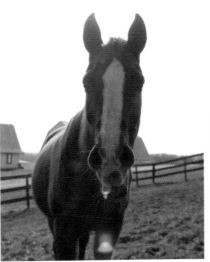

7.10 A Not having a lens hood on when shooting into a bright light source caused the lens flare visible in the bottom portion of this image.

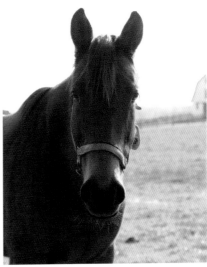

7.10 B Using a lens hood when shooting into a bright light source can eliminate lens flare.

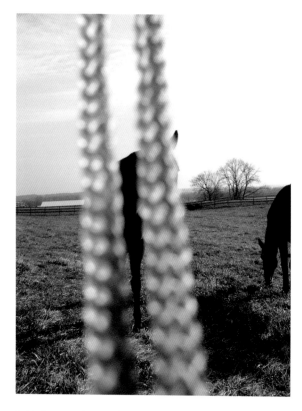

7.11 Because the viewfinder on this point-and-shoot camera is not the same lens that exposes the image, I did not see the strap hanging down in front of the lens. Always make sure you know where straps and jewelry are in relationship to the lens of your camera.

camera. With all the advanced technology in today's cameras, it is important to make sure that your lenses are 100 percent compatible.

Problem 13: Straps, Bracelets, and Fingers

Have you ever taken a picture of your camera strap, a loose dangling bracelet, or your finger? This common problem occurs particularly with disposable and range-finder point-and-shoot cameras. This is because when you look through the viewfinder of these cameras, the

scene you see comes through a different lens than the camera uses to expose the picture (Photo 7.11).

The same problem can occur with SLR cameras as well. It sometimes happens when using longer focal length lenses, because the strap is so close to the lens that the light waves wrap around the strap. The image in the viewfinder might look a little darker and not as sharply focused as it should.

FIX: Before you take the photo, be aware of your camera strap, clothing, and your hand placement to keep this mistake from happening.

Flash Problems

Problem 14: Syncing the Flash with Your Camera

The most common problem when using a flash happens when you use a shutter speed that is higher than your camera's sync speed. *Sync speed* refers to a camera's optimum exposure time for flash photography. If your shutter speed is out of sync with the duration of the flash, your photograph will have a black or very underexposed area along one side of your image (Photo 7.12).

FIX: Consult your owner's manual to find the correct sync speed for your camera. This may also be indicated on the shutter speed dial by a different color or an "X" placed next to the sync speed.

The typical shutter sync speeds for the focal plane shutters found on most 35mm cameras are: 1/30, 1/60, 1/125, and 1/250. A sync speed is rarely higher than 1/500.

Some higher end camera systems have the ability to sync at almost any shutter speed. To achieve this, you need to have a camera and flash that are designed to work together at these speeds. You usually have to go into the custom settings to activate this feature, but it is very helpful when shooting on bright, sunny days and you want to use a fill-flash to brighten the shadowed areas of your subject (such as the rider's face under the brim of a hat) or illuminate fast moving objects.

Problem 15: Images Too Bright

Another common problem when using flashes is having images that are too bright. A leading cause of images being too bright is something blocking the flash's sensor that reads the light output reflecting off the subject.

Standing too close to your subject for the flash settings you are using is another cause of overly bright images.

FIX: Your finger, the camera strap, or any other object might be blocking the flash sensor. Remove the object in question from the proximity of the flash sensor and the problem will disappear.

Problem 16: Images Too Dark

When an image is too dark, it is typically because you were too far away from your subject to effectively light it. Most flash units have a scale indicating the effective range of the flash for a given setting (Photo 7.13).

FIX: Moving closer, increasing the ISO, slowing the shutter speed, and opening the aperture can help put your images in the right light.

Double-check the settings on your flash and camera to see that they are set correctly. Also, make sure your batteries have a "ready" light before you take the picture.

Carefully read the owner's manual. Understand how each of the settings works and know the limits of your flash unit to correct lighting inconsistencies.

Problem 17: Red Eye

Red eye—or "green eye" in the case of horses and other animals—occurs when light from the flash reflects off the retina. When the ambient room light is low, our pupils dilate. Because the flash is usually close to the axis of the

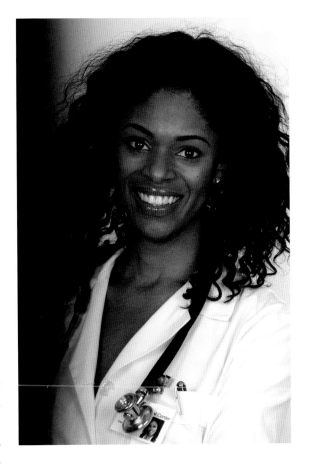

7.12 This image shows a dark area along the left side where the shutter was already closing before the flash fired.

camera lens, the light from the flash bounces off the retina and right back at the camera, which is then recorded on the film or digital media.

FIX: To help eliminate red-eye from your photos, use the red-eye reduction setting on your camera or flash, if it is available. This sends out a pre-flash, before the main flash, that makes the pupils constrict and lessens the chances of the flash reflecting off the retina.

Moving the flash off the camera lens axis is another way to correct the problem. If the flash is moved far away from the center of the lens via an extension cord or

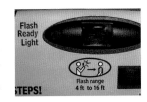

7.13 Know the range of your flash. On this disposable camera, the icon shows a working distance of from 4 to 16 feet.

strobe lights, the light cannot reflect off the retina directly back to the camera.

As a last resort, you can always buy a correction pen at the photo lab to cover up the red eye in your prints, or learn how to correct it in a graphics program such as Photoshop.

Problem 18: Bright Reflections

Have you ever taken a picture in a glass-enclosed lounge or viewing room and found nothing but a bright reflection of the flash in the window on the final image? Using a flash with glass or any other very shiny surface behind your subject—or between you and the subject—can be a problem. The bright reflection happens because you are standing perpendicular (90 degrees) to the glass or shiny surface, and pointing the flash directly at it. The flash of light is then reflected straight back to the camera.

FIX: To prevent capturing the flash on film, move so you are not shooting at a 90 degree angle to the glass or shiny surface.

Color Issues, White Balance, and Color Temperature

Problem 19: Color Cast to Entire Image

Images with a color cast to them have been taken with the wrong film—or the wrong white balance setting on digital cameras—for the light source that illuminated the subject.

The *color temperature* of daylight is constantly changing as the day goes on. It can be very warm, or red, at sunrise and sunset. It can also be very cold, or blue, when a thick cloud passes in front of the sun. The light under a shade tree or in the shade of a barn will be "cooler" than that of direct sun.

When you are dealing with artificial light sources, there are nearly limitless color temperature possibilities.

FIX 1: Plan ahead before you make your film purchase, or have several types of film and filters with you if you are not sure what sort of light will be available.

The most commonly used film is balanced for sunny daylight or for use with a flash. It also can be used on partly cloudy and overcast days, but the use of filters is then required for accurate color reproduction. (For more information on this, see "Color Temperature" on p. 43.)

If you are shooting indoors in a stall or an office, under a tungsten light source, such as an incandescent household lamp, make sure you use film balanced for tungsten light.

You will need additional filtering on your lens if you are shooting under fluorescent lighting, which gives your images a green cast when no filters are used.

When shooting under stadium lights or in an indoor arena, some of the high-speed print films will do a good job without additional filters on the lens, but your colors may still be slightly off or a little flat.

Fixing the problem digitally is much easier, because you have the option of changing the white balance as you go.

For consistent, accurate color rendition, remember to select the correct white balance for your situation. Don't always rely on the auto white balance setting to give you accurate color for horses, because your camera can be fooled by large amounts of color in a scene.

Some cameras allow you to take custom white balance readings and save them to use later. This feature can be very useful when shooting in an indoor arena or outdoor stadium. Consult your owner's manual to see if your camera has this option and to learn the procedures for taking custom readings.

FIX 2: Correcting the light source can correct the color temperature of your situation. Applying a color-correction filter to the light source can change its color temperature to match the film type you are using. Color-correction filters come in either sheets or tubes that slide over fluorescent bulbs. They can be found at camera stores or theatrical light shops.

Problems with Film and Prints

Problem 20: Fogged Film

Fogged film occurs when it is exposed to X-rays such as those at airport screening areas. This can produce a grainy, overexposed image with dark areas that appear green. The effects of X-rayed film cannot be corrected in the printing process.

FIX: Properly transporting your film through security checkpoints will help prevent X-ray damage. You can purchase lead-lined film bags to protect your film as it goes through the machines, but you will more than likely be asked to have your bag hand-checked.

Some international airports are not very accommodating about hand-checking film. If possible, it is a good idea to have your exposed film processed *before* you travel.

When I was shooting film, I would take all my film out of the boxes and canisters it came in, place it in clear plastic bags, and hand it to the screeners for a "hand check" before I went through the metal detector. This procedure worked well at most security screenings.

Kodak has a service bulletin that addresses the problem of X-ray damage when traveling. For more information, visit the Web site http://www.kodak.com/global/en/service/publications/tib5201.jhtml.

Problem 21: Heat and Humidity

Most consumer films are designed to be used and processed by the expiration date noted on the package (Photo 7.14). And, processing the film as soon as you use

it will produce the best color rendition. Remember that changes in heat and humidity can shorten a film's usable life span.

Professional films are manufactured with a tighter expiration tolerance and are typically refrigerated until used. They are no less susceptible, however, to atmospheric conditions.

FIX: Always follow the manufacturer's recommendations for storing your film. Never leave film in the glove box of your car or truck. Keep it away from heaters. After shooting your photos, process your film as quickly as possible.

Problem 22: Scratches and Dust

Scratches on your film are permanent scars that will show up when you have that image printed or scanned.

FIX: Scratches can sometimes be corrected digitally with photo manipulation software. You can also try having the film scanned by a newer generation scanner with built-in software that can remove most scratches and dust. The easiest way to protect your film, however, is to store it correctly.

Problem 23: Color, Density, and Contrast

Poor color, density, or contrast is related to whether or not you properly expose your film.

If you overexpose your negative film, the image will look very dense or thick. This makes it hard for the light from the printer to pass through the negative, resulting in a poor quality print that looks very light.

An underexposed negative is one that looks very thin or clear. When printed, the light from the printer easily passes through the negative, making a dark print with very little detail.

A negative with a lot of contrast has both overexposed and underexposed areas of the film, which makes it harder to reproduce well.

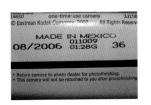

7.14 All film products have an expiration date. Changes in heat and humidity will greatly shorten a film's usable life span. Use and process the film before this date for the best results.

FIX: Using the proper exposure for the situation or location is the best line of defense for images that lack color, density, and contrast. If problems with color and density persist, then you might want to have your camera meter checked to make sure it is accurate.

The speed of the film you use can affect the quality of your final images. Higher speed films typically have a larger grain than slower speed films. A large grain can produce a less than satisfactory print if enlarged or cropped into a small area. Whenever possible, try to use slower speed film.

Problems with Prints from Digital Files

Problem 24: Visible Pixels, or Lack of Detail

When digital prints lack detail and sharpness, or show signs of pixilation, it usually means that the resolution was not high enough for that printer or printing process.

When making prints from digital files, it is critical that you know the proper resolution for the output device. This can be your own printer, the photo lab, or any other device that will reproduce your images.

FIX: Most photo labs that make prints from digital files have a resolution guide to let you know what size prints you can make from a particular digital file. Check with your lab before you make any changes to your digital files for printing.

Problem 25: Quality Issues in Prints from Inkjet Printers

The inkjet printer manufacturers have made it very easy to make prints at home. To produce consistent quality and color prints on your own, however, you need to follow the manufacturer's directions.

If you do not maintain your inkjet printer correctly, your prints will not be as sharp as they should be. You could have a line though your prints because the print heads are clogged. You could even have prints in which one color is totally missing.

The following images illustrate several problems that you might encounter with your inkjet printer (Photos 7.15 A – F):

FIX: Set up the printer and take into consideration any color management requirements for your software (see "Color Management," on p. 89). Make sure that the inks and papers are compatible with your machine.

Clean and align the print heads from time to time.

Also, don't leave the printer on for months at a time. Most inkjet printer directions instruct you to turn the printer off when it is not in use. Leaving it on for long periods, with nobody using it, can result in all the print heads clogging.

Finally, if you work in a room or office where cat, dog, or horse hair might be present, cover the printer to prevent those hairs from sticking to the print head, and then smearing ink all over your prints. (Trust me—I learned the hard way!)

Don't leave an inkjet printer on for months at a time. Turn the printer off when it is not in use. Leaving it on for long periods of time, with nobody using it, can result in clogging all the print heads.

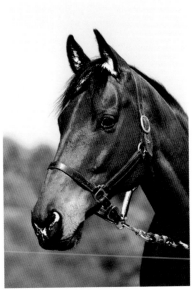

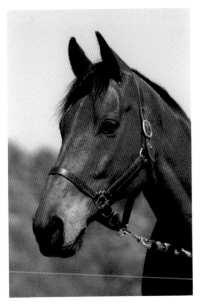

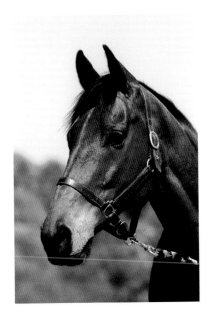

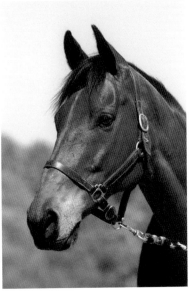

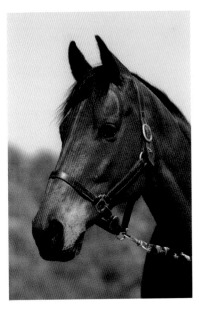

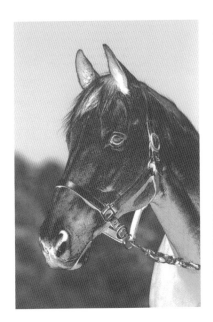

7.15 A Printing correctly.

B Running out of black ink.

C Yellow ink low.

D Yellow and black ink completely gone.

E Missing some yellow and black ink, possibly clogged ink jets.

F Low on yellow ink, and possibly clogged yellow and black ink heads.

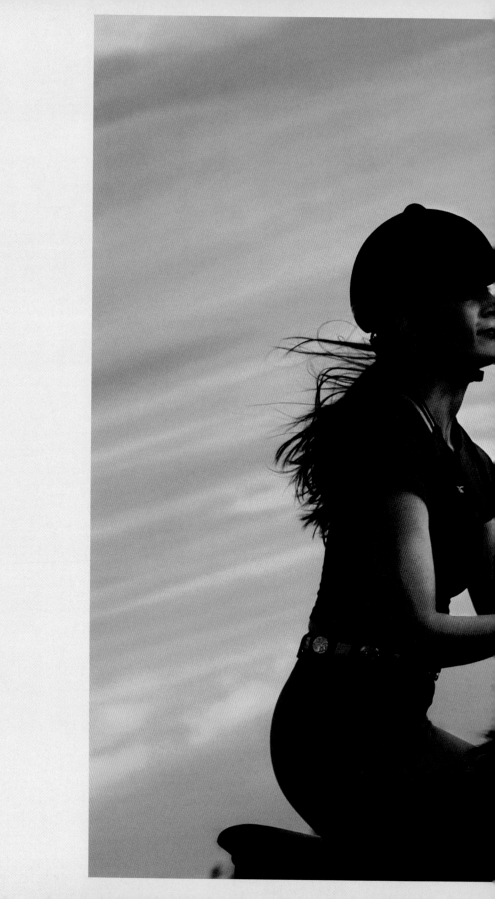

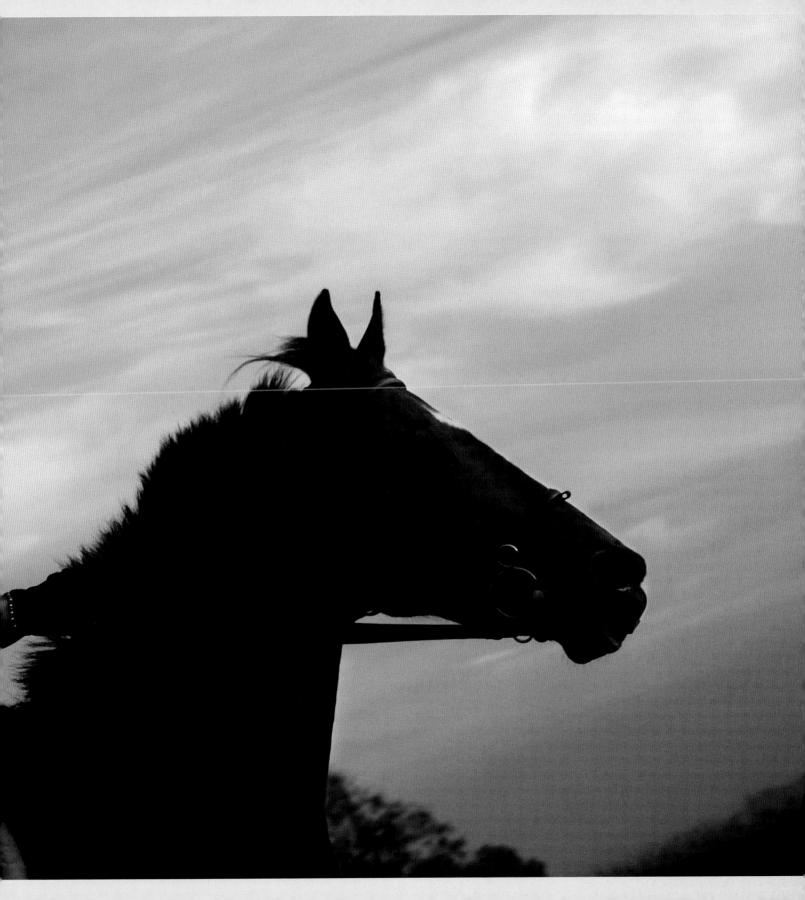

8

Turning Pro—
Handing in Your Amateur Card

You may eventually reach the point in your horse photography when people start telling you that you should take pictures for a living. If the thought appeals, there are several things to consider.

Selling your photos can be very rewarding. The first time you pick up a magazine or newspaper and see one of your photos printed, along with your credit line, is a memorable occasion. As a professional equine photographer, you have the opportunity to attend important events, meet top horses and riders, and record history in the making (Photo 8.1). But before that can happen, you must first understand the business and legal end of photography.

To begin with, you must realize that actually taking photos is going to be the smallest part of your business. The professional photographer wears many hats. He is a businessperson, accountant, lawyer, bill collector—and don't forget the janitorial duties!

Moving from a Hobby to a Business

Before you hang out your shingle, you need to know what licenses, permits, and zoning regulations are required to run a business in your area. You also need to investigate what type of business you wish to set up.

You need to answer some basic, but important, questions. For instance:

▶ *Will you operate best as a sole proprietor, a partnership, or a corporation?*

▶ *Do you need an office and, if so, where will it be located?*

▶ *Will you need to hire someone to help you?*

▶ *How will you advertise your business?*

As you can see, if you want to make a leap into professional photography—even part-time—there is a lot more work to doing it right than when taking pictures was just a hobby.

Several photography organizations exist that can help you understand the business. These include the American Society of Media Photographers (ASMP), Editorial Photographers, Professional Photographers of America, Advertising Photographers of America, and Equine Photographers Network, among others. In addition to these, there are many Web sites and online forums to help you find the necessary information and support to conduct your business. (See the "Resources," p. 182, for contact information.)

Model Releases

One of the most misunderstood aspects of professional photography is whether or not you need a *model release* from someone in order to take his or her picture.

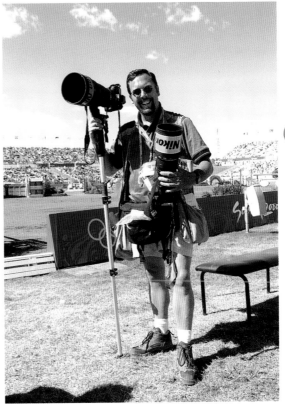

8.1 The author at work at the 2000 Sydney Olympics.

If you go pro, you must realize that actually taking photos is going to be the smallest part of your business.

A model release is a document that both you—the photographer—and your subject (or the parent, guardian, or legal owner of your subject) sign. It clearly defines how you may use an image that features the subject in question. Model releases typically outline whether or not the photographer may profit from the images taken, and whether or not the subject is entitled to notification or compensation from the use of those images.

There is no standard "boilerplate" form for a model release. It can say how much, or how little you want it to say. The most important thing about a model release is that both parties agree to its terms and sign it.

Certain conditions—such as whether or not the subject is identifiable within the shot, whether the image constitutes photojournalism, how the image will be used, whether the subject received compensation for appearing in the image, where the image was taken, and under what conditions the shoot occurred—must be taken into account before determining whether or not a model release is required. It is in your best interests to familiarize yourself with what the law has to say on this matter.

There is no need to worry over whether or not you need a model release when shooting your pictures. Releases may be retroactive. Photographers often shoot the images they want, and only get a model release when an opportunity to use the picture arises.

Licensing Your Images

When you "sell" a photo to a client, you are actually only *licensing* that image for a *particular* use. This is a very important distinction.

Licensing images is like running a car rental company. When someone needs a vehicle for short-term use, he goes to a rental company. He says when he needs to pick up the car, when he will drop it off, what kind he needs, and whether or not he will be taking it out of state. He also discusses who will pay for things like insurance and gas. The rental contracts include who can drive the car, which party is responsible for damage, mileage allowances, fees for overdue returns, and other considerations. The person that rents the car does not own it.

The same sort of thing happens when you license an image to a person or company. You allow the use of an image, at a certain size, for a designated period of time, within a given geographical area. Your contract also states the penalties that will arise from misusing or straying from

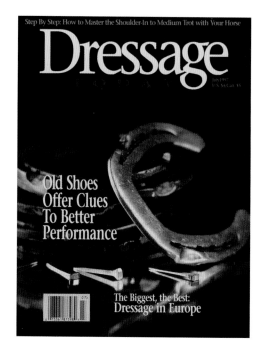

8.2 A These layouts for *Dressage Today* magazine took quite a bit of time to complete...

the original terms of the agreement.

Even when you sell a print to a rider, trainer, breeder, or owner, you should have terms stating what he can and cannot use the image for. This could include whether or not you allow its use for a sale ad, Web site, or other commercial means.

Put a Value on Your Work

Deciding what to charge is probably the trickiest part of going professional. Charging too little can set a precedent that you work "for cheap." Charging too much can drive potential clients away. Knowing your market and

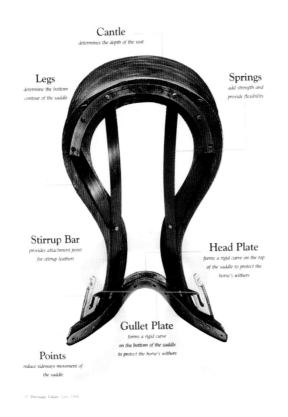

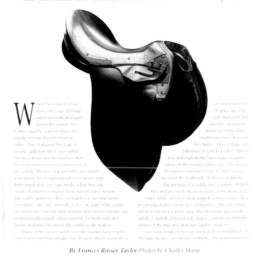

> Licensing images is like running a car rental company — the person who rents the car does not own it.

8.2 B…much longer than I expected when I bid out the job.

the value of your images is important when setting up your pricing structure.

Sometime during your photography business, you will be asked to photograph something that you do not typically do (Photos 8.2 A & B). This might be an interesting challenge you are willing to try, but you need to know how you price your studio time as opposed to what you charge for spending time at a horse show.

If your business involves supplying images to advertising and publishing companies, one price doesn't fit all situations. Before you can come up with the final asking price, you need to know things such as the circulation of the piece or publication, the size of the image that will be printed, where, and for how long the image will be used.

When renting a car, you know that a luxury model costs more than a compact or economy car. The cost of licensing images varies as well. A national, high profile product ad or cover image will demand a higher licensing fee than a regional ad, a ½ page inside image, a local ad, or a 1/8 page inside image. They are all your photos. They all do essentially the same thing. But the fee to license them is very different, depending on the advertiser or publisher.

The first thing you need to do before you license an image to a publisher or advertiser is understand the value of your photography. When your image is used as a commercial tool to sell a product or a service, your image is—for all intents—a spokesperson for that company. In turn, it is worth more money because it is being used to draw people to that ad or Web site.

There are several good books on the market to help you determine photo pricing, but the one I use as my bible is *Negotiating Stock Photo Prices* by Jim Pickerell. Pickerell explains the value of photography in today's marketplace. In addition, he walks you through the process of negotiating a proper licensing fee for the use of your images. He also gives you a list of average prices for just about every conceivable use.

Know Your Copyright

Copyright is a federal law that protects the creator of art such as drawings, paintings, photographs, literary works, screenplays, movies, and music. Copyright protects you from people stealing your work and selling it as their own. It also prohibits them from selling your work for you without your permission.

By law, when you take a photograph you own the rights to that image as soon as you take it—even before it is processed into a print, slide, or digital file.

To help protect your investment in your photography and your rights under the copyright law, you must conduct your business in such a way that your clients understand how they may and may not use your images, and what the penalties are if they misuse your photos. This means having the proper paperwork to conduct your business, including delivery, assignment, stock photo, and editorial photo contracts with terms and conditions. Also, don't forget to stipulate the terms and conditions of prints that you sell to a client. This lets the client know what he can and cannot do with the image.

> When you take a photograph you own the rights to that image as soon as you take it—even before it is processed into a print, slide, or digital file.

Part of the process to get full protection under the copyright law requires you to register your images (both published and unpublished) with the Library of Congress (LOC). Registering your images with the LOC allows you to seek larger damage amounts, punitive damages, and lawyer's fees should a copyright case end up in court. Without registration, your images are still protected but your maximum damage amount is much less and you cannot collect punitive damages or lawyer's fees in the case of copyright infringement.

The ASMP has lobbied hard to make the process of registering your images very easy. You simply burn a CD or DVD of all the thumbnail images and 5 x 7-inch JPG files at 72 DPI that you can fit on a disc, fill out the application, and send in the registration fee. Some companies will do this for you, but the cost is much greater than if you were to do it yourself. You can also send copies of the material to be registered. These will not be returned to you.

Once the LOC receives your package, your images are registered as of that date—even though it may take up to six months for you to get the final paperwork.

A key phrase to know when talking about copyright law is the term "work-for-hire." Agreeing to do work-for-hire can strip you of all rights to the images you create. If you sign a work-for-hire contract, every photo you take for your client becomes the property of the person or company you have contracted with and you have no rights to those images, even though you created them.

Contracts

As you can see, the legal issues of photography are many. But understanding the legal aspects of copyright law, invoices, contracts, purchase orders, model releases, terms,

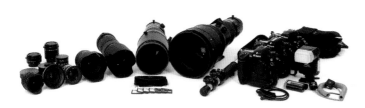

8.3 Quality photographic equipment is far from inexpensive. Insurance is good peace of mind when I am carrying such a sizeable investment around with me—especially when traveling.

and conditions is vital to running a successful photography business.

Protect your company and yourself. Make sure you have all the proper legal documents and use them every time you make a transaction.

A little homework can help you find the necessary information. Consult Web sites, lawyers, organizations, and books that address the legal issues photographers face. Some books even include sample documents that you can use. In addition, you can find several books on how to price and license your images. (See the "Resources," p. 182, for more information.)

Avoid the Most Common Pitfall: Giving Images Away

Many photographers who are just starting out make the grave mistake of giving away images to "get their foot in the door." This rarely works in the long run. Once you give away even just *one* photo to someone, you have set a precedent for that person (and all his friends) to come to you and expect to get future photos for free.

I am not saying that you should *never* give or donate images, but you should always get something in return, such as advertising space of comparable value, or a tax statement for your donated images so you can deduct their costs from your taxes.

The bottom line is: how would you feel if you found out that you licensed an image to a client for $50, while that client paid $500—or even $5,000—for another image from another photographer for the same use? I have seen this happen more than once.

Insurance

An important consideration is having the proper insurance to cover you and your equipment (Photo 8.3). Consult your insurance agent for advice on covering your equipment and on getting liability insurance for your clients.

How would you pay for a $500,000 hunter champion if your photographing him somehow caused his injury or death? You don't want to be stuck with the vet or hospital bills if you take a picture and spook a horse that then injures himself or the rider. Liability insurance can help guard against such a disaster. (It can also cover you against property losses such as might occur as a result of a strobe light you were using breaking and causing a barn to be set on fire.)

Don't forget about health care insurance for yourself. Though insurance premiums have skyrocketed in recent years, lack of insurance is a very risky undertaking. Remember: you are working around animals that can be very dangerous. What happens if you have no insurance and get kicked by a horse? Who will pay the bills while you are laid up? When out on a job, the last thing you want to worry about is, "What if something happens to me?"

Do Your Homework

Many of the photography organizations that I have referred to (see p. 125) have group insurance options that are included with their memberships. This includes property, liability, and health care. Do the research and have the correct policies to protect you.

As I said earlier, running a photography business is not just about taking pictures. I find that I only shoot about 25 percent of the time. I spend the other 75 percent doing administrative and office duties.

No matter what type of equine photography you plan on pursuing, knowing your legal rights and the rights of others helps you protect yourself. This includes knowing what documentation you need to conduct a successful business. So be prepared, educate yourself, and be willing to keep learning.

If you sign a work-for-hire contract, every photo you take for your client becomes the property of the person or company you have contracted with and you have no rights to those images, even though you created them.

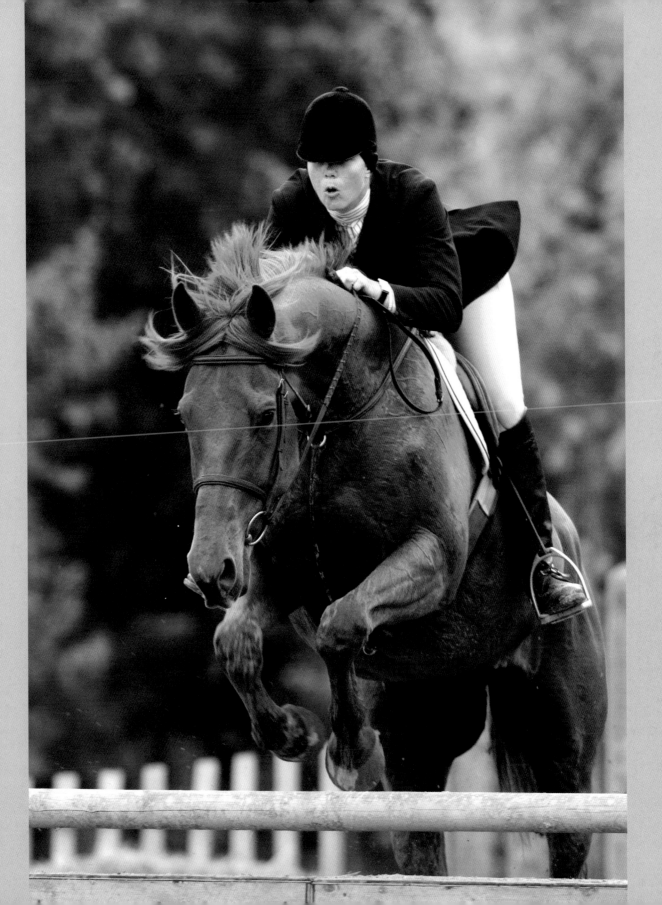

9

Tips for Success

P hotography is not something you will excel at overnight. You have to put many hours into it before you can be consistently good at it, but it is still a constant learning experience.

You might see something unusual or read about a different approach and say to yourself, "I can do that," or "I would like to give that a try." But it may take some time to master a new technique. Since both the world of photography and your subjects are always changing, you should always be learning and working to improve.

Finding different things to photograph in an interesting way is always a challenge. It is an ongoing, never-ending process of looking at things in different ways and trying different approaches until you get the right shot.

No matter how far you want to go with your photography, you must know how to use your equipment. This is true whether you are just a weekend picture-taker or an aspiring professional.

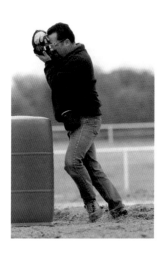

9.2 A I am always thinking of new angles from which to shoot.

The more comfortable you are with the equipment you have, the more of a "second nature" it will be to use. This translates into better photographs, because you will eventually reach the point where you do not have to think everything through for every photo—taking photographs will just become instinctive.

You could never learn everything about photography over the course of one lifetime. Mastering your craft means constantly learning and experimenting. It means taking *lots* of photos and then seeing what works and what doesn't.

Bill Stultz was one of my mentors when I was growing up. He was a father figure to me and owned the hardware store where I got my first job at fourteen. Bill always said, "Make sure that you learn from your mistakes."

He reinforced this concept nearly every day when he would tell me, "You are never too old to learn. You should learn something new everyday."

Bill's advice certainly holds true in photography. Constantly look for new angles to shoot and new things to try (Photos 9.2 A – D).

I am never satisfied with my work. I'm always looking to improve the quality of my photographs. During the learning process, the mistakes you inevitably make aren't as important as understanding *why* something did not work.

Stay current. Learn from others. Read voraciously. Keep up with the latest photographic technology such

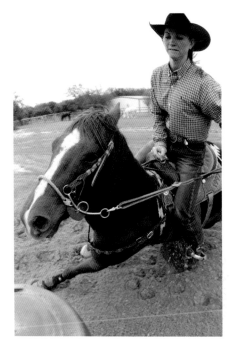

9.2 B New angles often necessitate quick thinking and extra legwork. Here I am "dancing" around the barrel as the rider and her horse make the turn.

9.2 C I had been thinking about this angle for barrel racers for a long time.

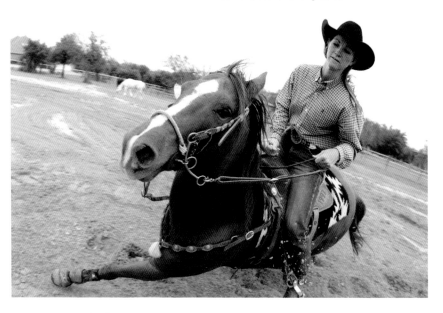

9.2 D On a couple of occasions, I was so close that the camera lens bounced off the horse's nose—which neither of us liked.

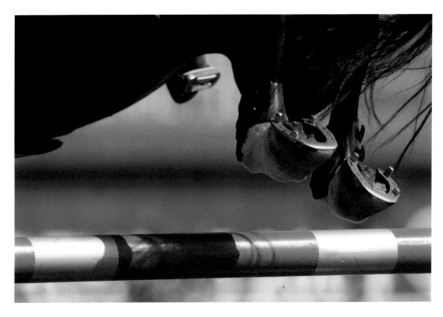

9.3 A During the 2004 Athens Olympics, the footing for the show jumping became an issue, so I decided to focus on the studs that riders use in the horse's shoes.

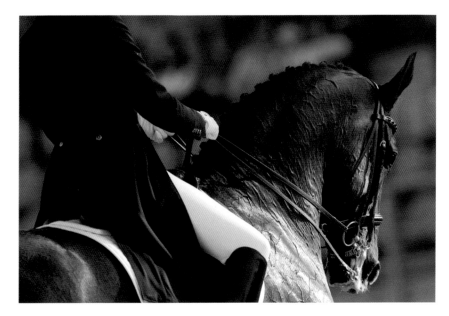

9.3 B During the freestyle dressage finals, I caught Germany's Ulla Salzgeber on Rusty in this narrow shaft of light. The light was gone the next time she came by this point.

as the newest cameras, lenses, and accessories. Be hungry to know about anything that might help you produce better photographs.

People often ask me why I take so many pictures. My answer is that I am not happy with the "okay" image; I am looking for that "great image." When I covered the 2004 Athens Olympics, I shot more than 26,000 pictures, which averaged around 1,238 images a day during my three weeks in Greece (Photos 9.3 A – C).

Of all those images, I am *really* happy with only 12 to 24 of them. This is not to say that the rest are not usable, because many of them have been used. It just means that I have set a higher standard for the work I want to produce.

The things you learned in this book are not just meant for photographing horses. They can be used in nearly any type of photography. Whether you are attending an equine expo, competition, school play, sporting event, going on vacation, or just playing around with your camera, the information in these pages should help you produce better photographs.

Before you venture out to capture those intimate moments, beautiful settings, or breathtaking action shots, let me leave you with a few final tips:

Ten Tips for Photography Success

1. Know your equipment.
2. Practice, practice, practice.
3. Envision your final image.
4. Practice your timing.
5. Be ready for anything.
6. Move around (this includes getting up and down).
7. Try different things.
8. Take chances.
9. Never stop learning.
10. Just go out and *play*!

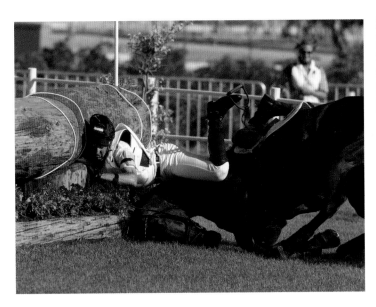

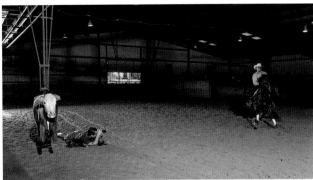

9.3 C In this dramatic image, Andreas Zehrer and his horse Raemmi Daemmi, of Austria, crash on the cross-country course. They both got up with no report of injury.

In the end, it all comes down to shoot, shoot, and shoot some more. Do things you've never done before. Look for ways to produce images no one has ever seen (Photos 9.4 A & B).

Finding different things to photograph in an interesting way is always a challenge. How can I make this stack of hay or these round bales look interesting? This horse in the snow? This horse and rider and their reflection? John Lyons? These hands and feet? It is an ongoing process of looking, and looking at things in a different way—trying it one way, then another (Photos 9.5 A–F).

Go out and experiment with new equipment, techniques, lighting, or different subject matters. Don't wait for the ideal conditions to shoot. Just go out, have fun, and enjoy!

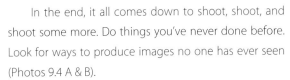

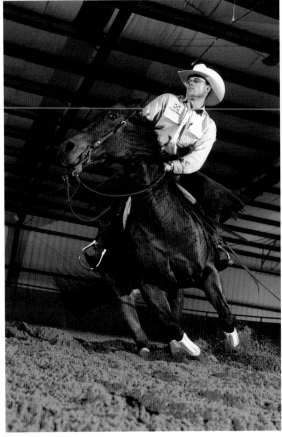

9.4 A & B On a trip to Texas I wanted to shoot some cutting horses. Here I am lying on the ground between the mechanical calf and the cutting horse. The unusual angle made for some interesting images.

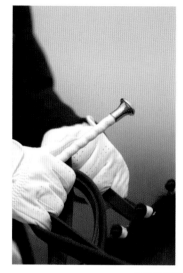

Photos 9.5 A–F Finding interesting ways to photograph images is a never-ending process.

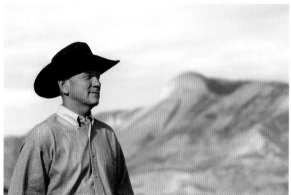

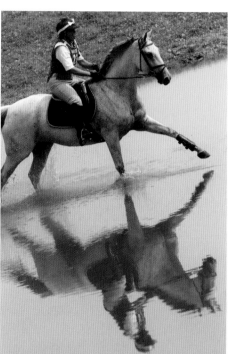

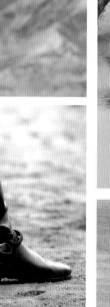

Do things you've never done before. Look for ways to produce images no one has ever seen.

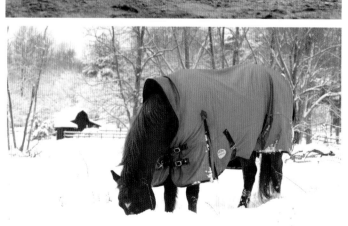

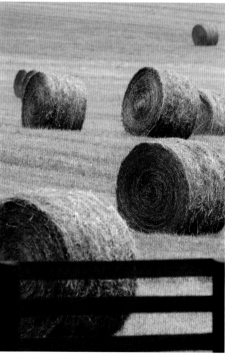

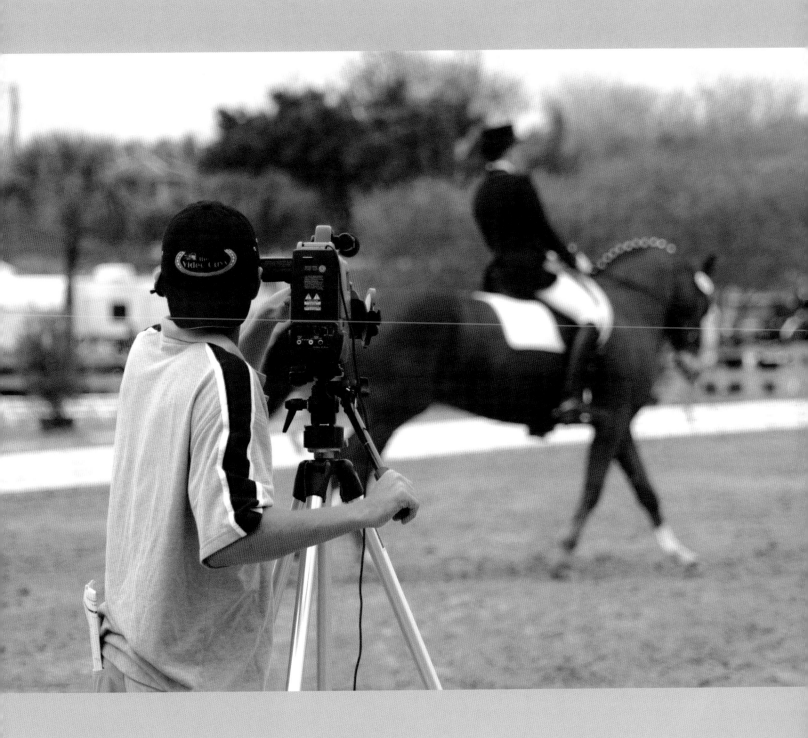

10

Equine Videography

by Stormy May

photos by Rhett Savoie

n many ways, taking successful video images is related to taking good still photos. Effectively recording a friend's lesson, capturing a class at a show, putting together a sales video, or producing a promotional video for your stallion or riding facility requires the right equipment, a little planning, and a bit of practice.

This section offers practical suggestions and advice for successful equine videography, from selecting the right equipment, to setting up your shots, to getting the sound, to completing the final edit.

The Right Equipment

A video camera (camcorder), extra battery packs, tripod, and some video editing software and hardware are the basic necessities for any video project (Photos 10.1 A & B).

Electronics get more sophisticated and less pricey every day. The only

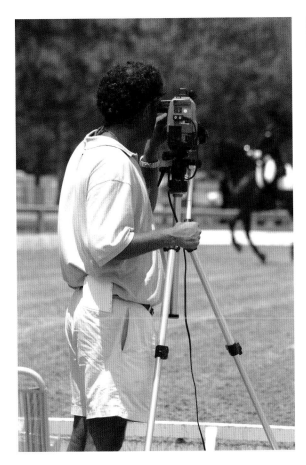

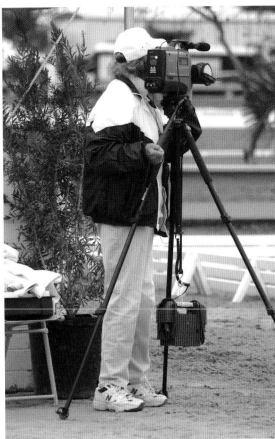

10.1 A & B You don't have to be a professional to record competent, useful video images. Much of what you know about still photography applies to video as well. Knowing how to capture a horse, lesson, or class on video can be a great complement to your still photography skills.

way to keep up with the latest trends is to educate yourself by looking at the Internet (see "Prices" on p. 141) and speak with a reputable sales person at a video equipment store.

With today's technology, you can get yourself up and running for under $600 with a broadcast-quality camera and a tripod good enough to make your palm-sized camcorder act like a full-sized movie camera. If you are not certain about the wisdom of investing in a particular piece of equipment, look into rental options in your area.

Rapid advances in technology quickly make "cutting edge" obsolete. When shopping for a video recorder,

know what you want to do with it before you start to shop. Be familiar with the options available, and don't allow extras to overwhelm you.

The Camcorder

If you are in the market for a new camcorder, look for a digital video with *three CCDs (Charged Coupled Devices —also called *three-chip technology*). Three CCD chips in the camcorder will separate the red, blue, and green colors, giving you vibrant "broadcast quality" colors. The color quality of video cameras with a *single* CCD chip is noticeably inferior.

Other specifications you will want in a camcorder for videoing horses are good backlight and/or manual exposure control, and at least a 10X optical zoom lens (20X or 30X optical zoom capability is even better).

Don't be fooled by camcorders with a large digital zoom number. Using the digital zoom will make your subject appear grainy and unstable. Use only the optical zoom for the best quality picture.

Low Light Specifications

If you know that you're going to be shooting in low light (such as nighttime events under lights or in indoor arenas anytime) it's important to start with a camcorder that does well in these situations. Otherwise, no matter how many chips your video camera has, your final video will have a grainy look, referred to as "noise," in the picture.

If your camcorder comes with an automatic light or flash, don't bother using it when videoing horses. It won't be powerful enough to help.

When choosing your video recorder, take the *LUX rating* into consideration. LUX measures the camera's light sensitivity. In low light situations, a camera with a low LUX rating will produce video of significantly superior quality than a camera with a higher LUX rating.

Three-chip video cameras that have a minimum illumination rating of 1 LUX should serve you well in all but the darkest of situations. If you're only going to be shooting outdoors during the day, you can afford to skimp on the low light rating.

Media Types

Consumer camcorders record onto a variety of media. Analog VHS, 8mm, and Hi8 tapes are all but obsolete (Hi8 tapes may be used as a digital medium, however. See "Digital8 tape," p. 141.) Digital video recording is the new norm.

Most digital media formats capture accurate, high-resolution images and record quality audio. Many camcorders also allow you to take still images. Bear in mind, however, that with current technology, the quality of still images from video recording equipment is noticeably inferior to the quality of photographs taken with a digital camera.

At this time, no standard digital video format or medium exists. The most common formats include:

▶   **Digital Video Disc (DVD).** Some camcorders record onto a miniature digital disc. Mini DVD-R discs may be recorded upon only one time. Mini DVD-RW and mini DVD-RAM discs allow you the option of re-recording on them. The DVD-R and DVD-RW discs may often be viewed on your home DVD player or computer DVD drive. DVD-RAM discs require a DVD-RAM drive for viewing.

Because the discs do not deteriorate with repeated viewing, as tapes do, and because the disc format allows for easy computer editing, many people consider the DVD format to have a distinct advantage over others.

▶   **MiniDV tape.** Camcorders that use MiniDV tapes can be very compact and produce video that is clearly superior to analog equipment. MiniDV tapes are capable of recording at a horizontal resolution of up to 500 lines (a standard television set delivers a picture of no more than 480 lines).

MiniDV tapes are somewhat limited, however, because of their composition. Since they are still tapes, they are subject to damage from heat, magnets, moisture, and other media hazards. But the relatively low cost, high compatibility, and ability to re-record over sections make MiniDV camcorders very popular.

> Using the digital zoom will make your subject appear grainy and unstable. Use only the optical zoom for the best quality picture.

MiniDV tapes are also used in high-definition (HD) camcorders. HD camcorders use the same technology found in HDTV to produce superlative image quality in a picture with at least 720 lines.

▶ **Digital8 tape.** Camcorders that record using this high-quality digital video format are often one of the most economical choices, though they may not be as compact as those of other formats. Digital8 camcorders use analog Hi8 recording media, but digitally encode the information recorded. A high-quality Digital8 camcorder can record at a horizontal resolution of more than 500 lines.

▶ **Microdrive.** With this disc-less, tapeless format, you can record digital video directly onto a flash memory card. It allows you to select the level of recording quality (the highest level is compatible with DVD quality), determine available recording time, and take still images. Microdrive camcorders are generally very compact. The Microdrive cards enable you to easily upload the video images into your computer. Since the transfer of information is digital-to-digital, no quality is lost.

A current drawback to these camcorders is the rather limited storage space. As technology increases, however, this will be less and less of a limitation.

Size Matters

It may be trendy to get a smaller camcorder, and there are several that weigh less than one pound, but unless you want your camcorder to double as a lightweight travel and home video camera, you will do better with a larger camcorder. A larger camcorder stays more stable and has larger, easier-to-use controls than a very small one.

Prices

Three-chip digital video camcorders vary in price from $500 to $5,000. "More expensive" doesn't necessarily mean "better quality" for what you want. It pays to read editorial and consumer reviews and find the best prices online at sites such as www.cnet.com.

Finding the Right Tripod

Whether you've just invested in a new camcorder or you want to use one you already own, the next investment to make is in a quality tripod.

Still cameras take a single frame in a fraction of a second. Very fast shutter speeds won't blur your pictures if you wiggle. But video cameras don't give you that same luxury. Using a video camera requires you to follow a horse's motion while minimizing extra movement for an extended period of time. A video segment may be only two to three minutes for a jumping round, or it may capture an entire one-hour lesson. Regardless of the length of the shot, a steady camera is essential.

As the camera operator, your work should be transparent. It should not leave the viewers feeling as if they need to reach for a motion-sickness patch.

Using a tripod allows the camera to move back and forth (and, to some degree, up and down) in a gliding motion. It will also minimize the videographer's fatigue.

Don't let video cameras with "image stabilization" fool you. Image stabilization does even out some of the smaller movements, but it doesn't come anywhere close to what even the simplest tripod can do.

When choosing a tripod, make sure it is designed to hold the weight of your camera. You may find that you get better results using a tripod that is built for a larger, heavier camcorder.

In any case, your tripod should have a *three-way fluid pan head*, in which each axis is self-controlled and moved

When choosing a tripod, make sure it is designed to hold the weight of your camera. You may find that you get better results using a tripod that is built for a larger, heavier camcorder.

When you record someone's ride at a show or in a lesson, you probably won't be able to choose an optimal location or time. It's up to you to find the best available angles, light, and sound conditions.

independently from the others. It will do wonders to smooth out any rough shots.

Before buying any tripod, try it with *your* camcorder:

- ▶ Practice setting up the tripod. See how complicated the legs are to adjust and operate.
- ▶ Make sure the camcorder mates well with the base and anchors firmly.
- ▶ See how easily you can attach and release the camera from the tripod.
- ▶ Practice recording while moving the camcorder. Evaluate the resulting video for smoothness and steadiness.
- ▶ If you're going to be carrying your equipment any distance, see how quickly and easily the tripod breaks down and sets up. Also make sure you are physically able to carry it wherever you will need to go.

A decent-quality tripod runs between $40 and $50 (or more), but even a $20 tripod is better than nothing.

Editing Software and Hardware

If you only want to take videos of lessons or shows on a non-professional basis, you can do without the added expense of editing software and hardware. However, if you want to produce sales tapes or promotional videos, editing equipment is a necessity.

The traditional form of editing is called *linear editing*. Linear editing refers to the manual stopping and starting of the camera to cut and paste the video onto the final format (usually VHS tape). Linear editing is what consumers learned to do in the 1980s when they wanted to transfer different home movies onto one tape.

The advent of digital technology has largely made

linear editing a thing of the past. You may, however, decide to try your hand at it. Most likely, if you own a VCR or DVD burner, your camcorder comes with all the cables and instructions you need to perform linear edits.

Non-linear editing is today's standard. Non-linear editing involves downloading the information from your camera into your computer or other non-linear editing device. This is usually done via *firewire*, a high-speed serial communications standard for attaching camcorders and other peripherals to computers. Then, using the editing program of your choice, you can cut and paste your video together. Editing programs make it simple to add titles, music, transitions, narration, and then transfer it all back to a new tape in your camcorder, send it to a Web site to show, or burn it onto a DVD for everyone to see.

Non-linear editing software varies in price from free (or included with your computer's software) to $700 or $800 dollars for full-function editing programs such as Adobe Premier Pro or Final Cut Pro.

If you are only going to be editing on an occasional basis, and you don't have the software already, editing programs for under $100 should serve you well. If you want to do more advanced or involved editing in the future, however, it might be worth your while to start learning the more advanced programs now, rather than having to learn a whole new program when you want to improve your capabilities.

Whatever software and hardware you choose, make sure they are all compatible with each other. When a software package lists the operating specifications (available RAM, hard drive space, operating system, available ports, etc.), make sure to have the recommended requirements and not just the minimums. This avoids late night hassles and computer crashes!

Shows, Lessons, and Schooling Sessions

When you record someone's ride at a show or in a lesson, you probably won't have much say about the location or time. It's up to you to find the best available angles, light, and sound conditions.

Background

When we watch a horse and rider in "real life," our mind is able to filter out a distracting background. With the two dimensional view of the camera, however, background becomes much more important. Passing cars and busy barns are just two examples of potentially distracting backgrounds. Trees, hills, or an arena wall are much better background choices to help focus the viewer's attention on the subject.

When you look for a spot from which to shoot, try to set up your tripod in a place that will give your shot a neutral background that contrasts with the horse's color. For example, a dark horse will show up best when framed by a light sky or a light grassy hill. A light horse will look best with dark foliage or dark mountains in the background.

If you can't find a background you like, try to find a way to elevate your video camera. If you can shoot from a little hill, bleachers, or even the back of a pickup truck bed, you will still be able to catch all the action, but the ground will fill most of the background (Photos 10.2 A & B).

Make sure whatever location you choose is still close enough for you to zoom in with your camera's optical zoom and fill about 80 percent of the frame with your subject—even when it is at the far end of the arena.

Pan and Zoom

Although you want to keep the horse in the viewfinder, try to avoid unnecessary *panning* back and forth of the camera. Panning is the sweeping motion the camera makes as

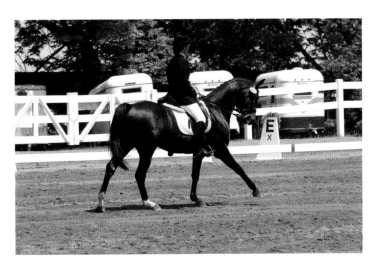

10.2 A If you can't find a background you like…

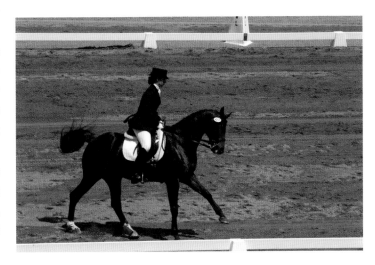

10.2 B … elevating your shooting position can often remedy the situation.

it moves from side to side to follow the subject.

If you are shooting a horse in a rectangular or oval-shaped arena, one way to minimize panning is to set up in a corner where the short and long sides come together.

Start recording a few seconds before the action starts and continue for a few seconds after it has finished.

EDIT FOR FREE

Editing programs often come pre-installed on your computer. If you've bought a new Mac or PC computer in the last few years, you may already have all the hardware and software you need.

Free *non-linear computer editing programs* include Windows Microsoft Movie Maker 2 (available for Windows XP users at www.microsoft.com). Apple's iMovie is already installed on new Macs or available for purchase at: www.apple.com.

If you want a free entry-level editing program that runs on Windows XP or Mac OSX, Avid's FreeDV is easily upgradeable to more professional grade applications if you decide later that you would like to make a career of video editing. Download the free version at www.avid.com.

If you want to be able to transfer your edited video to DVD, make sure you also have a DVD burning program and a DVD-R or DVD-RW drive in your computer. iDVD is an easy DVD burning program for Macintosh users that is included with newer Macs. For PC users, a program such as Sonic's MyDVD works well.

There, you will only need to make small movements with the camera to keep up with the action. The disadvantage to being at the end of an arena is that you will need to use the zoom feature more often.

If your camcorder's optical zoom isn't strong enough to get all the action from the far side of the arena, or if you like the lighting and background better from the long side, try positioning yourself at least 10 to 20 feet away from the closest point the horse will pass by. This way, as the horse goes by, you can still get the entire horse and rider in the frame (as opposed to a close-up of the rider's boot).

If an arena rail obstructs your view, find some way to get above it.

Practice smoothly zooming in and out until it becomes easy to keep the subject in the viewfinder.

Although a good general guideline is to have the subject fill 80 percent of the viewfinder, there may be times when you want to focus in more closely or zoom out farther. If the instructor is reminding the rider to keep her hands steady or put more weight in her heels, zooming in on that body part for several seconds may help the rider when she is reviewing her tape. In addition, zooming in on the horse and rider from a wide-angle view at the beginning of your shot, or zooming out at the end of a ride can give the video a professional flair.

Make sure you start recording a few seconds before the action starts and continue for a few seconds after it has finished. These extra seconds will allow you to make smooth transitions if you decide to edit your tape later. They will also allow you to compensate if your camcorder takes a few seconds to start up after you press the "record" button.

Lighting

If you have the luxury of planning the time of day that you are shooting, the light in the early morning or late afternoon will give you the most vibrant shots. Midday sun will flatten out even the most interesting subject.

Ideally, you want the light source (in most cases the sun), at your back. If you must shoot toward the sun, you may need a special *matte box* (a container that holds filters and attaches to the front of the lens) or another type of sun shade over your camera to prevent sun flares from showing up on your video.

Watch out for areas that have sections of bright sun and deep shade (e.g. partially covered arenas or areas surrounded by trees with dense foliage). If these can't be avoided, position your video camera so that the background is mainly comprised of the dark areas—such as trees or an arena wall. Remember, you can shoot from bleachers, a hill, or the back of a pickup bed. This enables you to block out the lightest part of the sky and make the ground become your background.

If your camera has a backlight feature or an adjustable exposure control, take some time before you start recording to test out these options and adjust them for the best picture.

The most difficult lighting situation for a consumer-quality video camera to handle is an open-sided, covered arena during the middle of the day. Unless you take steps ahead of time, the horse and rider will end up looking like a silhouette against a bright background (Photo 10.3 A). The same tricks you used when shooting in patchy shade (changing the backlight or exposure settings, or getting an elevated shooting angle) should help (Photo 10.3 B). The more bright sky you can leave out of the shot, the better the camcorder will be able to self-adjust to the light and give you a much better looking video.

If you are shooting in a completely enclosed arena, you often won't need to make any special adjustments with your camcorder other than making sure the camcorder itself is good enough to handle the low light situation.

Sound

Once you have taken the camera angles and lighting into consideration, you might need to start again at square one

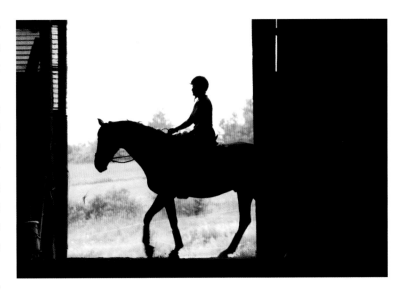

10.3 A A covered, open-sided arena makes for a very tricky lighting situation. If you don't plan ahead, you are bound to end up with poor images.

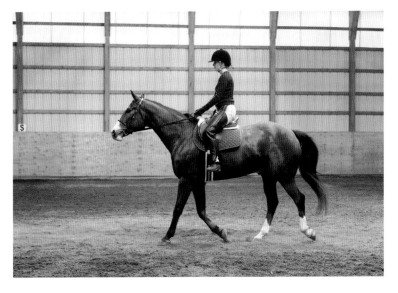

10.3 B Shooting from a higher vantage point, eliminating much of the bright light coming from outside the arena, and adjusting the camcorder's exposure and backlight settings can yield acceptable results. *Photo Charles Mann*

as you consider the sound. Often, the ambient sounds you get when videoing horses are not the ones you are going to keep in the final edit. However, preserving the sound is very important when you're taping a lesson or a musical ride.

If the sound of the music or instructor's voice is amplified by a speaker system, try to locate yourself near one of the speakers and away from other people talking.

If the instructor isn't using a sound system, you may want to ask if you can record from the instructor's location, whether it is in the center of the arena or on the side. At this point, you need to ask the person you're videoing if it's more important to get a good visual shot or to hear the instructor's comments. Rarely can both be achieved from one location unless the instructor uses a sound system.

One very important point to remember is that a camcorder's built-in microphone will *not* give you the best quality sound. Professional videographers clip a small microphone (called a *lavalier* or *pin microphone*) on the instructor's clothing. This microphone transfers sound directly to the camera via a wireless signal.

If sound is crucial to your projects, make sure the camcorder has a place to hook up an external microphone. Most importantly, remember that your own voice is only a few inches from the camcorder's microphone. Unless you are the instructor, stay quiet!

> **Remember that your own voice is only a few inches from the camcorder's microphone. Unless you are the instructor, stay quiet!**

Logging

For lessons, schooling sessions, or shows, you may want to *log* your videos—add a title, date, and time to them— if your camera has the capability to do so.

Most camcorders have a function that allows you to decide whether or not you want to leave the date and time on for the whole recording. Generally speaking, unless you're filming a speed event, or you have another reason for leaving the date and time on, display them briefly (up to a minute) at the beginning of the video and then turn them off. This method of logging can be very useful for riders when they want to save and catalog their videos.

If your camcorder records directly onto DVD-R format, you can just pop out the DVD after recording and your work is finished. If it records onto a digital or analog mini tape, however, you will probably want to transfer it to another format for easier viewing.

VHS tapes and players are still widely available. Any camera that records onto such tapes will probably have output jacks to transfer the video from the camera to your home VHS recorder. If you decide not to use the sound from your recording, just plug in the yellow (video) jack to your VHS recorder to transfer the video. The white and/or red jacks are for sound. If you don't transfer the sound, you may want to make a note on the final copy that the recording contains no sound. This saves viewers from wondering what might be wrong with their equipment.

Recording and Producing a Sales Video

Sales videos can serve one of two purposes. Most often, a sales video is something that a horse's owner or trainer can send to potential buyers who, upon viewing it, decide if it's worth their time to come and look at the horse.

There are times, however, when the potential buyer might decide to buy the horse without seeing it in person. This may happen when the buyer lives far enough away to make such a trip impractical. This may also be the case when buyers are looking for a breeding animal and are relying heavily on bloodlines and proven progeny. In both cases, the video, along with the seller's good reputation might be all it takes to sell the horse and have him shipped to the buyer.

A word of advice: when shooting a sales video, be sure to represent the horse as fairly as possible. Although it might be easy to edit out undesirable aspects, sooner or later prospective buyers will come to know the truth.

For example, if your hunter routinely knocks rails, don't edit out all of his mistakes when showing his jumping. In the end, the buyers will decide for themselves if the trait is something they can live with or improve through training.

On the other hand, a sales video is not the time to call attention to situations where the horse is being disciplined, or being trained to do something new. You want to show your horse in the best possible light, without misrepresenting him.

Turnout

Video can hide some of the dust on a horse that hasn't been bathed, but the difference on camera between a horse that's just been brushed and one that has been thoroughly bathed is like the difference between a horse in average health and one in excellent health. The cleaner horse will have that extra sparkle, especially in the early morning or late afternoon sun. Adding oil to his hooves and a little baby oil on the horse's clean nose and around his eyes will help show him off and make him look well cared for.

Of course, all tack and equipment—including the halter—should be clean, well fitted, and nicely show off the horse's features.

The handlers and riders in the video will look best if they dress in a casual, professional manner. Slacks, blouses, and riding attire are appropriate. Avoid having the handler or rider show too much skin. Also avoid having anyone wear bright stripes, patterns, or excessive jewelry. These tend to distract from the horse. If at all possible, handlers should not wear the colors white or red, which are difficult to film without "flaring" or "bleeding."

Finally, riders with long hair should tie it up so it doesn't bounce and make the horse appear rough to ride. Likewise, women are well-advised to wear a good sports bra when being filmed while riding or handling the horse.

Time and Location

For a sales video, you probably have more flexibility to choose both time and location than when filming at a show or a lesson. Carefully consider when and where to shoot your video.

If the location is outdoors, early morning or late afternoon sun will give a better look to your finished video than filming in harsh midday sun.

The time of year is an important consideration as well. If your horse is clipped or kept under lights for the winter, then it's possible to video year-round. If your horse is out of work for the winter—especially if he gets a fuzzy winter coat—it might be best to postpone the video until after spring shedding. (Fortunately, if you *must* video your horse in his winter coat, most knowledgeable potential buyers will probably be sympathetic and try their best to look past the fuzz.)

Videoing the horse in his home environment may be most comfortable for both horse and handler. There are some instances, however, when you may consider trailering to an alternate location to get the shots you need.

If you decide to go off-site, look for the following:

▶ An area with footing that is good enough to show off the horse's gaits.

▶ A background that is not distracting and contrasts well with the horse's color (or an elevated position from which to shoot).

▶ An area that is large enough to show what the horse can do (e.g. a full jumping round, carriage driving course, trail course, or reining pattern).

If you decide to use your horse's home location, try to look at it with a fresh perspective. In what condition are the fences? Is there a junk pile or dilapidated barn in the background? Are the weeds out of control? Factors like these will attract the viewer's attention and may affect the potential buyer's overall impression of your horse.

A gorgeous estate in the background isn't necessary. Just try to use the elements you have to your best advantage. When all else fails, remember: the camera only sees what's in front of it—not what's behind it.

Suggested Sales Shots

A sales video of a *riding* or *driving horse* should include:

▶ Front, hind, and side conformation shots of the horse untacked.

▶ Shots of the untacked horse being walked and trotted, both toward and away from the camera.

▶ Brief shots of the horse being groomed and tacked in his usual environment.

▶ The horse being ridden or driven in the style(s) for which you are marketing him.

The video could also include:

▶ Trailer loading and unloading.

▶ Clipping.

▶ Bathing.

▶ At liberty in a pasture or corral.

▶ Longeing.

▶ Round penning or other groundwork that the horse does well.

▶ Being handled or ridden by children (only if appropriate!)

▶ Shots on the trail, around traffic, or other distractions.

▶ Footage from a show.

A sales video for a *broodmare* should include:

▶ Front, hind, and side conformation shots of the mare untacked.

▶ Shots of the untacked mare being walked and trotted, both toward and away from the camera.

▶ Shots of the mare in her home environment.

▶ Shots of any offspring or relatives, if available. (You can edit in still pictures if you get a little creative. More on this in "Adding Stills," p. 151.)

▶ Show the mare under saddle, if she is being sold as a rideable horse.

A sales video for a horse *not yet started under saddle* should include:

▶ Front, hind, and side conformation shots of the horse untacked.

▶ Shots of the untacked horse being walked and trotted, both toward and away from the camera. (Show a foal with his mother if he is not yet weaned.)

▶ Shots of the horse in his home environment.

▶ Shots of the parents, if available. (Still pictures are acceptable.)

▶ Brief shots of any training the horse has had, such as leading, tying, clipping, bathing, trailer loading, round penning, longeing, backing, etc.

Voiceovers

A *voiceover*, or narration that can be heard while the viewer is watching a video, works very well in sales videos.

If you will be editing the video on a computer, voiceovers are very easy to add to the project. For the best quality, don't try to record your own voice while you are videoing the horse. It will end up sounding as if you are very distracted and you may say things that you don't want to end up in the final copy.

The easiest way to get a good voiceover is to record a

person talking about the horse at the end of the day's video shoot. Since you will only be using the audio portion, you won't need to aim the camera anywhere in particular, so just hold it quietly while the person talks near the camera.

The best place to get narration for a horse video is in a quiet space outdoors, away from traffic, barn sounds, and other people talking. Occasional bird sounds in the background are fine, but don't sit next to a tree full of squawking or tweeting birds.

If you can't find a quiet spot outdoors, your next best choice is to do the voiceover indoors. The viewer may subconsciously think it sounds a little unnatural when they hear a voice talking indoors and they are watching the visuals of a horse outside, but it shouldn't be distracting enough to stop you from doing it when necessary.

If all else fails, most computer editing programs will allow you to add a voiceover while you're sitting at your editing computer and watching the video. This will work in a pinch, but it won't sound as natural as a recording from your video camera taken in a quiet outdoor location.

If you want to add a voiceover but won't be doing any non-linear editing, you have two primary options. Either have someone behind you say some preplanned lines about the horse while you're showing the first few shots, or show somebody on camera talking before, or immediately after, the video footage of the horse. (For more, see "Sound Editing," p. 150.)

Editing the Sales Video

Consumer-level, non-linear editing software is widely available, affordable, and surprisingly easy to learn. Many of these programs are designed as a way to edit together home movies and photos, but they can be easily tailored to fit your equine video needs.

If you taught yourself how to edit videotapes from one VCR to another in the 1980s or 90s, then you can probably figure out these editing programs even without the instructions. If you're young enough that you don't remember the 80s, you'll still be able to edit on your computer in a couple of hours.

Most of the tips in this section are for non-linear editing systems. However, if you are doing linear editing, you'll discover some hints as well.

What to Leave In; What to Take Out

In a well-edited sales video, shorter is almost always better. If your purpose in putting together a sales video is to get the potential buyers to come out and see your horse, you want to show them enough so they will be interested, but not so much that they will have time to get bored as they watch the horse trot around the arena for the seventh time.

A general guideline for a video of a ridden horse is to show no more than one minute at each gait. The walk might only need 30 seconds. If you have a particularly good video from a show, you may want to incorporate parts of that in your sales video—especially if your horse ended up winning the class.

Once you add in the conformation shots, tacking, leading, and other footage (try for no longer than one minute for each segment), you may end up with a video about 10 minutes long, which is plenty to showcase one horse.

If you look at your footage and only come up with 3 or 4 minutes of really good footage, just use that. Don't think you need to pad the video for the buyers. If you are the owner or the rider, you may fall in love watching your horse go around and around, but potential buyers will be able to tell whether or not this is a horse they want to see more of after the first few minutes. Any more than that, and you risk the viewer fast-forwarding or getting distracted.

DO'S AND DON'T'S OF VOICEOVERS AND NARRATION

DO

▸ Have a plan. Better yet—have a script.

▸ Say only what you must.

▸ Speak clearly and with enthusiasm.

▸ Be as professional as possible.

▸ Practice until you like the way you sound.

▸ Tell the truth.

DON'T

▸ Add fillers such as "um," "now," "you know," or "like."

▸ Make sarcastic or flippant remarks.

▸ Laugh nervously when you speak, or laugh at your own jokes.

▸ State the obvious ("He's trotting here…" "Now, he's going over the oxer…")

▸ Mumble, chew gum, eat, smoke, or drink while narrating.

Sound Editing: Voice and Music

More than likely you won't use any of the sound that your camera captured while you were recording. The exception would be if you have some voiceover material that you recorded in a quiet location.

If you're using a non-linear editing program, you will be able to add the voiceover to any part of the video. You can also edit what was said if you want to leave some of it out. If you're using the voiceover function and recording voice straight to your editing program, follow your program's instructions for recording your voice and adding it.

Computer editing makes it simple to add *music* to your video. Well-chosen music will seem to enhance your horse's performance and may leave your viewers humming a catchy tune that reminds them of your horse long after the video is over. Instrumental music is almost always a safe choice, but songs with appropriate lyrics can also work well in the final edit.

Don't just run out and copy your favorite song to your computer's hard drive, however. Copyright laws cover almost all commercially recorded music. Unauthorized duplication, or use without the proper license release, could lead to penalties.

If you use commercially recorded music, check with the music publisher (you can usually find contact information on the CD case) and ask about synchronization or "sync" licensing for your project. Alternatively, there are places where you can buy "royalty free" or "buyout" music. Once you pay for these songs (usually about $40 per song or $150 per CD) you are licensed to use them in any small-scale project for your entire lifetime or 99 years. A quick Internet search for "royalty free" or "buyout" music will get you headed in the right direction.

All the non-linear editing programs will allow you to add titles, still pictures and transitions between clips. These standards of the editing industry will add the finishing touches to your video and make it stand out from the rest. Pretty soon, you might feel like tackling your home movies!

Linear Editing

If you don't have access to a computer, but you do have your camcorder with video and audio output jacks, you can do a decent job transferring video footage directly from your camcorder to a VHS tape or DVD.

Some digital video cameras offer minimal editing functions such as transitions, fades, and titles right in the camcorder. Read the owner's manual and practice with these functions before you start videoing valuable footage.

If you want to output your camcorder's recording to a DVD, make sure you have a DVD burner and follow the instructions that come with the camcorder about how to transfer the information while performing linear editing functions. If you're going from a video camera to VHS, you will also want to spend some time making a linear edit.

In either case, first watch the original recording a few times, making notes about which parts you want to keep and what you want to edit out. Organize your shots into a logical order and then transfer your clips, one by one, onto the VHS tape or DVD. Keep in mind that no sound is better than bad sound—you may want to unplug the audio jacks when you're transferring.

When linear editing, try to keep your cuts to a minimum, but don't do it at the expense of adding excessive length to your video. Remember, 10 minutes is more than enough time for a video of one horse.

Adding Stills

To add still pictures to your presentation without going through a computer, mount a picture on a well-lit wall or a stiff board propped vertically in front of the camera, far enough away so the camera can focus on it. With the camera sitting very still on a tripod, zoom in on the picture until the picture edges disappear from the corners of the viewfinder.

Once the picture is properly centered in the viewfinder, let the camera record for several seconds. Now you have the picture on the same format as the rest of your video. You can edit it in with the rest of the footage to make it part of your final sales presentation.

Producing a Promotional Video

Once you've tackled lessons, shows, and a sales video or two, it's time to let your creative juices flow and put together an eye-catching video promoting a stallion, a boarding facility, a trainer, or any sort of equine program.

Stallion Videos

The best way to start is to find some other stallion videos that you really like and determine if they have elements that you'd like to include in your own video.

For stallion videos, think about the potential clients. What are they looking for? What can this particular stallion contribute to the breed or type? What are people saying about him and his offspring? What types of mares make the best crosses?

As you plan to showcase the horse's talents, consider his breed, type, and training. For example:

▶ Arabian videos tend to focus on the stallions' natural beauty and fire.

▶ Quarter Horse videos generally emphasize the horse's tractability, versatility, and work ethic.

▶ Warmblood and sporthorse videos often highlight a sire's athleticism and grace.

▶ Gaited horse videos illustrate the comfort and rideability of the horse's gaits.

▶ Driving horse videos show the stallion's obedience and elegance.

▶ Racehorse videos show the horse's power and heart, along with his records, his winnings, and the winnings of his offspring.

Don't let these examples limit you. Consider building your video around whatever characteristics your stallion excels in. Choose music, locations, and other elements that enhance these characteristics.

When shooting a sales video, be sure to represent the horse as fairly as possible. Although it might be easy to edit out undesirable aspects, sooner or later the potential buyers will come to know the truth.

You'll definitely want to include footage of some of your stallion's offspring if they are available. Even if it's just one foal with his mother, potential clients will want to get an idea of what your stallion has been producing. Showing footage of good quality offspring under saddle or at shows will help strengthen your stallion's reputation even more.

If you have the opportunity to interview satisfied clients, judges, other breeders, or trainers, they all can help you fill in the story you want to tell about your stallion.

For the final touches, get some location shots from around your farm. Perhaps include a shot of the sign guests see as they drive in, broodmares with foals resting in a pasture, or your stallion being ridden into the sunset.

Coming up with a list of shots you'd like to get before you start videoing will help ensure that you end up with all the shots you'll need once you sit down to edit them together. You may even want to get creative with your editing software—like doing a slow motion shot of your stallion galloping by, or scrolling your horse's achievements over a still picture of him taking a victory lap.

Other Promotional Videos

These videos can be as individual as your operation. You can style them after a commercial, an infomercial, a documentary, or even a fictionalized story. If you're really ambitious, the sky's the limit. Come up with the information you'd like to convey and then figure out how you want to put it all together.

Questions to ask before you begin shooting include:

▸ *Who is your audience?*

▸ *Will the video be showing during a horse show, career day, or at a trade show?*

▸ *Will it be sent out to current or potential clients?*

▸ *Will it be sent to a local television station or news service?*

The answers to these questions will help you determine length, content, and presentation.

Finished Length

Stallion or other promotional videos can be longer than sales videos because the creativity you put into them will help hold the viewer's attention. Still, limit each video to no more than 30 minutes, as a rule. This holds true unless you can tell a really good story that takes longer than 20 or 30 minutes, are putting together a video with multiple stallions, or are combining a stallion and sales horses in the same video.

The Final Edit

The new affordability and ease of using powerful, quality video equipment allows the average horse owner and lover to record and edit right alongside professionals. However, even the most sophisticated equipment requires an operator with a discerning eye to bring out the best in the equine subjects.

With the guidance from this book, practice, and feedback from your friends and clients, you can create what you want, from the first shot to the final edit.

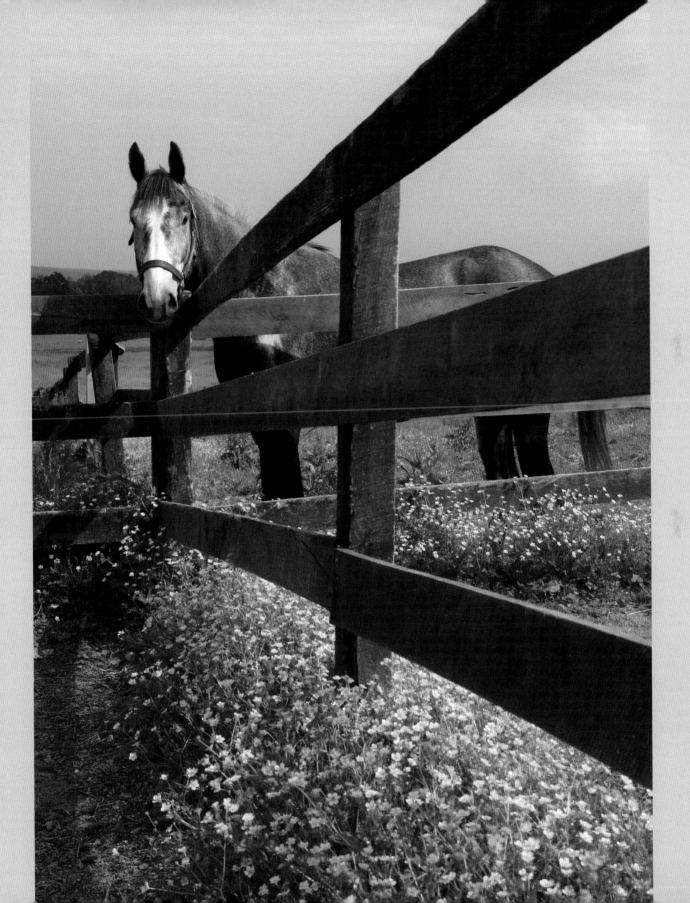

11

Sales and Promotion:
Essential Photography

by Ami Hendrickson

photos by Rhett Savoie

Throughout this book, much has been made of the merits of indulging your artist's eye, playing with the images you take with your camera, and exploring your creativity. Remember, however, that when it comes to sales and promotional photography, quality often takes precedence over creativity (for an illustration, see "Quality Sells" on p. 81). Sometimes, the success of a shoot will depend more upon showcasing a horse's merits than your artistic ability.

Photographing the Posed Portrait

No matter how much you may enjoy finding new and different angles for shooting horses, horse people will generally prefer to see images from a tried-and-true perspective, rather than an overly arty one. This does not mean that shooting posed portraits of horses standing is easy, or that the resulting images fall into the "if you've seen one, you've seen them all," category.

The straightforward shot of a standing horse is an important element of the horse industry. Horse owners, breeders, and trainers can tell a lot about an animal from a photograph. A picture is often a potential breeder's or buyer's introduction to the horse. It can give an experienced professional considerable insight. In fact, a single picture can provide the information needed to determine whether or not the horse in question is suitable for a particular breeding or training program.

Prospective breeders, trainers, and buyers will look at a posed portrait with an eye for certain aspects of a horse's conformation. Owners and riders will appreciate the same sort of picture as a tangible validation of their hard work, and as confirmation of their success.

Since a photograph of a horse standing still often serves to illustrate a win, a horse for sale, or a breeding prospect, the horse's owner wants to show the horse in the most flattering way possible. You also want potential clients to be able to learn what they need to from the picture. For these reasons, and others, a basic protocol has evolved that dictates how an image of a standing horse should look.

No one can tell you where to stand, how to shoot, and how to take a photograph. No one should try to do so. A huge part of the joy of photography is continuously developing your eye for balance, composition, and detail. Furthermore, no two photographers will ever take the same picture, even if given identical equipment, subjects, and lighting.

That said, however, there are some general rules for shooting a portrait of a horse that will enable you to show off its assets and downplay its weaknesses.

When photographing a horse at rest, with or without a rider, remember:

▸ Proportion
▸ Parts
▸ Balance
▸ Attitude

Your image may be technically perfect, but failure to take any one of these four aspects into consideration can ruin the overall effect.

Granted, the situation may arise when you deliberately neglect to follow the general guidelines outlined on the following pages. If and when that happens, you may even end up taking an exquisite photograph. It stands to reason, however, that you must know "the rules" before you can break them.

Proportion

The traditional pose for a portrait involves photographing the horse from the side, in order to show off the animal's conformation.

The average riding horse is 7 to 8 feet long from his nose to his tail. He weighs 1,000 to 1,200 pounds and stands approximately 15 hands (5 feet) high at the withers.

Averages can be deceiving, however. Delicately built miniature horses are less than 3 feet high at the shoulder and weigh a few hundred pounds. A draft horse can stand over 19 hands tall and top the scales at more than a ton. You must have an approach that allows you to relate equally well with specimens at both ends of the size spectrum.

Aim for the Shoulder

A common mistake many equine photographers make is that of taking pictures of various animals from the same vantage point. This point is generally the "default" position

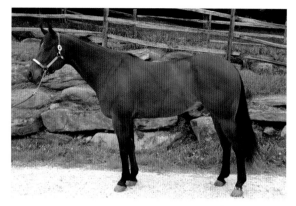

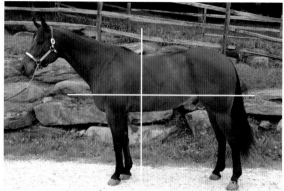

11.1 A A great deal of thought goes into composing the familiar standing portrait. Here, the horse is standing on level ground with the photographer shooting him from the side. All four legs are visible, he is balanced evenly on all four legs, his ears are up, and he is simultaneously relaxed, poised, and alert.

11.1 B Imagine a plumb line that starts behind the withers and falls straight to the ground. Imagine a second line that starts at the horse's point of shoulder and runs along the length of his body, parallel to the ground. Composing your image so that the intersection of those two lines becomes the center of your photograph will allow you to keep the horse's body parts in proper proportion.

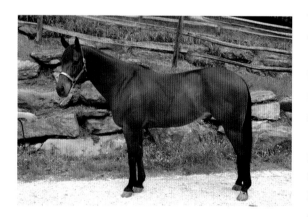

11.2 This is what can happen when you remain standing, holding your camera at eye level to take a picture of an average-sized horse. With the lens aimed at the withers, rather than further down the shoulder, the horse may appear short-legged or unnaturally squat. You also run the risk of making the body look too large, or too heavy for the legs.

that occurs when you stand up, raise the camera to your eye, and snap the picture.

In most cases, however (except when photographing extremely tall horses), standing in such a position will result in a photograph that makes the horse's body seem disproportionately heavy with respect to his legs.

When setting up a formal portrait shot, your position must be relative to the horse you are shooting. All other things being equal, aim the camera lens just behind the horse's shoulder. This holds true whether the horse is shown in hand, with a rider, or standing alone without a handler visible in the picture (Photos 11.1 A & B).

1. To begin, face the horse squarely from the side. Then move so that you are *slightly* more in line with the front legs than with the horse's barrel.

2. The horse should be standing on level ground, or very slightly uphill.

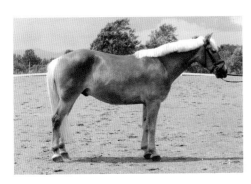 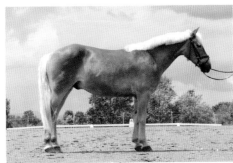 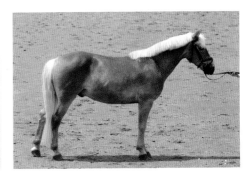

11.3 A A good starting point, as far as where to aim the camera is concerned. The pony's body is in proportion with his legs. His ears are up, and all body parts are visible. From here, the next steps might include positioning the pony to make better use of the natural light, eliminating distracting reins and background, draping the tail over the closest hock (rather than having it hang between the hind legs), and producing a more polished turnout.

11.3 B This is the result of shooting from a vantage point that is too low. The pony's legs look disproportionate to his body and the angle makes his hindquarters appear weak.

11.3 C The smaller your equine subject, the more pronounced the problem of a too-high vantage point becomes. Here, aiming too high has made the pony appear more lightly built than he really is.

3. Your camera should be horizontal—level with the ground, with the lens on a plane parallel with the horse.

4. Point the camera lens just behind the center of the horse's shoulder (or where the flap of the saddle would fall, if a saddle were on the horse).

Parts

As far as an owner, breeder, or trainer is concerned, the ideal pose of a standing horse illustrates all the major body parts. It highlights the horse's strengths and enables viewers to make informed decisions about the animal based upon what they see in the photograph.

An unwritten, but generally accepted way of presenting a standing horse had evolved long before cameras

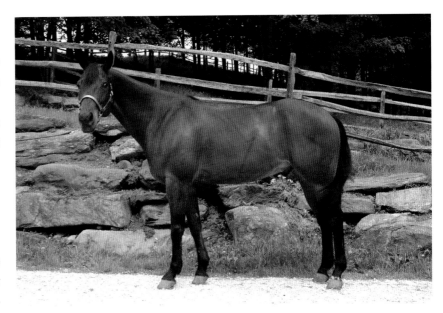

11.4 Composing your image so that the bulk of the horse's body is above your sight-line results in a neck that appears disproportionate and a head that is too small for the rest of the horse. It also tends to make the hindquarters appear weak and poorly constructed. The overall appearance is of a gangly horse.

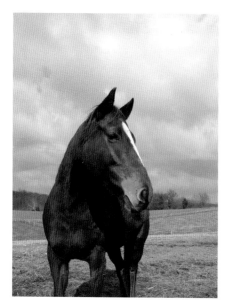

11.5 A Shooting more from the front than the side foreshortens the body and can make the hindquarters appear too small in proportion to the rest of the horse. *Photo Charles Mann*

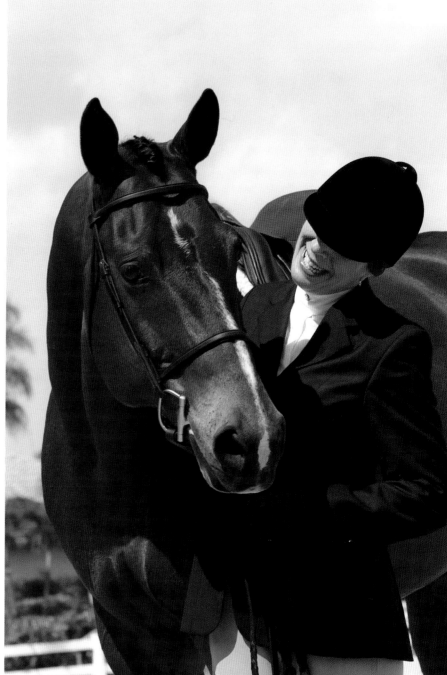

11.5 B However, the advantage of standing more toward the front is that it allows you to shoot an image that shows the whole chest, which may be advised when photographing a horse with his handler. The handler's body can obscure some of the difficulties with proportion. *Photo Charles Mann*

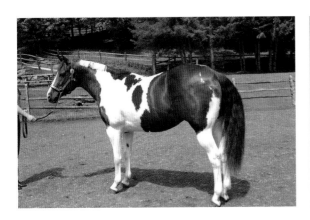

11.6 Some breeds are intentionally shot from different angles. Heavier breeds, most notably Quarter Horses and drafts, are often photographed slightly from the rear in order to emphasize the power in their hindquarters. When shooting from this angle, however, note how easy it is for the hindquarters to appear implausibly large and for the horse to seem to "run downhill."

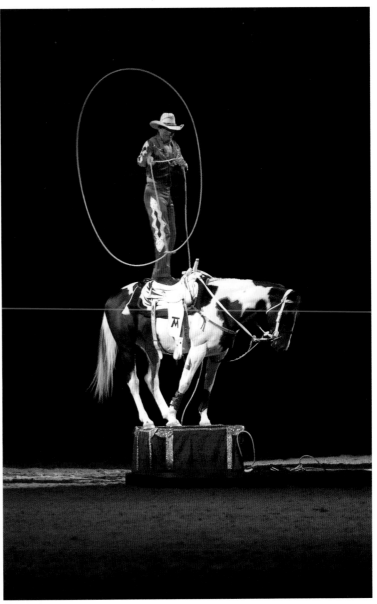

11.7 The addition of a person mounted on the horse does not change the location of where to aim the camera lens. Continue to aim just behind the horse's shoulder (see Photo 11.1 B). Take care not to angle the camera upward to focus on the rider, or you may end up with unfortunate problems with proportion. *Photo Charles Mann*

were around to capture the image. When it was more common to commission a painter, rather than a photographer, to document a horse's qualities, the rules of posing a standing image were already well established.

Though there are stylistic differences in the professional presentation of various breeds and types of horses, any photographer is advised to take the following into consideration:

▸ **Legs:** All four legs should be visible. The two legs closest to the camera are the farthest apart, so they "frame" the other two legs between them.

▸ **Ears:** Both ears should be visible, pricked up and alert.

▸ **Tail:** The horse's tail should either hang straight, or be draped slightly over the hock closest to the camera.

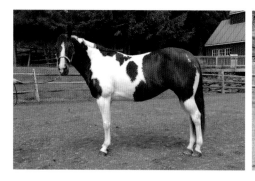

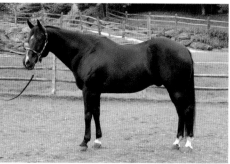

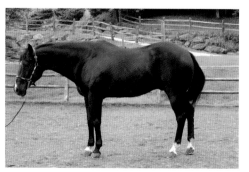

11.8 If a horse is standing "square" in front or behind, when photographed from the side his opposite leg is hidden from the camera's view. The resulting image of a three-legged horse "feels wrong" even to non-horsemen.

11.9 A The horse should be balanced, with his weight evenly distributed on all four legs. The two legs closest to the camera should be slightly farther apart than the two legs away from the camera. The end result is that all four legs are readily visible.

11.9 B When the legs nearest the camera are closest together and "framed" by the outside legs, rather than presenting a pleasing image, the horse looks undeniably off-balance. In this shot, the horse has also been allowed to carry more of his weight on his front legs than on his hindquarters, making him appear front-heavy (see also Photo 11.15).

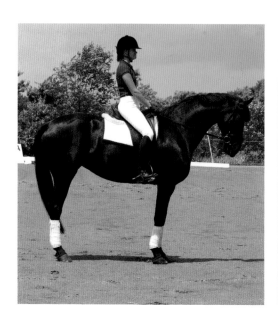

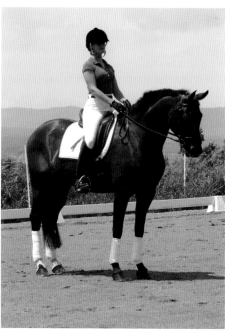

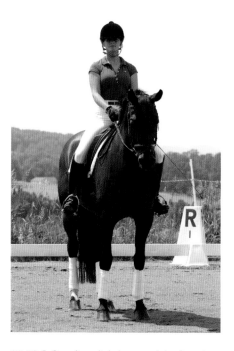

11.10 A As you can see, if a horse stands truly square, only two legs will show in any image shot from the side.

11.10 B If it is important for the horse to be shown standing absolutely square, you are generally better advised to shoot him more from the front than the side.

11.10 C Standing slightly toward the front in order to shoot a horse standing squarely doesn't guarantee that all four legs will be visible. The pose carries its own risks of photographing a "three-legged" horse.

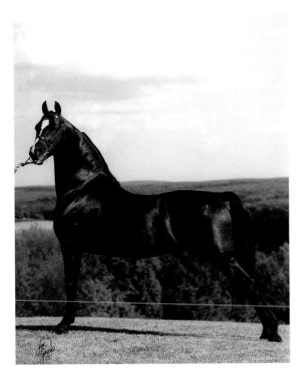

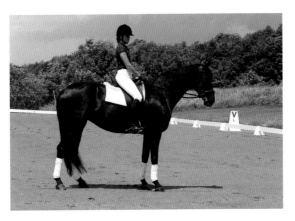

11.12 A A horse with unpricked ears appears bored, dull, or distracted. Lazy ears can ruin an otherwise lovely shot, even if the rest of the photograph is posed to perfection.

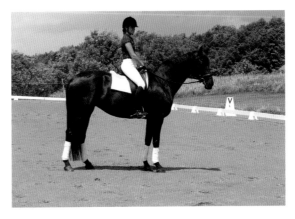

11.12 B What a difference the ears make in the feel of the overall shot. Notice how the horse appears more focused and more alert. Pricked ears immediately bring more energy to the image.

11.11 When photographing breeds and types of horses that are typically shown in a "parked out" or "stretched" position, such as Saddlebreds, Morgans (such as the stallion in this photo), Hackneys, Tennessee Walking Horses, and others, it may not be necessary to depict all four legs. *Courtesy of the American Morgan Horse Association*

Find Four Legs

As just mentioned, the front and hind leg closest to the camera should "frame" the other two legs, which should be only slightly staggered so that the horse is not standing truly "square."

Ears Up!

With rare exceptions, a horse with pricked, alert ears makes for a much more pleasing photograph than a horse with ears that are relaxed and unfocused.

When photographing a horse with a rider, bear in mind that the ears indicate the horse's attention. Though many riders like to have the horse's ears focused on them while they are riding, it does not make for a desirable standing shot (Photos 11.12 A & B).

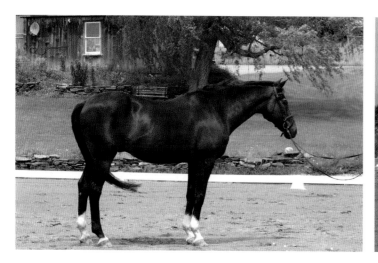

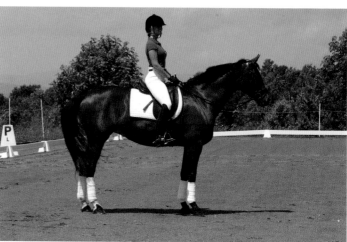

11.13 A Horses will instinctively turn their hindquarters to the wind. This often results in a tail blowing through the hind legs in an unsightly way.

11.13 B Draping the tail over the nearest hock takes advantage of the wind to hold it in place while you snap the shot.

Turning Tail

The horse's tail should be visible, but not blown between his hind legs (Photo 11.13 A). If wind is an issue, either position the horse so the wind blows the tail away from, rather than toward, the body, or drape the tail over the hock nearest the camera (Photo 11.13 B).

Balance

A horse carries two-thirds of his weight in the front half of his body. This means that if you drop an imaginary plumb line at the withers of a 1,200 pound horse, roughly 800 pounds will be carried in front of that line.

Many otherwise acceptable photographs of horses are marred because the photographer did not compensate for the horse's natural tendency to be front-heavy. The end result is a horse that either looks as if he is about to walk forward out of the picture, or one that simply appears ungainly.

Once a horse's legs are positioned, he will often hold himself well balanced for a short while (Photo 11.14). If much time passes, however, even if the horse's legs don't move, his natural inclination to rest more of his weight in the front will take over (Photos 11.15 & 11.16).

If the horse starts to get a bit front-heavy, it is often useful to have the handler create some energy to attract the horse's attention just before taking the picture. Waving a whip, rattling keys, or crinkling a plastic bag can be useful ways to encourage the horse to shift his weight more evenly, without startling him into moving or tempting him to walk forward.

Attitude

Though a posed shot follows certain general guidelines, what keeps each image from becoming a generic photograph of a standing horse is the horse himself.

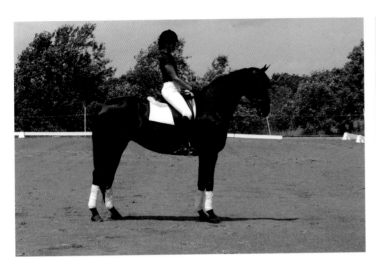

11.14 The horse's weight should be balanced and evenly distributed over all four legs. This means that he must carry as much weight in his hindquarters as on his forehand.

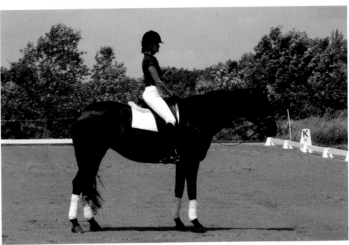

11.15 If the horse is allowed to stand for any length of time, he will naturally settle more of his weight over his front legs. This results in making the hindquarters appear less engaged—and less powerful. It adds an overall appearance of heaviness to the front of the horse.

When preparing to take a photograph, ask yourself what qualities the horse exhibits. Is he bold? Fiery? Athletic? Inquisitive? Honest? Or regal? Then consciously look for ways to capture those qualities in your lens. A show champion will have a very different attitude than a child's pony. Likewise, a broodmare with a young foal will exhibit significantly different attributes than either a young stallion or an older gelding.

Ideally, you want the horse alert, with bright eyes and an engaged look on his face.

Encouraging a little attitude can make for a good picture. But the photography session should never become something that frightens or irritates the horse. Take care that any "attention getters" such as keys, plastic bags, shaker cans, or squeaky toys don't startle a horse into bad behavior.

His muzzle should be soft and relaxed—with no tension in the lips, and no teeth or tongue showing. If he is wearing a bridle, the reins should be relaxed, regardless of whether or not a rider is astride. If he is in a halter, the lead line should be loose.

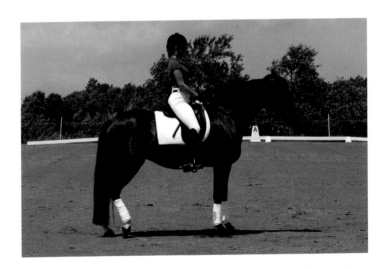

11.16 When the horse's weight is not evenly distributed over all four legs, he will have a tendency to rest a hind leg while the minutiae of the shot is arranged. Shifting the horse's weight back toward his hindquarters will generally correct the situation.

Your goal is to capture the horse's spirit, his personality, and his individuality. For instance:

▶ A reliable gelding won't exude the fire and verve of a breeding stallion—and he doesn't need to. Challenge yourself to find a way to illustrate his can-do attitude, his confident demeanor, or his capability.

▶ Innocence, curiosity, and boundless energy are hallmarks of young horses. When photographing foals, look for the opportunity to let their simple charms shine through.

▶ A breeding stallion holds the promise of improving his breed or type. It's up to the handler to show the stallion effectively—but it's up to you to capture an image of the horse that will give prospective breeders a feel for what he has to offer them.

With practice, you'll soon find that working within the structure of the posed shot liberates you to use your creativity to show each horse in the best possible light.

When shooting a portrait featuring only the horse's head, look for opportunities to spark the horse's interest and appeal to his sense of curiosity.

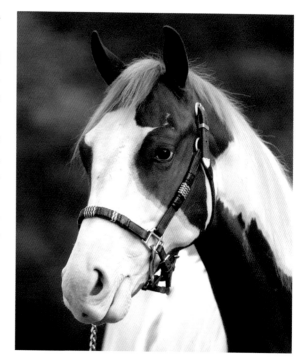

11.17 When the horse's opposite eyelash is just visible, all parts are "accounted for." The overall picture is visually balanced, and generally depicts the horse the owner knows and loves. *Photo Charles Mann*

Posing the Head Shot

When shooting a portrait featuring only the horse's head—with or without a human in the image—capturing the horse's attitude becomes even more crucial. Look for opportunities to spark the horse's interest and appeal to his sense of curiosity.

When photographing a horse's head, remember the "show all parts" rule—it applies here as well. If at all possible, arrange the shot so that the horse's opposite eyelash is *just* visible (Photo 11.17). Be sure that both ears are pricked forward and visible before taking the image (Photo 11.18).

Compose the head shot to emphasize the horse's eye, and to minimize the size of both the muzzle and the ears (Photos 11.19 & 11.20). A telephoto lens will enable you to minimize the background and focus the viewer's attention only on the horse.

Aiming the camera lens at the eye closest to you, and composing an image where the center of the forelock and each eye form three "points" of an equilateral triangle is a good place to start. Experiment with shooting the broad front plane of the horse's face at various angles until you find the angle that accentuates the horse's good qualities.

Knowing how to shoot a quality, posed portrait is an important part of every equine photographer's repertoire. The rules, such as they are, are few, and with practice, you'll be able to consistently turn out good photographs.

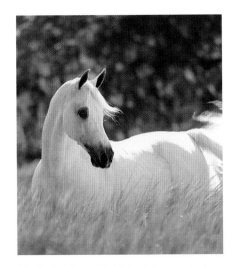

11.18 Arabians with "dished" faces and other horses with strong, clean lines in their profiles are often photographed from the side in order to accentuate their exquisite bone structure. When shooting from this angle, however, take care to avoid capturing a one-eared horse! *Photo © Mark J. Barrett*

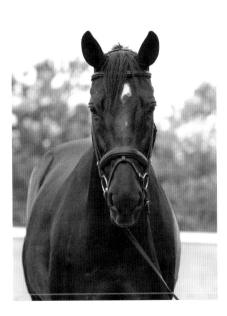

11.19 When the lens is parallel to the plane of the horse's face, the ears—and not the eyes—take center stage in the photograph.

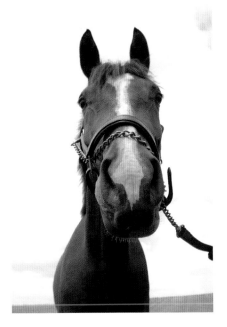

11.20 A horse's head can be nearly 2 feet long. Don't forget the laws of focal length and perspective!

Shooting Effective Action

In chapter 2, you learned about shutter speed and explored how it relates to motion and action. Taking images that capture a horse at his best requires not only an understanding of the technical aspects of photography but also a working knowledge of how the horse moves.

To many people, a moving horse is poetry in motion (Photo 11.21). To the camera, however, certain aspects of each gait are more aesthetically pleasing when frozen in a static shot than others. Developing an eye for the "sweet spot" of each gait takes some time. A little practice, patience, and timing, however, will soon reward you with action shots that leap from the page.

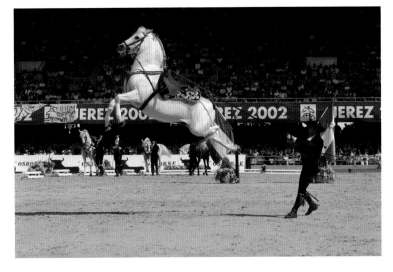

11.21 Horses' superb athleticism and grace provide enough visually compelling material to supply an army of photographers with images for a lifetime. *Photo Charles Mann*

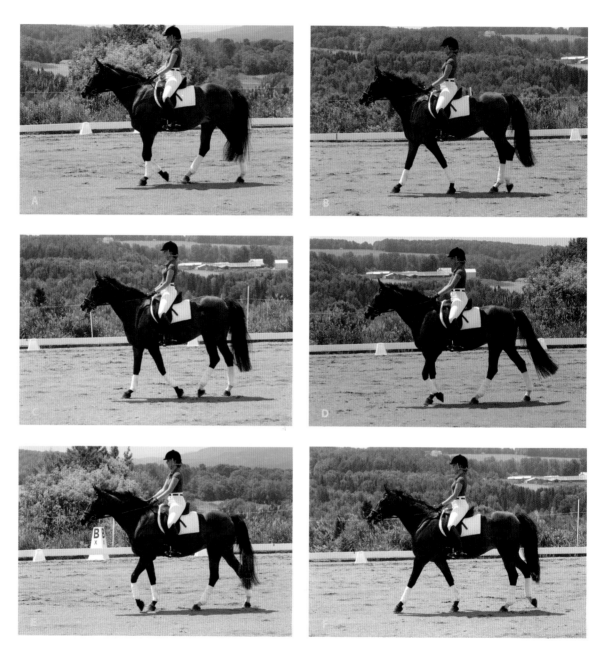

11.22 A – F When a horse walks, each foot falls on the ground independently. Whenever one foot is raised to swing forward and take a step, the other three feet remain in contact with the ground.

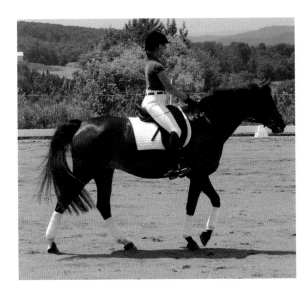

11.23 To show balanced animated movement at the walk, the best time to capture the gait is when either front foot is raised and starting to step forward.

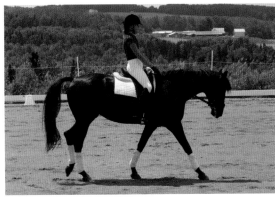

11.24 A horse captured after pushing off his hind foot, with a hind leg extended behind him, looks less poised, less balanced, and presents a less pleasing overall effect.

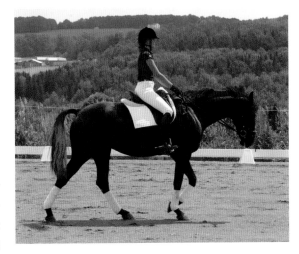

11.25 Many riders allow themselves, as well as their horses, to get a bit lazy at the walk. It is not uncommon for horses to drag their feet or become heavy in the bridle and lean on the rider's hands. Such faux pas are often more obvious in photographs than in "real life." Here, the horse is clearly moving with a lack of enthusiasm. The resulting image, even though taken at the right time in the stride, is rather lackluster.

All Power Comes from the Rear

Regardless of a horse's gait—whether he is moving forward at a walk, trot, pace, rack, canter or gallop—remember that the hindquarters are his source of power. Almost without exception, if the horse is pushing off the ground with his hindquarters, he will appear to be in balance.

The Walk

The walk is a four-beat gait. Each foot hits the ground independently of the others (Photos 11.22 A – F).

The ideal time to capture a horse at the walk is when both hind legs are engaged, and one fore foot is raised and swung forward in the stride (Photos 11.23 & 11.24).

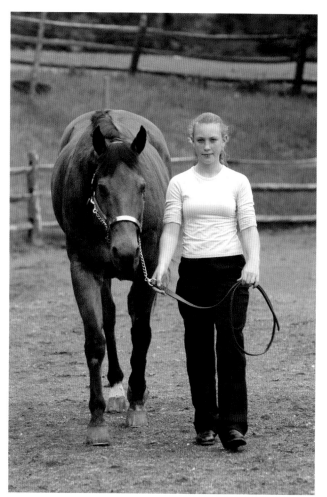

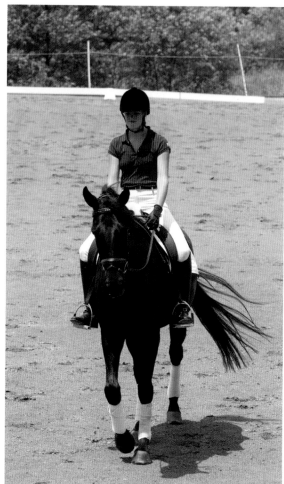

11.26 A Photographing a walking horse from the front can be preferable to a shot from the side. The photographer provides an item of some interest, and as a result, the horse's head often comes up and he may even walk with a bit more animation than usual. Photographing the walk from the front also makes it less important to time the shot to capture a raised front foot.

11.26 B When shooting a moving horse from the front, a too high vantage point, or failure to take the horse's overall length into consideration will result in an image such as this where the horse appears to be traveling downhill.

The Trot

Because of its predictability and relatively slow speed, the trot is the gait favored by many in-ring photographers at horse shows.

The trot is a two-beat gait, as rhythmic as a metronome (Photos 11.27 A – C). It is an easy gait for both horse and rider to maintain—so there is no reason not to practice until you can capture the perfect moment of the horse's stride every time.

There are two "sweet spot" moments of a trot that lend themselves to great images.

One is *the moment of suspension* when the horse is airborne (Photos 11.27 B & C). At this point in the stride, one foreleg and the opposite hind leg stretch forward. The other diagonal pair of legs extends back after pushing the horse off the ground. This is the moment favored by hunt seat enthusiasts to showcase a horse's scope and ground-covering ability. These images are most striking when the horse is moving well forward.

The second ideal trotting shot occurs when the horse is *pushing off the ground with his hind leg*. The easiest way to gauge this, however, is often by paying close attention to the opposite foreleg. When one foreleg is perpendicular to the ground, the opposite hind leg will be fully engaged. The opposite foreleg will also be at its highest point in the stride. This portion of the gait highlights a horse's knee action, "flash," and power (see Photo 11.29).

Western-style and dressage riders generally sit the trot. English-style riders—both hunt seat and saddle-seat equestrians—typically post at the trot, rising out of the saddle with every other stride the horse takes (Photos 11.28 A & B).

Western riders sit in the saddle at the jog. A Western-style horse's jog often has a short, easily missed moment of suspension during each stride. You may find it preferable to time your photographs to capture the horse with

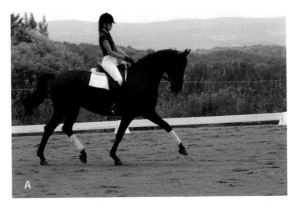
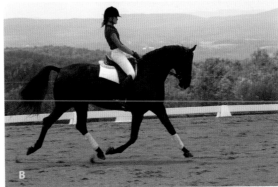
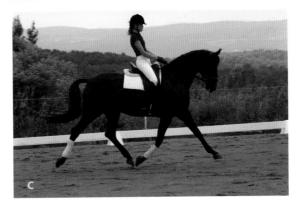

11.27 A– C At the trot, a two-beat gait, the front and back legs move in diagonal pairs. The left front and right hind legs rise and fall in unison, as do the right front and left hind legs. Each stride has a moment of suspension (Photos B & C) when the horse is airborne.

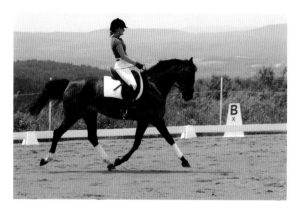

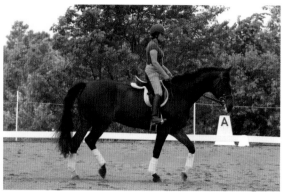

11.28 A When photographing a rider posting, the ideal image is one in which the horse's feet are suspended between strides, with the rider seated in the saddle.

11.28 B As you can see, the visual effect of the horse's trot is somewhat diminished when the rider is captured out of the saddle while posting.

one foreleg perpendicular to the ground while the other foreleg is lifted and moving forward.

When photographing gaited horses, such as Tennessee Walkers, Missouri Foxtrotters, Peruvian Pasos, five-gaited Saddlebreds, and the like, the same rules of action and animation apply. If the horse's weight is in his hindquarters, if he is light and stylish in the front, and if you angle the camera so he seems to be moving slightly uphill (Photo 11.29), you can't go wrong.

When a horse is shown in hand, in a halter class, no tack or rider obscures his conformation and movement. Generally speaking, it is better to get a great shot of the horse than a good shot of both horse and handler. Since the handler leads the horse from the left side, you should shoot horses shown in hand from the right (Photo 11.30).

Standing slightly in front and to the left of a horse being shown in hand allows you to get a nice shot of both horse and handler, but it does little to illustrate the horse's movement. Such a shot can be useful, however, if photographing a showmanship competitor or some

other instance where the handler's skill is an important aspect of the image.

The Canter and Gallop

The canter, or lope, is a three-beat gait with a moment of suspension. The horse pushes himself off the ground with a single hind leg. The other hind and the opposite foreleg land together and propel him forward. He then lands on the remaining foreleg.

In general, a horse tracking clockwise will begin a canter stride on the left hind leg and complete the stride on his right foreleg. Traveling in this manner, he is said to be on the right lead. Conversely, a horse traveling counterclockwise will canter on the left lead.

After a horse lands on a single foreleg, he gathers his legs underneath him while his body goes airborne and continues forward.

The ideal time to take a photograph of a horse cantering is when the single hind leg is in contact with the ground at the first "beat," or the beginning of each stride.

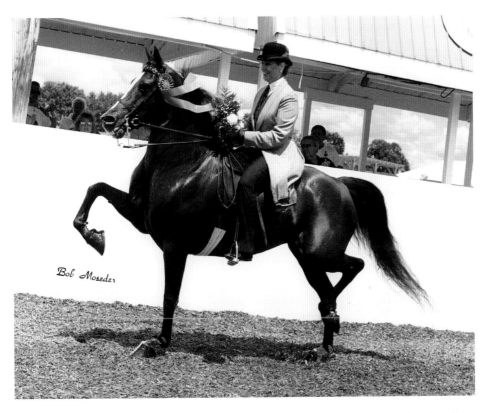

11.29 For certain types of saddle, roadster, and fine harness horses, more importance is placed on their knee action than on the suspension of their stride. Such horses are often photographed when one foreleg is perpendicular to the ground, and the other foreleg is raised as high as possible. When photographing such types of horses, the ideal image is one that highlights the horse's elegance, style, and grace. Angling the camera so the horse appears to be trotting slightly uphill helps to emphasize the gait's animation. *Courtesy of the American Morgan Horse Association*

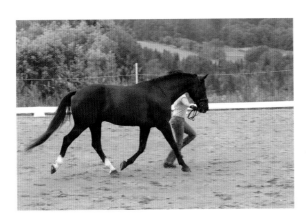

11.30 When a horse is shown in hand, the handler leads him from the left side. Shooting the right side of the horse, then, is the only way to assure a shot of the whole animal in motion.

At this moment, the horse's weight is in his hindquarters. His front end is elevated, and he looks most poised and balanced. Snapping the picture at any time during this beat—up until the first foreleg hits the ground—will probably result in a good image (Photos 11.31 A – C).

Furthermore, when a rider is present, the upper part of the rider's body is closest to the horse's head and neck at the first beat of the gait, making for a pleasing visual composition.

The second "beat" of the gait, when both a hind and a foreleg hit the ground together makes for adequate images. However, the concussion with which many horses hit the ground at this stage in the canter often causes their pasterns to flex so much that it results in an undesirable, flattened effect (Photos 11.31 D – E).

During the third "beat" of the canter, the horse's body rocks forward to land on a front leg. No matter how poised, how balanced, or how agile the horse, snapping the photograph at this moment of the canter will not result in a flattering image. The horse will appear to be ungainly, front-heavy, off balance, or pitching forward. If a rider is present, this moment of the gait also results in an awkward-looking, open angle between the horse's neck and the rider's body (Photos 11.31 F – I).

Taking a photograph of the canter's moment of suspension can be visually interesting. Because the horse's legs tend to "curl up" underneath his body as he gathers himself in the air, images of this moment in the stride sometimes have an odd feeling of weightlessness to them.

In the gallop, the horse's body extends and stretches forward. Each foot hits the ground individually—first the two hind legs and then the two forelegs. Guidelines for photographing the galloping horse are the same as for taking shots of the cantering horse. Because of the gait's speed, however, sometimes the tradeoff to an image of a perfectly balanced horse is one of an animal reveling in his athleticism and power.

The ideal time to take a photo of a horse cantering is when the single hind leg is in contact with the ground at the first "beat," or the beginning of each stride.

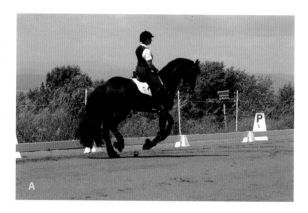

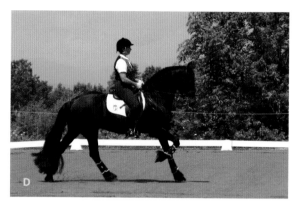

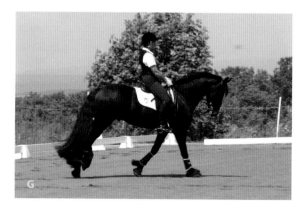

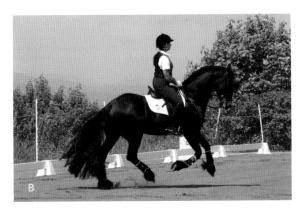

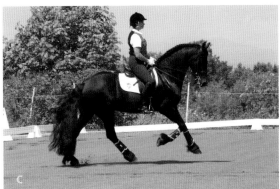

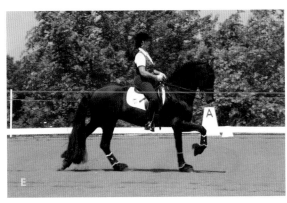

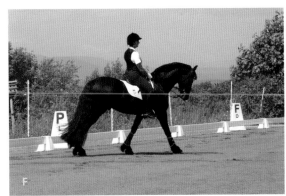

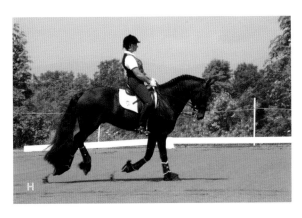

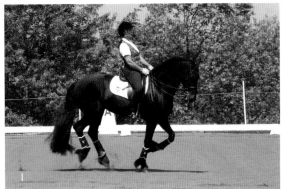

11.31 A–I The canter is a three-beat gait in which the horse moves forward in a rocking motion. When on the right lead (illustrated here), the horse pushes himself off with his left hind leg. The right hind and left fore legs land simultaneously, followed by the right foreleg. All legs will then leave the ground for a moment before the horse takes the next stride.

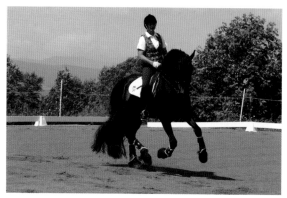

11.32 Photographing the horse from the front or from the rear can create visually compelling images, but you still need to time the shot to capture the first beat of the canter stride.

The Horse at Work

Just as there is an art to knowing when to snap the photograph to capture an image of a balanced horse at any gait, a similar talent is required to take memorable images of horses "on the job."

Every equine discipline—be it dressage, eventing, jumping, racing, driving, reining, cutting, roping, show riding, vaulting, or trick riding—has moments that hold special appeal to enthusiasts and aficionados. If you are going to spend any amount of time photographing a particular equestrian sport or riding style, you owe it to yourself and to your subjects to learn all you can about it, and to study the work of those photographers who excel within that sphere.

That said, however, here are a few simple guidelines for some of the more common equine activities.

Horses in Dramatic Action
From circus performances to *haut école* dressage maneuvers, from Western-style events such as cutting, calf

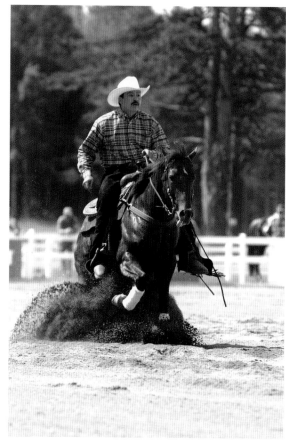

11.33 A One of the hallmarks of a good reining horse is a sliding stop. Sometimes the best "action shots" happen when the action stops. *Photo Charles Mann*

roping, and team penning to the quintessentially English work of the foxhunter, show hack, and native pony, one of the equine photographer's greatest challenges is to highlight the talents of a horse performing a specific job.

A good practice is to strive to compose images that capture the split second when the horse best performs his duties.

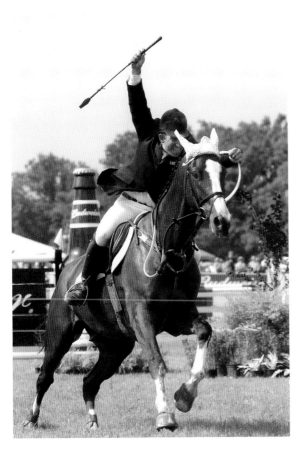

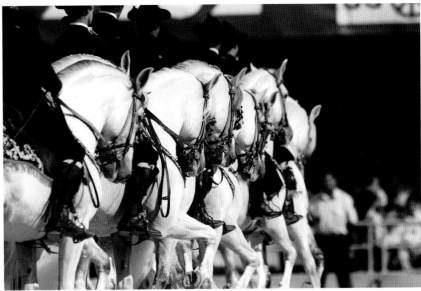

11.33 C How else would you illustrate the cohesive unity of a quadrille of horses and riders who have spent hours choreographing and practicing their routine to perfection? *Photo Charles Mann*

11.33 B Not all the action happens over fences. Moments such as these, when both the rider and the horse know they've done a great job, are worth capturing. *Photo Charles Mann*

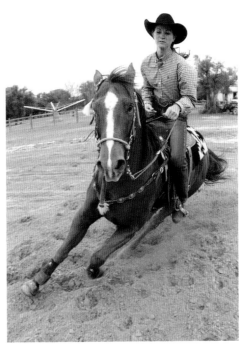

For instance, when photographing a cutting horse, look to document the moment when he suddenly changes direction in response to a particular cow. A reining horse in the middle of a rollback or a sliding stop can be visually riveting (Photo 11.33 A). And a jumper exerting himself to cleanly clear a fence makes for a compelling composition. A horse that knows his job and does it well almost always makes for an interesting image (Photos 11.33 B – D).

11.33 D The barrel is unimportant. The barrel racer's attitude, however, is all about the job at hand. *Photo Charles Mann*

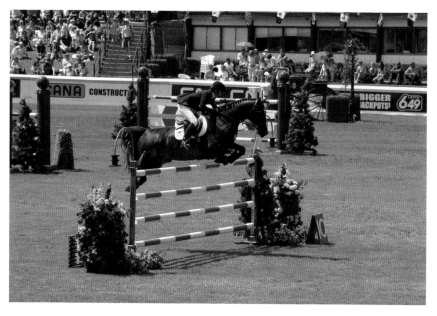

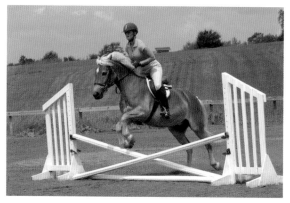

11.35 A Low jumps have very little leeway between the horse's "rise" and "fall." When photographing ponies, beginning riders, and other low jumpers, it is often advisable to snap the shot at the moment of takeoff, while the hind legs are still on the ground.

11.34 Ideally, the image of a jumping horse captures a moment when he is airborne, with his front end still on the rise. This photo would be more dramatic with fewer distractions in the background—hard to achieve in a show arena (see Photo 11.36 A for a solution).

Hunters and Jumpers

A horse that jumps with good form traces an arc, or *bascule*, with his topline as he clears the fence. He lifts his forelegs and tucks them neatly under him. He then stretches his head and neck forward while he rounds over the jump (Photo 11.34).

As long as the horse's front end is going *up* over the fence, the chances of your snapping a good jumping picture are excellent.

As soon as the horse's hindquarters come even with his front, and he begins his descent, however, your odds of taking a picture that will appeal to jumping fans diminish. As the horse comes over the obstacle, his head and neck come up, his front legs start to drop, and his overall frame flattens.

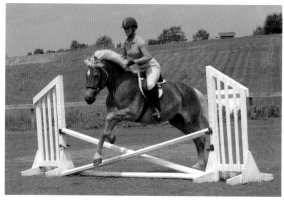

11.35 B It is more important for the low jumper to be dependable and safe than for him to have great form. Still, hanging front legs are not attractive. Taking the shot a split second sooner probably would have resulted in a more pleasing picture.

The exception to the general rule of taking a picture of a horse on the rise comes when snapping shots of cross-country fences. Sometimes a horse landing from a sizeable drop makes for an arresting picture—regardless of the horse's high head and the often ungainly appearance of the rider in the saddle (Photo 11.40).

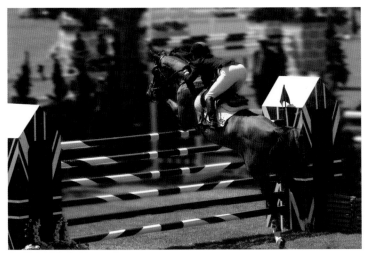

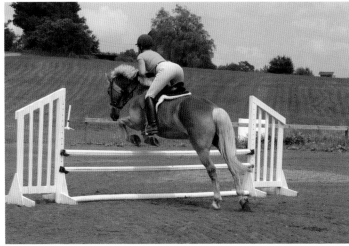

11.36 A Shooting the jumper slightly from the rear can dramatically highlight the incredible power in his hindquarters as he launches himself over a big vertical. This picture was manipulated in Photoshop to lessen the distracting background clutter.

11.36 B The technique of shooting the jumper slightly from behind at the moment of takeoff is effective even when the obstacle is hardly an imposing one.

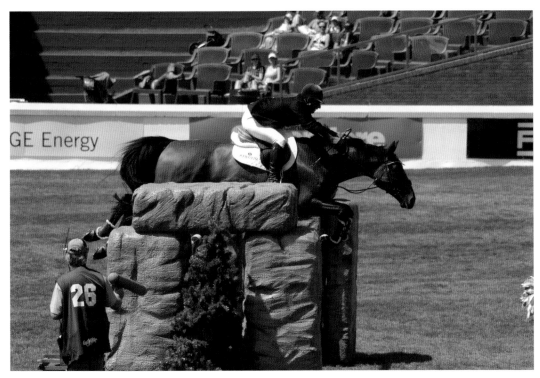

11.37 Shooting from the side of a wide fence emphasizes the spread of the jump.

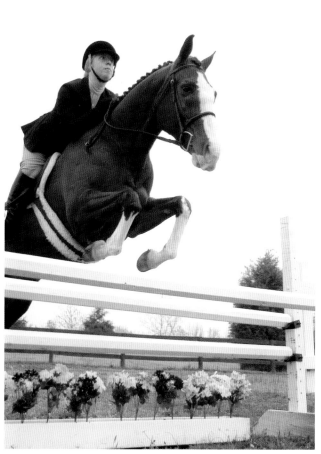

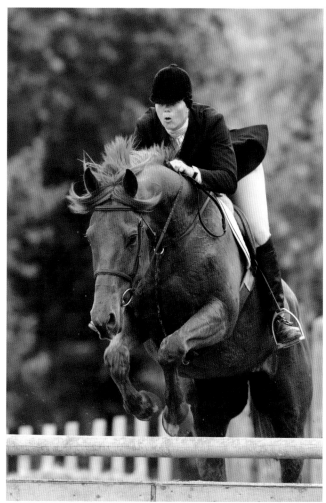

11.38 Shooting slightly from the front of the fence brings the rider's face more into view. Shooting from below adds a dramatic element. It creates an image that places as much emphasis on the rider as on the horse. *Photo Charles Mann*

11.39 Shooting a jump head-on loses the arc of the bascule, but can render a strong, bold image of the horse and rider working as a team. *Photo Charles Mann*

The Horse In Harness

Any time you are photographing horses in harness, you must pay close attention to your focal length. The larger the carriage, and the more horses there are pulling it, the more an awareness of the technical aspects of your photography come into play.

When photographing horses in harness, remember that the blinders on the bridles obscure up to 80 percent

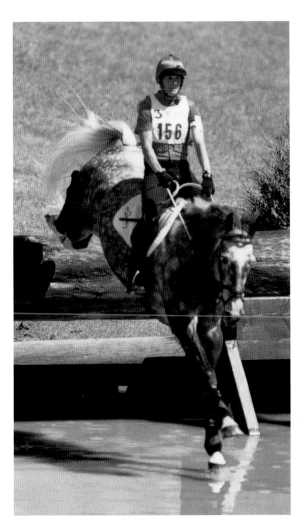

11.40 The landing is rarely the most beautiful aspect of a jump. Still, there is undeniable appeal in an image that captures the horse alighting from a "drop." *Photo Sport Horse Studio*

A few suggestions for making the most of some situations involving horses in harness:

▸ When photographing heavy horses pulling a considerable load, shooting slightly from the rear will draw attention to the team's power. A lower vantage point also helps. When the horses begin to pull, the sooner you can snap the shot, the more explosive the action will appear.

▸ Photographing a lengthy hitch (such as a four-in-hand, a six- or an eight-horse show hitch) as it rounds a slight turn can give you plenty of time to focus on various aspects of the turn-out (Photo 11.41A).

▸ When shot from the side, longer hitches with many horses often lose the feeling of harnessed energy that permeates a more head-on shot. A benefit of this angle, however, is the element of perspective it lends to the team as a whole.

Gymkhana Classes, Mounted Games, and Other Speed Events

Barrel racing, pole bending, speed and action, down-and-back, keyhole races and other events where speed is a factor offer exciting opportunities for action shots.

Before shooting a race, gymkhana class, or other speed event, it behooves you to familiarize yourself with the rules of the game.

In barrel racing, for instance, the horse must run a "cloverleaf" pattern that includes tight turns around three barrels before he heads for the finish line. In these classes, a horse's speed on the flat is often less important—and certainly less visually interesting—than his ability to negotiate the barrels. It makes sense, then, to set yourself up to capture the barrel action (see p. 133).

In pole bending, the horse must weave back and forth between a series of poles or posts in a line before turning for home. The lightning-fast lead changes down the line generally make for much more compelling

> Every equine discipline has moments that hold special appeal to enthusiasts and aficionados.

of the horses' vision. The horses will only be able to see you if you are immediately in front of them—and such a position is rarely advisable. Take special care not to spook a horse in harness. If in doubt about the safety of a set-up for a shot, always check with the driver.

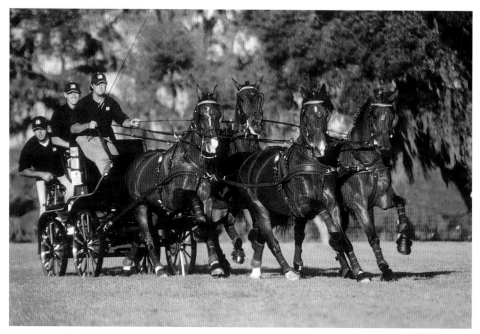

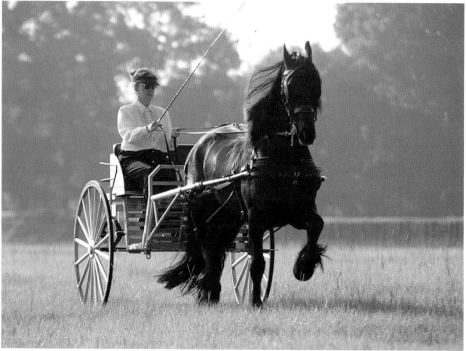

11.41 A & B Shooting harness horses obliquely, or slightly from the front can be a good way to "compress" all the important elements—horses, driver, carriages, and passengers—into an interesting image. A long focal length is essential for such shots. *Photos © Mark J. Barrett*

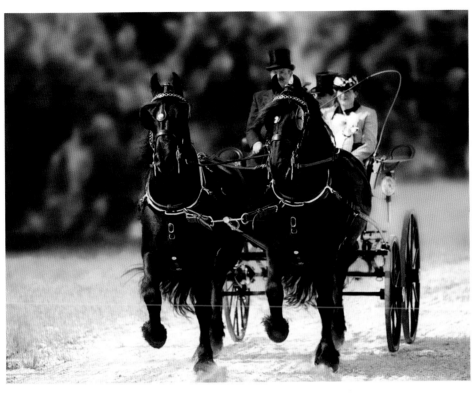

11.42 A head-on shot, with the horses coming straight at you, can be quite dramatic. But you often sacrifice the ability to see the drivers, passengers, and other elements of the rig. *Photo © Mark J. Barrett*

photographs than shots of a horse running beside a line of white uprights.

A race is an event where action is king. Many individual stories play out during any given horse race. Sometimes a leader will leave the pack behind. At others, the horses form a sort of flying mob. The object is always the same, however—to get from Point A to Point B as fast as physically possible.

If in doubt about the viability of a shot, remember the cardinal rule of action: all power comes from the rear. Snap the picture when the horse's hindquarters are engaged and chances are you will have an image that works.

When it comes to photographing horses in motion, all the tips and "tricks" in the world cannot make up for the time you spend practicing. Learn your camera's shutter lag (see "Shutter Lag" on p. 15) and get comfortable with its idiosyncrasies. Become intimately familiar with the equine gaits. Take a *lot* of pictures. You'll soon discover that you've developed a sort of sixth sense that tells you when a great shot is about to occur—and you'll have honed the skills that allow you to capture it.

Resources

Groups and Organizations

Advertising Photographers of America (APA)
PO Box 250
White Plains, NY 10605
Tel: 800.272.626
Fax: 888.889.7190
www.apanational.com

American Society of Media Photographers (ASMP)
150 North Second St.
Philadelphia, PA 19106
Tel: 215.451.2767
Fax: 215.451.0880
www.asmp.org

Cameras.co.uk
Andy Needham
Supreme Software Ltd
PO BOX 565
Weybridge
KT13 9WF
Tel: (01932) 828 496
www.cameras.co.uk

Editorial Photographer (EP)
PO Box 591811
San Francisco, CA 94159
www.editorialphoto.com

Equine Photographers Network (EPNet)
White Hill Road
Walton, NY 13856
Tel: 607.865.5215
www.equinephotographers.org

Gary Elsner and Associates, Inc.
455 Windham Court North
Wycokoff, NJ 07481
Tel/Fax: 201.847.0048
www.garyelsener.com

New Rider
Priors Court
Callow End
Worcester
WR2 4TJ
www.newrider.com

PonyPics.co.uk
Parkfield House
Park Street
Stafford
Staffordshire
ST17 4AL
Tel: (01785) 878 045
www.ponypics.co.uk

Professional Photographers of America (PPA)
229 Peachtree St. NE
Suite 2200
Atlanta, GA 30303
Tel: 404.522.8600
Fax: 404.614.6400
www.ppa.com

Rob Galbraith
Digital Photography Insights
www.robgalbraith.com

Sports Shooter
PO Box 5124
Pleasanton, CA 94566
www.sportsshooter.com

Online Stores

B&H Photo Video
420 Ninth Ave
New York, NY 10001
Tel: 800.221.5743, 212.239.7765
Fax: 212.239.7549
www.bhphotovideo.com

Burrard - Lucas Photography
www.burrard-lucas.com

Equine Media
Cleveland House
39 Old Station Road
Newmarket
Suffolk
CB8 8QE
Tel: (01638) 601 709
Fax: (0870) 444 6051
www.equinemedia.co.uk

Horses-In-Motion
79 Tollgate Road
Salisbury
Wiltshire
SP1 2JP
Tel: (01722) 321 306
Mob: 07798 923 294
www.horses-in-motion.com

Penn Camera
Washington, DC
Tel: 800.347.5770
www.penncamera.com

Roberts Distributors
255 S. Meridian St.
Indianapolis, IN 46225
Tel: 800.726.5544, 317-636-5544
www.robertsimaging.com

Rural Portraits
Reddings
High Street
Maiden Bradley
Wiltshire
BA12 7JG
Tel: (01985) 845 106
Fax: (01985) 844 170
www.rural-portraits.co.uk

Samy's Camera
431 S. Fairfax Ave.
Los Angeles, CA 90036
Tel: 800.321.4726
Fax: 503.297.1768
www.samys.com

XCPhotos
M & J Freeman
Brierley Hill
Staunton
Gloucester
GL19 3QR
Tel: (01452) 840 336
www.xcphotos.co.uk

Camera Manufacturers and Equipment

Canon USA, Inc.
One Canon Plaza
Lake Success, NY 11042
Tel: 800.692.7753
www.usa.canon.com

Canon (UK) Ltd
Woodhatch
Reigate
Surrey
RH2 8BF
Tel: (01737) 220 000
Fax: (01737) 220 022
www.canon.co.uk

Fuji Film
850 Central Ave.
Hanover Park, IL 60133
Tel: 800.800.FUJI (3854)
www.fujifilm.com

Fuji Film (UK) Ltd
Unit 10A
St Martins Business Centre
St Martins Way
Bedfordshire
MK42 0LF
Tel: (01234) 217 724
Fax: (01234) 572 652
www.fujifilm.co.uk

Hasselblad USA
15207 NE 95th St.
Redmond WA 98052
Tel: 425.861.6434
www.hasselbladusa.com

Ilford Imaging
W 70 Century Road
Paramus, NJ 07652
Tel: 201.265.6000
www.ilford.com

Kodak
343 State Street
Rochester, NY 14650
Tel: 800.235.6325
www.kodak.com

Kodak (UK) Ltd
Hemel One
Boundary Way
Hemel Hempstead
Herts
HP2 7YU
Tel: (01442) 261 122
Fax: (01442) 240 609
www.kodak.co.uk

Konica Minolta Photo Imaging USA
725 Darlington Ave.
Mahwah, NJ 07495
Tel: 201.574.4000
www.minolta.com

Lexar Media
47421 Bayside Parkway
Fremont, CA 94538
Tel: 510.413.1200
www.lexar.com

Light Impressions
PO Box 787
Brea, CA 92822
Tel: 800.828.6216, 714.441.4539
Fax: 800.828.5539, 714.441.4564
www.lightimpressionsdirect.com

LowePro
1003 Gravenstein Hwy North
Suite 200
Sebastopol, CA 95472
Tel: 707.827.4000
www.lowepro.com

Nikon USA
1300 Walt Whitman Road
Melvin, NY 11747
Tel: 800.645.6687
www.nikonusa.com

Nikon (UK) Ltd
380 Richmond Road
Kingston Upon Thames
Surrey
KT2 5PR
Tel: (0871) 2001 964
www.nikon.co.uk

Olympus America Inc.
3500 Corporate Parkway
PO Box 610
Center Valley, PA 18034-0610
Tel: 800.645.8160, 484.896.5000
www.olympusamerica.com

Olympus (UK) Ltd
2-8 Honduras Street
London
EC1Y 0TX
Tel: (020) 7253 2772
Fax : (020) 7251 6330
www.olympus.co.uk

Pentax USA
600 12th Street
Suite 300
Golden, CO 80401
Tel: 800.877.0155, 303.799.8000
www.pentax.com

Phase One
24 Woodbine Avenue
Suite 15
Northport, NY 11768
Tel: 888.742.7966, 631.757.0400
www.phaseone.com

Polaroid Corp.
1265 Main Street
Bldg. W3
Waltham, MA 02451
Tel: 800.343.5000, 781.386.2000
www.polaroid.com

Polaroid (UK) Ltd
800 The Boulevard
Capability Green
Luton
LU1 3BA
Tel: (01582) 409 800
Fax: (01582) 409 801
www.polaroid.com/uk

SanDisk Corp.
140 Caspian Court
Sunnyvale, CA 94089
Tel: 888.726.3475, 408.542.0500
www.sandisk.com

Sigma Corporation of America
15 Fleetwood Court
Ronkonkoma, NY 11779
Tel: 800.896.6858, 631.585.1144.
www.sigmaphoto.com

Sony Corporation of America
550 Madison Avenue
New York, NY 10022
Tel: 212.833.6800
www.sony.com

Sony (UK)
The Heights
Brooklands
Weybridge
Surrey
KT13 0XW
Tel: (0870) 6060 456
www.sony.co.uk

Speedotron Corp.
310 South Racine Avenue
Chicago, IL 60607
Tel: 312.421.4050
Fax: 312.421.5079
www.speedotron.com

Tamron USA Inc.
12 Austin Boulevard
Commack, NY 11725
Tel: 800.827.8880, 631.858.8400
www.tamron.com

Vivitar Corp.
520 Graves Avenue
Oxnard, CA 93030
Tel: 805.988.0463
Fax: 805.981.2421
www.vivitar.com

Computer Hardware and Software

ACDSee®
PO Box 36
Saanichton, British Columbia
Canada V8M 2C3
Tel: 250.544.6700
Fax: 250.544.0291
www.acdsystems.com

Adobe PhotoShop
345 Park Avenue
San Jose, CA 95110
Tel: 408.536.6000
Fax: 408.537.6000
www.adobe.com

Adobe Photoshop Systems Ltd
3 Roundwood Avenue
Stockley Park
Uxbridge
UB11 1AH
www.adobe.com/uk

Alien Skin Software Inc.
1111 Haynes Street
Suite 113
Raleigh, NC 27604
Tel: 888.921.7546
Fax: 919.832.4065
www.alienskin.com

Apple Computers
1 Infinite Loop
Cupertino, CA 95014
Tel: 800-MY-APPLE, 408.996.1010
www.apple.com

Apple Computers
Hollyhill Industrial Estate
Hollyhill
Cork
ROI
Tel: (+44) 6895 89343
www.apple.com/uk

AutoFX Software
141 Village Street
Suite 2
Birmingham, AL 35242
Tel: 205-980-0056
Fax: 205.980.1121
www.autofx.com

Bibble Labs Inc.
11940 Jollyville Road
Suite 115-N
Austin, TX 78759
Tel: 512.345.3480
Fax: 512.345.3485
www.bibblelabs.com

Blu-Ray Disc Association
10 Universal City Plaza
T-100
Universal City, CA 91608
Tel: 818.301.1891
Fax: 818.301.1893
www.blu-raydisc.com

Canto Cumulus
221 Main Street
Suite 460
San Francisco, CA 94105
Tel: 415.495.6545
Fax: 415.543.1595
www.canto.com/pro/

ColorVision®
5 Princess Road
Lawrenceville, NJ 08648
Tel: 800.554.8688, 609.895.7430
Fax: 609.895.7447
www.colorvision.com

Dell Corp.
2401 Greenlawn Boulevard
Round Rock, TX 78682
Tel: 888.560.8324, 512.255.1568
www.dell.com

Dell Products
C/O Milbanke House
Western Road
Bracknell
Berks
RG12 1RD
Tel: (0870) 908 0800
www.dell.co.uk

Epson America, Inc.
3840 Kilroy Airport Way
Long Beach, CA 90806
Tel: 800.463.7766, 310.782.0770
www.epson.com

Epson (UK) Ltd
Campus 100
Marylands Avenue
Hemel Hempstead
Herts
HP2 7TJ
Tel: (08702) 416 900
www.epson.co.uk

Extensis Portfolio
1800 SW First Avenue
Suite 500
Portland, OR 97201
Tel: 800.796.9798, 503.274.2020
Fax: 503.274.0530
www.extensis.com

FotoStation
Lille Grensen 5
0195 Oslo
Norway
Tel/Fax: +47 22 00 30 20
www.fotoware.com

GretagMacbeth
617 Little Britain Road
New Windsor, NY 12553
Tel: 845.565.7660
Fax: 845.565.0390
www.gretagmacbeth.com

Hewlett Packard
3000 Hanover Street
Palo Alto, CA 94304
Tel: 650.857.1501
Fax: 650.857.5518
www.hp.com

Hewlett Packard
Amen Corner
Cain Road
Bracknell
Berkshire
RG12 1HN
Tel: (0870) 013 0790
Fax: (01344) 363 344
www.hp.com/uk

iMatch
Pestalozzistrasse 6-12
61250 Usingen
Germany
Tel/Fax: +49 6081 12535
www.photools.com

iView
30-40 Elcho Street
Battersea Park
London SW11 4AU
England
Tel: +44 20 7223 8691
Fax: 44 20 7223 8712
www.iview-multimedia.com

LaCie, Ltd.
22985 NW Evergreen Parkway
Hillsboro, OR 97124
Tel: 503.844.4500
Fax: 503.844.4508
www.lacie.com

Lexmark International
740 New Circle Road NW
Lexington, KY 40550
Tel: 800-539-6275
www.lexmark.com

MonacoEZcolor
X-Rite Photo Marketing
8Westchester Plaza
Elmsford, NY 10523
Tel: 914.347.3300
Fax: 914.347.3309
www.xritephoto.com

Neato
250 Dodge Avenue
East Haven, CT 06512
Tel: 800.984.9800, 203.466.5170
www.neato.com

Pantone® Inc.
590 Commerce Boulevard
Carlstadt, NJ 07072
Tel: 888.726.8663, 201.935.5500
Fax: 201.935.3338
www.pantone.com

Powerfile
3350 Thomas Road
Santa Clara, CA 95054
Tel: 866.838.3669
www.powerfile.com

Quark Inc.
800 Grant Street
Denver, CO 80203
Tel: 303.894.8888
www.quark.com

Quark Systems Inc
1 Northumberland Avenue
London
WC2N 5BW
Tel: (00800) 1787 8275
Fax: (00800) 4647 8275
www.quark.com

Quantum Mechanics
4055 NW Columbia Avenue
Portland, OR 97229
Tel: 503.531.8430
Fax: 503.531.8429
www.camerabits.com

Roxio Inc.
455 El Camino Road
Santa Clara, CA 95050
Tel: 408.367.3100
www.roxio.com

ViewSonic Corp.
381 Brea Canyon Road
Walnut, CA 91789
Tel: 909.444.8888
www.viewsonic.com

Wacom Technology Corp.
1311 SE Cardinal Court
Vancouver, WA 98683
Tel: 800.922.9348
Fax: 360.896.9724
www.wacom.com

Business Books

Crawford, Tab. *Business and Legal Forms for Photographers*. 3rd ed. New York: Allworth Press, 2002.

Duboff, Leonard D. *The Law (in Plain English) for Photographers*. Revised ed. New York: Allworth Press, 2002.

Pickerell, Jim, and Cheryl Pickerell. *Negotiating Stock Photo Prices*. Edited ed. Rockville, MD: Stock Connection, 1997.

Angle of View: The amount of a scene (notably the horizon) visible through a given lens. In general, the shorter the focal length, the wider the angle of view.

Ansel Adams: (1902 – 1984) American master photographer, especially known for his black and white photography of landscapes in the West.

Aperture: The opening that lets light into the camera to expose the image. (See also *F-stop*.)

Attention Getter: Any device used to get a horse's attention and to keep his ears up.

Autofocus: A system that lets the camera automatically bring a pre-indicated point on a lens into sharp resolution.

Brightness: The whiteness of a piece of paper. Typically expressed on a scale of 1 to 100. The higher the number, the brighter the paper.

Browsers: Software that easily allows you to view and access the digital images from a photo CD, camera, or scanner. A sort of digital filing system.

Buffer: Internal memory in a digital camera that temporarily stores information for a certain number of frames before writing the image information to the storage media.

Bundled Software: Programs that are included with a camera, computer, printer, or other piece of hardware. Bundled software is generally easy to learn and use, and is compatible with the equipment it accompanies. It is often less powerful than software available for independent purchase.

Burn: Recording data on a CD or DVD.

Camera Shake: The movement of an unsupported camera at slow shutter speeds that produces a blurry image.

Cavalletti: A series of low poles or groundpoles used for a variety of equine exercises.

CCD: Short for Charged-Couple Device. The sensor used in some digital cameras and camcorders that captures the image. The CCD converts the light exposed on it into a digital image. The "film" of a digital camera.

Color Management: A system to reproduce color in a consistent, predictable manner.

Color Space: The range of colors that a camera, printer, monitor, or other piece of hardware can recognize and accurately reproduce.

Color Space Profile: The color ranges available through a particular type of software. Profiles are device-independent. They provide a consistent medium for editing images.

Composition: The visual elements that make up a photograph.

Copyright Law: A federal law that protects the author of original works including literary, dramatic, musical, artistic and certain other intellectual works. To read the full law, visit www.copyright.gov.

Crop/Cropping: Enlarging a small portion of an image, or removing extraneous portions of an image in order to produce an image with better composition.

Depth of Field: The area of acceptable sharpness that is in front of and behind your point of focus. As a general rule, this area is 1/3 in front and 2/3 in back of your point of focus.

Diffuser: A device that evenly distributes lamp, or other artificial light.

Digital Video: A means of capturing and storing video images using a digital, rather than an analog, medium.

Digital Zoom: In some digital cameras, a means of "cropping" in on a smaller portion of the image. This can make the image larger in the frame, but the quality may be poor because it is a sampling from a smaller portion of the CCD.

Discharge Lights: Types of commercial lighting fixtures that are commonly used for light streets, parking lot lighting, and lighting on the outside and inside of large buildings. Common types of these lights are Metal Halide, High Pressure Sodium, and Mercury Vapor.

Disposable Camera: An inexpensive camera that is purchased for a single use. Once all the images are exposed and the camera is turned in for processing, the camera cannot be used again.

DPI (or dpi): Short for dots per inch. A means of measuring the number of pixels, dots, or other components in a linear inch. An electronic image at 72 dpi, will measure 72 pixels high by 72 pixels wide. It will contain 5184 pixels in a square inch.

Emulsion: Fine grains of silver bromide in a gelatinous suspension that form a light-sensitive coating on film stock.

Exposure: The amount of light reaching the film or digital sensor to produce an image. Both shutter speed and aperture control exposure.

Exposure Compensation: Increasing or decreasing the amount of light reaching the film or digital sensor as a means of overriding the auto exposure.

Film: A recording media made up of acetate and emulsions. The three most common types are black-and-white negative, color negative, and color transparency.

Filters: Colored glass, plastic, or gels that alter the light passing through them. Filters can change the color, enhance the colors in an image, add special effects, block ultraviolet (UV) rays, correct for color temperature, or change the contrast of black-and-white images.

Firewire: A high-speed serial communications standard for attaching camcorders and other peripherals to computers.

Fish-Eye Lens: An extreme wide-angle lens with an exaggerated angle of view, which produces a recognizable curvature of the final image.

Focal Length: The distance between the center of the lens and the focus point on the focal plane. The longer the focal length of a lens, the larger the image is on the focal plane and the narrower the angle of view.

Focal Plane: The plane that passes through the focus that is perpendicular to the axis of a lens or mirror. The plane containing the film or digital sensor.

F-Stop: The number derived from dividing the focal length by the diameter of the aperture. The resulting numbers are calibrated to known values known as f-stops. As the numbers get higher, less light is let through the lens. A focal length of 100mm divided by an aperture diameter of 25mm equals four—or f/4.

Gamma: The measurement of contrast in photographic material, such as film and other recorders of photographic images like computer monitors. The higher the number, the more contrast in the material or device.

Gig: Short for gigabyte, which is 1,073,741,824 bits of computer information.

Glossy Paper: A photographic paper having a smooth, shiny, glass-like surface used to print photographic images with great detail.

Grain: Granular texture of silver-halide used in photographic material. Clumping of the silver-halide crystals is more noticeable in higher speed films. Slower speed films are said to have "less grain."

Grid Spot: A honeycomb-shaped device placed over a light source to control the spread of light into an area. Grid spots come in varying degrees, which allows you to change the size of the spot of light.

Hard Light: A small light source resulting in a direct light that produces hard shadows. Similar to the effect of the sun on a clear day.

Highlights: The bright areas of a photograph or on a subject.

Inkjet: A type of printer that sprays ink droplets through very small nozzles to produce an image.

Inverse Square Law: A physical law that states when you have a point source of light, the intensity of light decreases by the square of the distance from the light source. Practically speaking, doubling the distance from a light source reduces the light to a quarter of its original intensity.

ISO: Abbreviation for International Organization for Standards. A worldwide organization that standardizes the values of film sensitivity. ISO 200 film purchased in one country is the same as ISO 200 film purchased in any other country.

JPG or JPEG: A widely used image format developed by the Joint Photographic Experts Group for digital images. It uses a "lossy compression" (see separate entry) that reduces a file's size, which makes it easier to send over the internet.

Kelvin (K): A unit of measurement to describe the color content of a light source in the continuous spectrum of light.

Keyword: A word or series of words used to describe an image in an electronic file, enabling digital asset management software to sort files efficiently.

Latitude Range: A range of tones that any particular photographic medium can record at a given exposure.

Lavalier Microphone: A small, portable microphone that clips on the speaker's clothing, which transfers sound directly to a videocamera via a wireless signal. Sometimes referred to as a "pin mike."

LCD Screen: A Liquid Crystal Display is a low powered monitor used to view images on the backs of digital cameras. Also utilized in computer monitors.

Linear Editing: Manually stopping and starting a videotape (usually VHS tape) on one machine while recording only the desired portions on another.

Log/Logging: Adding a title, date, or time stamp to a photograph or video.

Lossy Compression: A data compression technique that permanently eliminates extraneous or superfluous data and significantly reduces the storage space needed for a graphics file. The lost information is usually unnoticeable to the user. Extrapolating information from the remaining file is the only way to recover data during decompression.

Luster Paper: An instant-drying paper produces vivid images. Print quality is said to rival that of traditional silver halide prints.

LUX: A means of measuring a videocamera's light sensitivity. The lower the LUX number, the more sensitive the recorder is to light.

Manual Focus: A camera system that requires the photographer to physically adjust the lens in order to improve image resolution.

Matte Box: A container that holds filters and attaches to the front of the lens to act as a sun shade.

Matte Paper: A nonreflective, nontextured paper with little or no glare, used to print photographic images.

Megapixel: One million pixels.

Non-Linear Editing: The ability to access, select, and duplicate any frame of a digitally recorded video with ease.

Opacity: A means of measuring a material's ability to prevent light from passing through it. The higher the opacity of a material, the less light passes through.

Panning: Moving the camera to follow along with a subject in motion, keeping the subject visible through the lens.

Panoramic: A format that produces a wider-than-normal photograph in relation to the height of the image. Especially useful for photographing landscapes.

Paper Weight (or basis weight): A means of measuring a paper's thickness. The weight of a ream (500 sheets) of paper measuring 17 x 22 inches. Measured in pounds (lbs). The higher the weight, the thicker each individual sheet of paper. (Common copier paper generally has a weight of 20 lbs.)

Photographic Activity Test (PAT): A worldwide standard for the archival quality of various photographic enclosures. The PAT predicts possible interactions between photographs and their storage enclosures.

Pixels: An abbreviation for Picture Elements, which are the small squares of light that are transmitted to make up a digital image.

Polaroid: A company that makes instant photographic materials and equipment. Sometimes used to refer to the instant photograph itself.

Postproduction: Work performed on a photograph after the image is taken. Photo manipulation, digital effects, cropping, and color correction all occur in post production.

Power Pack: A device for supplying power or converting a power supply to a required voltage.

Printer Paper: Any paper specifically manufactured for use in computer printers. Some paper is specially developed for optimum use in laser printers, while other paper is better suited for inkjet printers.

Program Settings: Preset parameters that allow the camera to automatically capture an image with little or no input from the user.

Prosumer: A term used to describe a photographer who is more than an amateur but not yet a professional.

RAW Image: A format or file that contains unprocessed or minimally processed data taken directly from a digital camera's sensor. RAW images must be converted to TIFF, JPG, or a similar RGB format, before they can be printed, edited, displayed, or manipulated.

Reflectors: Devices used to reflect light onto your subject. These may be made of any material that will reflect light.

Resampling: Permanently changing the pixel dimensions of an image when editing.

RGB: Short for Red, Green, Blue. The color system used in most digital cameras and computer systems consisting of red, green, and blue light to create a full color image.

Rule of Thirds: A popular rule in art and photography that divides a frame into nine equal parts. The artist places the image's point of interest at one of the intersecting lines.

Scrim: A translucent material used to soften or reduce the amount of light on your subject.

Sharpness: Relating to an image's distinction or clarity.

Shot List: An inventory of ideas, poses, props, and other specifics to help you plan and organize a photo shoot.

Shutter Lag: The amount of time that lapses between pressing the shutter release and when the camera actually exposes the image.

Shutter Release: A button or lever that the photographer presses in order to open the shutter, expose the film or digital sensor, and take a picture.

Shutter Speed: The amount of time, measured in fractions of a second, that the shutter is open to expose the film or digital sensor.

SLR: Single Lens Reflex camera. One of the most popular camera designs on the market today, designed so that you can see the same image that the camera lens sees.

Softbox: A device placed on the front of a light source to soften the light emitting from it.

Soft Light: A large, curved light source that bounces light from all directions and has little or no shadows. A light source that emits light similar to a cloudy day.

Standard Lens: A lens with a 50mm or 55mm focal length, intended to capture an image similar to the human perspective. Best suited for taking general, informal photographs.

Strobe: An electronic flash system that stores up energy and once released produces a bright light.

Sync Speed: A camera's optimum exposure time for flash photography. If the shutter speed is out of sync with the duration of the flash, the resulting photograph will have a black or very underexposed area along one side of the image.

Telephoto Lens: Lenses with longer focal lengths that magnify the image. Telephoto lenses are necessary for getting good shots from long distances.

Testimonial Portrait: A photograph in which the subject looks into the lens with a confident look or expression.

Thumbnail: A very small image to use as an organizational aid.

TLR: Twin Lens Reflex camera. This is the second most common camera design. It uses two lenses, one for taking the picture and a second for the viewing lens. You will find this type used in some of your point-and-shoot and disposable cameras.

TTL: Short for Through the Lens. A means of metering by measuring the light that passes through the lens.

Variable F-Stop: An f-stop that changes in conjunction with the focal length of a lens (i.e., a zoom lens).

Voiceover: Narration that accompanies a video.

Waterproof Disposable Camera: A camera purchased for a single use around wet conditions or even underwater. Once all the images are exposed and the camera is turned in for processing, the camera cannot be used again.

Wide Angle Lens: A lens with a wider angle of view than a standard lens, thus including more of the horizon in the final image.

Zoom Lens: A lens with a narrow angle of view and a variable focal length.